T0214091

Lecture Notes in Computer Science　12121

More information about this series at http://www.springer.com/series/7410

Luís Antunes · Maurizio Naldi ·
Giuseppe F. Italiano · Kai Rannenberg ·
Prokopios Drogkaris (Eds.)

Privacy Technologies and Policy

8th Annual Privacy Forum, APF 2020
Lisbon, Portugal, October 22–23, 2020
Proceedings

 Springer

Editors
Luís Antunes 🄳
University of Porto
Porto, Portugal

Maurizio Naldi 🄳
LUMSA University
Rome, Italy

Giuseppe F. Italiano 🄳
LUISS
Rome, Italy

Kai Rannenberg
Goethe University Frankfurt
Frankfurt am Main, Germany

Prokopios Drogkaris 🄳
ENISA
Athens, Greece

ISSN 0302-9743   ISSN 1611-3349   (electronic)
Lecture Notes in Computer Science
ISBN 978-3-030-55195-7   ISBN 978-3-030-55196-4   (eBook)
https://doi.org/10.1007/978-3-030-55196-4

LNCS Sublibrary: SL4 – Security and Cryptology

This Springer imprint is published by the registered company Springer Nature Switzerland AG
The registered company address is: Gewerbestrasse 11, 6330 Cham, Switzerland

Preface

With this volume we introduce the proceedings of the 2020 edition of the Annual Privacy Forum (APF), that took place in Lisbon, Portugal. APF 2020 was organized by the European Union Agency for Cybersecurity (ENISA), the Directorate General for Communications Networks, Content and Technology (DG CONNECT), and Católica University of Portugal, Lisbon School of Law.

This conference, already in its 8th edition, was established as an opportunity to bring together key communities, namely policy, academia, and industry, in the broader area of privacy and data protection while focusing on privacy related application areas. This edition coincided with the first evaluation and review of the General Data Protection Regulation (GDPR). Unfortunately, it also coincided with the global COVID-19 outbreak which lead the organizers to postpone the organization of the APF from June to later in 2020, in order to ensure the safety of the participants.

There were 59 submissions in response to the APF call for papers. Each paper was peer-reviewed by three members of the International Program Committee (PC). On the basis of significance, novelty, and scientific quality, 12 papers were selected (a 20% acceptance rate) and are compiled in this volume. The papers are organized across four thematic areas, namely:

- Impact Assessment ("The Data Protection Impact Assessment as a tool to enforce non-discriminatory AI", "Processing operations 'likely to result in high risks for the rights and freedoms' - Lessons to be learned from national authorities' DPIA 'blacklists'", and "Analysing the Impacts of Facial Recognition - Towards a Rigorous Methodology")
- Privacy by Design ("Privacy through data recolouring", "Privacy by Design Identity Architecture Using Agents and Digital Identities", and "Preliminary remarks and practical insights on how the Whistleblower Protection Directive adopts some of the GDPR principles")
- Data Protection and Security ("Webs of Trust: Choosing Who to Trust on the Internet", "Italian National Framework for Cybersecurity and Data Protection", and "Operationalization of privacy and security requirements for eHealth IoT applications in the context of GDPR and CSL")
- Transparency ("Measuring the usage of purposes for data processing and their legal basis in IAB Europe's Transparency and Consent Framework", "Towards Transparency in the Internet of Things", and "Tracking without Traces—Fingerprinting in an Era of Individualism and Complexity")

Any conference is the fruit of the efforts of many people, and APF is no exception. We wish to thank the European Data Protection Supervisor, for continuing an established tradition of supporting the APF and the Portuguese Data Protection Authority. Further, we wish to thank the members of the PC, for devoting their time to reviewing the submitted papers and providing constructive feedback, the authors, whose papers make up the bulk of the content of this conference, and the attendees, whose interest in the conference is the main driver for its organization.

May 2020   Luís Antunes
                                                   Maurizio Naldi
                                              Giuseppe F. Italiano
                                                Kai Rannenberg
                                              Prokopios Drogkaris

Organization

Program Committee

Agrafiotis Ioannis	ENISA, Greece
Banavara Harsha	Signify North America Corporation, USA
Berendt Bettina	Katholieke Universiteit Leuven, Belgium
Castelluccia Claude	Inria, France
D'Acquisto Giuseppe	Garante per la protezione dei dati personali, Italy
Del Álamo José M.	Universidad Politécnica de Madrid, Spain
Dell'Amico Matteo	NortonLifeLock, France
Dimitrova Diana	FIZ Karlsruhe, Germany
Efstathopoulos Petros	Symantec Research Labs, USA
Fabian Prasser	Technical University of Munich, Germany
Ferreira Ana	University of Porto, Portugal
Fischer-Hübner Simone	Karlstad University, Germany
Friedewald Michael	Fraunhofer, Germany
Gruschka Nils	University of Oslo, Norway
Irion Kristina	University of Amsterdam, The Netherlands
Jensen Meiko	Kiel University of Applied Sciences, Germany
Kalloniatis Christos	University of the Aegean, Greece
Kamara Irene	VUB, TILT, The Netherlands
Kardasiadou Zoi	European Commission, Belgium
Kasem-Madani Saffija	University of Bonn, Germany
Katsikas Sokratis	Open University of Cyprus, Cyprus
Lambrinoudakis Costas	University of Piraeus, Greece
Lauradoux Cedric	Inria, France
Le Métayer Daniel	Inria, France
Limniotis Konstantinos	Hellenic Data Protection Authority, Greece
Malatras Apostolos	ENISA, Greece
Mantelero Alessandro	Politecnico di Torino, Italy
Mitchell Chris	Royal Holloway, University of London, UK
Mitrakas Andreas	ENISA, Greece
Moulinos Konstantinos	ENISA, Greece
Olejnik Lukasz	EDPS, Belgium
Pape Sebastian	Goethe University Frankfurt, Germany
Pierce Robin	TILT Tilburg Law School, The Netherlands
Polemi Nineta	University of Pireaus, Greece
Roßnagel Heiko	Fraunhofer, Germany
Schiffner Stefan	University of Luxembourg, Luxembourg
Schweighofer Erich	University of Vienna, Austria
Silva Fernando	CNPD, Portugal

von Grafenstein Maximilian	Alexander von Humboldt-Institut für Internet und Gesellschaft, Germany
Zanfir-Fortuna Gabriela	Future of Privacy Forum, USA

General Co-chair

Antunes Luís Filipe	Coelho University of Porto, Portugal

Program Co-chairs

Naldi Maurizio	LUMSA University, Italy
Italiano Giuseppe	LUISS Guido Carli University, Italy
Rannenberg Kai	Goethe University Frankfurt, Germany
Drogkaris Prokopios	ENISA, Greece

Additional Reviewers

Schunck Christian H.	Fraunhofer, Germany
Sanchez-Rola Iskander	Symantec, USA
Sellung Rachelle	Fraunhofer, Germany
Schmitz Sandra	University of Luxembourg, Luxembourg
Karaboga Murat	Fraunhofer, Germany
Sellung Rachelle	Fraunhofer, Germany
Karkala Smaragda	ENISA, Greece

Contents

Transparency

Impact Assessment

The Data Protection Impact Assessment as a Tool to Enforce Non-discriminatory AI

Yordanka Ivanova[1,2](✉)

[1] Law Faculty, Sofia University "St. Kliment Ohridski", Sofia, Bulgaria
d_mintcheva@abv.bg, yoivanov@vub.be
[2] Law Faculty, Vrije Universiteit Brussel, Brussels, Belgium

Abstract. This paper argues that the novel tools under the General Data Protection Regulation (GDPR) may provide an effective legally binding mechanism for enforcing non-discriminatory AI systems. Building on relevant guidelines, the generic literature on impact assessments and algorithmic fairness, this paper aims to propose a specialized methodological framework for carrying out a Data Protection Impact Assessment (DPIA) to enable controllers to assess and prevent ex ante the risk to the right to non-discrimination as one of the key fundamental rights that GDPR aims to safeguard.

Keywords: EU fundamental rights · Non-discrimination · Data protection · GDPR · DPIA · Algorithmic impact assessment · Algorithmic bias · AI fairness

1 Introduction

Artificial Intelligence (AI)[1] is the new game-changer in the global technological race as it enables more efficient and cost-effective processes and promises to solve some of the big challenges of our time. These exciting prospects are, however, overshadowed by recent research [14–18] showing that algorithms tend to be explicitly or implicitly biased against certain protected groups – a serious risk that can affect adversely individuals' fundamental rights and the society at large when biased automated systems are deployed at scale.

Despite these shortcomings, the research community has recently examined AI not only as a problem, but also as a potential solution to discrimination and have looked reflexively to identify the sources of bias and develop measures to identify and correct them. The use of data to inform decisions could be also a positive development, given its

---

The author is thankful to Laurens Naudts who provided very useful comments on the draft. The paper reflects author's personal opinion as a researcher and is in no way representing EU institutions' position on the subject.

[1] Under this paper, the term AI is used to cover primarily machine and deep learning techniques that aim to simulate human intelligence and support or replace human decision-making. Still, the methodology proposed could be also relevant for other AI fields such as natural language processing, reasoning and other fields of AI application.

© Springer Nature Switzerland AG 2020
L. Antunes et al. (Eds.): APF 2020, LNCS 12121, pp. 3–24, 2020.
https://doi.org/10.1007/978-3-030-55196-4_1

potential for more objective and informed decisions [7]. Big data analytics could also find correlations and provide the necessary statistical evidence that is highly indispensable in the court to prove *prima facie* significant discriminatory impact across groups. AI has also the potential to limit discriminatory treatment based on human decision-making similarly proven to be tainted with prejudices that are even harder to detect. As argued by Barocas and Selbst [15], if AI bias problems are properly detected and corrected at early stages, its use can in fact limit individual human biases in important decision-making processes and thus protect civil rights, even where it fails to completely root out discrimination altogether.

This paper tries to explore the novel tools under the General Data Protection Regulation (GDPR) as an effective legally binding mechanism for enforcing non-discriminatory AI systems. Building on relevant guidelines [1–9], the generic literature on impact assessments [10–13] and algorithmic fairness [14–35], this paper places potential solutions for AI fairness in the context of EU data protection law and aims to fill a practical need by proposing a specialized methodological framework for carrying out a Data Protection Impact Assessment (DPIA) to enable controllers to assess and prevent ex ante the risks to the right to non-discrimination as one of the key fundamental rights that GDPR aims to safeguard.

2   Enforcing Equality and Non-discrimination Through GDPR

The General Data Protection Regulation (GDPR) is the modernized secondary data protection legislation whose primary objective is to ensure the protection of natural persons when their personal data are processed. Article 1 GDPR states that it aims, in particular to protect individuals' right to data protection, but also all other rights and freedoms, including equality and non-discrimination that could safeguard us against the risks posed by biased AI systems. These equality rights are enshrined in the EU Charter of Fundamental Rights, in particular Article 20 of the Charter which corresponds to the principle of equal treatment, which requires comparable situations to be treated equally and different situations to be treated differently. Article 21 of the Charter is, in addition, a specific expression of the equality principle that prohibits discrimination on the basis of a non-exhaustive list of protected characteristics such as 'sex, race, colour, ethnic or social origin, genetic features, language, religion or belief, political or any other opinion, membership of a national minority, property, birth, disability, age or sexual orientation'.

The CJEU has ruled that the EU data protection legislation must be interpreted and applied in the light of the fundamental rights, enshrined in the Charter, and that data protection should play an instrumental role for the protection of the right to non-discrimination in particular[2]. Arguably, such interpretation of the GDPR in the context of the fundamental right to non-discrimination could integrate the equality principles into the much wider scope of personal data processing, well beyond the limited scope of

---

[2] CJEU Opinion 1/15 on Draft agreement between Canada and the European Union — Transfer of Passenger Name Record data from the European Union to Canada, ECLI:EU:C:2017:592; Case C-524/06 Heinz Huber v Bundesrepublik Deutschland, ECLI:EU:C:2008:724.

the existing secondary EU equality directives applicable only to certain contexts (e.g., employment, education, access to good and services).

In particular, the protection of the right to non-discrimination can be operationalized in the GDPR through a number of principles incumbent on controllers (e.g. fairness, accuracy, minimization, purpose limitation, accountability) and data subjects' rights (e.g. right to information, access, correction, deletion or the right not to be subject to solely automated decisions with legal and similarly significant effects). Furthermore, there are not only provisions for restricted processing of certain sensitive categories of data, largely overlapping with the protected grounds (Article 9 GDPR), but also more systemic and collective safeguards such as public enforcement powers of supervisory authorities (e.g. audits) and new obligations for data protection impact assessments and data protection 'by design and by default', which shift the focus from ex post correction to ex ante prevention of unfair and discriminatory data processing.

3   The DPIA as an Ex Ante Tool to Prevent Discrimination

The Data Protection Impact Assessment (DPIA) is one of the key innovations in the GDPR as a tool for operationalizing the novel risk-based approach [10, 11], which obliges controllers to assess *ex ante* the risks of the processing activities to the individuals' fundamental rights and freedoms. Given that Article 35 requires prior assessment of the risks posed by the data processing to all fundamental rights, it could be argued that it obliges controllers to carry out a veritable human rights algorithmic impact assessment as a systematic, collective and precautionary safeguard to individuals' rights and the society at large [12, 13, 40].

Article 35(3) GDPR obliges data controllers to carry out a DPIA for high risky processing, in particular always when using AI and other new technologies to profile or extensively evaluate citizens with legal or similarly significant effects, when public accessible area is systematically monitored or sensitive data are processed at large scale. Article 29 Working Party (WP29) [1] has further stated that the processing is high-risky and controllers must carry out a DPIA, if two or more conditions included in a long list are met, thus subjecting to prior assessment practically every AI system intended to process personal data. Considering the extensive research, cited above, which shows the high risk of algorithmic bias, this paper argues that the assessment of the specific risk of discrimination should be an obligatory step in the design and use of every AI system, be it as part of solely automated or partially automated decision-making process(es).

To help controllers comply with their obligation, the next section will propose a methodological framework for the assessment of the risk of discrimination as part of the DPIA, building on the requirements in Article 35(7) GDPR, the WP29 guidance [1] and the relevant generic literature on DPIA and algorithmic fairness. Accordingly, the framework includes three consecutive steps: (a) assessment of the necessity and proportionality of the processing; (b) assessment of the risks to the right to non-discrimination; (c) the measures envisaged to address these risks. In addition, Article 35(7)a requires controllers to start the DPIA with a systematic description of the envisaged processing operations and the intended purpose left uncovered here as this will depend concretely on the AI model and its intended application.

3.1 Necessity and Proportionality Assessment

The first step is to assess the necessity and proportionality of the intended data processing, which the WP29 [1] has advised to be done, considering: (a) the specified, explicit and legitimate *purpose(s)* of the processing; (b) the *lawfulness* of processing, and (c) the principle of *minimization*, which requires the data to be adequate, relevant and limited to what is necessary for the objective. To assess the necessity and proportionality, this paper suggests to distinguish between two main stages when personal data are used: 1. Model's Training and Testing and 2. AI System's Application to end users, including continuous machine learning.

For the data processing in the **Model's Training and Testing stage,** it is suggested that the *overall purpose* that could be relied upon is scientific research given its broad definition in Recital 159 GDPR, including technological development, applied and privately funded research. The *legal basis* of the processing could be arguably the same on which the training personal datasets are originally collected at the first place by the controller given that research is considered per se a compatible re-use subject to the safeguards under Article 89(1) GDPR, including minimization, anonymization and pseudonymization where possible to achieve the research purpose. Such guidance has been given by the Norwegian DPA [6], advising AI developers to rely on the research exemption in the context of machine learning that could apply even for sensitive data, still highly indispensable to test and correct the algorithms for biases [18, 21]. Contrary to what Veale [21] and Hacker [14] opine, this paper also suggests that in the AI model's construction and evaluation phase Article 22 GDPR is not applicable. This provision applies only to solely automated decision-making with legal and similarly significant effects, but at the AI development stage the individuals whose personal data are used to train and test the model are not yet subject to such individual decision-making with real-life consequences. In all cases of research, ethical considerations should be, however, taken thoroughly into account, including consideration of ethical research codes and the EU Ethics Guidelines for Trustworthy AI [8]. In relation to the *minimization* principle, safeguards for the data subjects' rights to privacy and data protection will be important, requiring machine learning to be based on new privacy preserving methods such as differential privacy, federated learning techniques or homomorphic encryption where feasible [6]. Furthermore, given that the purpose and means of the data processing in the application stage are determined already at the design and development stages, the European Data Protection Board (EDBP) [3] has underlined controller's responsibility to assess the risks and integrate safeguards for algorithmic fairness already at these early stages to comply with the new data protection 'by design' obligation under Article 25 GDPR, even if no personal data are yet processed (e.g. models trained with anonymized or synthetic data).

For the AI Application Stage, the *legal grounds* under Articles 6 and 9 GDPR will vary depending on the context and the intended purpose/use. Contrary to Veale and Binns [21] who consider that GDPR requires explicit consent for processing sensitive data for bias detection purposes, recent CJEU case-law[3] suggests that even at this application stage it may be possible for controllers to process sensitive data when strictly necessary

---

[3] CJEU, C-136/17 *GC and Others v CNIL*, ECLI:EU:C:2019:773, para.68.

for the sole purpose of bias detection and correction on the basis of Article 9(2)g) substantial public interest, so as to safeguard the fundamental right to non-discrimination, if sufficient safeguards are taken to protect data subjects' privacy and other rights (e.g. encryption/hashing of the sensitive data to ensure security and technical limitation of re-use). Still, solely automated decision-making, including profiling, with legal and similarly significant effects will always require a special legal basis under Article 22(2) and (4) GDPR.

With respect to the intended application, the *legitimate objective* pursued may normally coincide with the purpose of the AI application (personalization of a particular service, assessing creditworthiness, preventing risk of fraud etc.), while the *suitability of the AI system as a measure* should be assessed on the basis of the predictive accuracy and efficacy of the model and the fact that there are no alternative less restrictive means to achieve the objective. If any protected characteristic(s) or proxy data which highly correlate with such characteristic(s) are envisaged to be used in comparable situations as part of the decision-making process, compliance with the *minimization principle* must be ensured and an objective justification for the differential treatment or disproportionate impact should be advanced - an exception explicitly allowed under EU equality law for direct discrimination (e.g. sex as a genuine and determining occupational requirement) or positive discrimination permitted by member states' law, while for cases of indirect discrimination the processing should be necessary and suitable to achieve a specific legitimate aim and proportionate, i.e. not going beyond what is strictly necessary [14]. Whether the *restriction is minimized and proportionate* to the legitimate objectives will largely depend on balancing the benefits and the adverse impacts, taking into account the suitability and the effectiveness of the mitigation measures (Sect. 3.3. below), which should limit 'by design' the risk of biases and unjustified discrimination and safeguard individuals' equality and privacy rights. In this respect, recent case-law[4] suggests that where the breath of differential impact on two groups is significantly disparate and appropriate mitigating measures are not taken "to limit the range and nature of the infringements', this could even violate the 'essence' of the right to non-discrimination, which can be restricted under no circumstances according to Article 52(1) of the Charter.

3.2 Risk Assessment

Having justified the processing, the second step covers the main object of the DPIA to objectively assess ex ante the potential "risks to natural persons' rights" - a novel concept in data protection law still subject to research and in need of more guidance from DPAs [10, 11]. In the context of algorithmic discrimination, the present framework proposes to assess the risks to the right to non-discrimination in terms of both direct and indirect discrimination, considering the fact that their respective justification differs under secondary equality law. As argued above, interpreting the obligations for DPIA in conjunction with the "by design" requirements under Article 25 requires this risk assessment to cover all stages of the AI process (design and programming/ training and testing/application and continuous learning). While the different stages are separately examined in this framework, it must be highlighted that the application stage may

---

[4] CJEU, C-528/13, *Geoffrey Léger v. Ministre des Affaires sociales*, para. 54.

externalize risks that have not been effectively mitigated in the previous stages, but it could also create emerging sources of discrimination even for AI systems that have been properly tested, validated and approved as non-discriminatory. Following the general risk management approach, the risk assessment must in principle identify the sources of risks, their likelihood and the impact on the individuals' fundamental rights [1, 10].

Classification of the Sources of Risks. The two main types of risks – direct and indirect discrimination – are covered with a suggested classification of the most common sources of risks for each stage of the AI cycle based on literature review [14–20] and relevant case-law. Direct discrimination is present where an individual is, has been, or would be treated differently 'on the grounds' of his protected characteristics in otherwise comparable situation[5] (discriminatory treatment) and indirect discrimination where seemingly neutral practice or criterion puts an individual from a protected group at a particular disadvantage[6] (discriminatory impact). The classification does not distinguish between intentional and unintentional sources of risks as intention is irrelevant under EU equality law[7].

Stage	Risk	Source of risk
Design and programming	Direct discrimination	Discriminatory values embedded in code (if not objectively justified)
		Biases or stereotypes in defining "Target Variable" and "Class Labels" (e.g. through notions of 'good employees', 'risky customer')
		Biases or stereotypes in feature selection/use of protected characteristics (e.g. sex, age, race, ethnicity) or blatant proxies ('redlining' e.g. postal codes)
	Indirect discrimination (if not masking)	Biases in feature selection/use of *proxies* that highly correlate with protected characteristics ('redundant encoding')
		Lack of special design measures to accommodate for the specific non-comparable situation of protected groups (such as children, disabled, elderly)[a] or protected groups suffering from structural discrimination[b]

(continued)

---

[5] E.g., Art. 2(2)(a) of the Race Equality Directive 2000/43/EC.

[6] Article 2(a) and (b) Racial Equality Directive 2000/43/EC.

[7] For example, in C-54/07, Firma Feryn NV, 10 July 2008, the CJEU did not treat discriminatory motive as relevant to deciding if discrimination had occurred. See also ECtHR, Biao v. Denmark (Grand Chamber), No. 38590/10, 24 May 2016, para. 103. ECtHR, D.H. and Others v. the Czech Republic [GC], No. 57325/00, 13 November 2007, para. 79.

(continued)

Stage	Risk	Source of risk
		Aggregation bias where a single model uses heterogenous data for different subgroups for drawing generalized conclusions or assumptions for all groups that can be eventually false or putting certain protected groups at particular disadvantage
Training and validation/Machine learning/	Direct discrimination	Tainted training datasets (e.g. unrepresentative/imbalanced sampling across protected groups, inappropriate, out-of-date, inaccurate or biased training data)
		Historic biased datasets (statistical discrimination from the past)
		Biases in labelling examples (in supervised learning)
		Evaluation bias (e.g. by using biased testing data or inappropriate metrics)
	Indirect discrimination (if not masking)	Training datasets include *proxies* that highly correlate with protected characteristics ('redundant training')
		Accuracy disparity of AI predictions across protected groups (if model and training data otherwise unbiased)
Application and continuous learning	Direct discrimination	Use of protected characteristics or blatant proxies as input or output of the AI process for decision-making purposes (e.g. sex, age, race, ethnicity)
		AI model creates or reinforces invidious stereotypes or 'discrimination by association' based on protected characteristics or blatant proxies (e.g. postal codes)[c]
		Biases injected through feedback loops (in continuous learning)
	Indirect discrimination (if not masking)	AI model is used in different context/for different purpose(s) from those it has been originally designed or trained for or AI outcomes have been misapplied/misinterpreted by human operators (correlation v causation)

(continued)

(*continued*)

Stage	Risk	Source of risk
		AI model creates or reinforces invidious stereotypes or 'discrimination by association' based on *proxy* indicators that highly correlate with protected characteristics
		Accuracy disparity of AI predictions across protected groups (if model, training and input data otherwise unbiased)

a See Articles 24, 25 and 26 of the Charter.

b E.g., ECtHR, *D.H. and Others v. the Czech Republic* [GC], No. 57325/00, 13 November 2007.

c Stereotypes have been condemned in the ECHR case-law where the behavior of one member of protected group was extrapolated from a stereotypical perception that the authorities had of the Roma community as a whole, see ECtHR, *Lingurar v Romania* App no 48474/14, paras. 75–76. The CJEU has also proclaimed the new concept of 'discrimination by association' which aims to protect persons who are not part of the protected group, but are treated less favourably because of the protected characteristics of other people. See CJEU, C-83/14, "*CHEZ Razpredelenie Bulgaria*" AD, 16 July 2015. Arguably, generalized predictive models used, for example, to decide allocation or levels of interests rates on loans by applying algorithmic generalized assumptions that 80% percent of people living in code Z-1900 pay their debts later also constitute 'discrimination by association' when this stereotyped prediction is in direct causation with membership in a protected group may be in fact incorrect for an individual who lives in the same quarter. If there is no causation, but simply correlation with a neutral proxy indicator, then this practice can amount to indirect discrimination, if it disproportionately affects certain protected groups.

Likelihood of Risks. The likelihood of risks includes the feasibility of their occurrence generally classified as low, medium and high. Accordingly, the methodological framework suggests:

– *High probability* where the source of risk is present and the direct or indirect discrimination is not objectively justified (as explained in Sect. 3.1 above) and the controller has not taken the necessary mitigating measures to safeguard individuals' rights to equality and non-discrimination. High probability of discrimination is present in all cases of stigmatization or offensive discriminatory practices as they cannot be objectively justified according to the CJEU case-law[8] as well as direct discrimination on the basis of ethnicity or race which cannot be tolerated in a democratic society[9].

  – *Medium probability* where the source of risk is present, but the controller relies on an objective justification for the discriminatory treatment or impact (see Sect. 3.1. above). It is suggested to classify probability as medium given that the proposed justification may not be accepted by the court as a strictly necessary and proportionate measure. Probability should be also classified as medium where the risk is still

[8] CJEU, C-83/14, *CHEZ*, para. 128.

[9] ECtHR, *Sejdić and Finci v. Bosnia and Herzegovina* [GC], Nos. 27996/06 and 34836/06.

likely to materialize because the controller has taken some mitigating measures, but these are not sufficiently appropriate and effective to mitigate all sources of potential discrimination in all stages of the AI cycle.

- *Low probability* where the source of risk is not present given that the controller does not seek to discriminate across individuals or groups and all appropriate and effective bias mitigation measures have been taken to illuminate or substantially reduce all sources of risks in all stages of the AI cycle.

Expected Impact. The expected impact on the data subjects' fundamental rights is also usually classified as high, medium and low. According to settled CJEU case-law[10], for a violation of the fundamental right to non-discrimination it is not necessary that any other rights or interests are simultaneously adversely affected, so the mere existence of an unjustified discriminatory treatment arguably suffices to qualify the discrimination as illegal and the impact as *high*. In addition, it is highly likely that the discriminatory practice, irrespective of whether it is legal or illegal, will further aggravate the impact because it will most often also lead to:

- Interference with other fundamental rights of the data subject (e.g. right to life, dignity, effective remedy and fair trial, presumption of innocence, security, integrity, personal liberty, property, free and fair elections, freedom of expression etc.);
- Allocation harms (e.g. rejection of credit or job application, promotion, admission to school, social security benefits, price discrimination etc.) or even exclusion from certain services/goods or from participation in the political and social life;
- Representation and personality harms, which may at the extreme lead also to harmful stigmatization, offensive treatment and/or subordination of protected groups;
- Non-material harms such as psychological distress or annoyance;
- Externalities for the society at large and/or adverse impact on wider societal or ethical values beyond the affected data subjects [8, 12, 39] (e.g. exacerbating inequalities, reinforcing collective bias, generating fragmentation and polarization of the society etc.).

It is, therefore, suggested that depending on the context, scope and purposes of processing and the applicable rules in the sector (e.g., law enforcement, employment), the impact of the various sources of algorithmic discrimination should be assessed concretely and should be always considered *high* given the potential violation of the right to non-discrimination unless bias mitigation measures are taken and objective justification given for the differential treatment. For cases of indirect discrimination (discriminatory impact), settled case-law[11] may possibly allow to set quantitative thresholds for lower impacts, e.g. *medium* impact, if 30 to 60% of a protected group are treated less

---

[10] CJEU, C-83/14, CHEZ, paras. 99–100.

[11] The CJEU has traditionally requested that the differential impact must be of a significant quantitative nature, certainly above 60%. See CJEU, C-33/89, *Maria Kowalska,* 27 June 1990. Still, in C-167/97 *Seymour-Smith,* para.61 the CJEU suggested that a lower level of disproportion could be accepted as a proof of indirect discrimination 'if it revealed a persistent and relatively constant disparity over a long period between men and women'.

favourably in comparable situations or *low* impact, if this figure is less than 30%. However, it is argued that even in these presumably low or medium impact cases of indirect discrimination, the side effects of the discriminatory practice on the affected individuals and the society (e.g. interference with other rights, allocation harms etc.) may aggravate the impact to *high*, depending on the context, purpose and scale and the severity of the consequences that may be unacceptable or disproportionate against the expected positive benefits.

Each source of risk must be assessed individually for its likelihood and expected long-term impact [22] and placed within the overall risk assessment matrix.

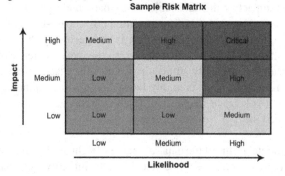

Sample Risk Matrix

High risk of discrimination in red colour should obligatorily trigger prior consultation with the DPA under Article 36 GDPR, if the residual risk is not reduced to acceptable levels and effectively mitigated by the measures (for example, because these are too costly or technically unfeasible, while the benefits of the processing ae deemed to prevail). This moves us to the next step of the methodology – examination of the mitigation measures.

3.3 Prevention and Mitigation Measures

The adoption of prevention and mitigation measures flows from the general obligation of the controller to ensure the data processing is risk-based and in compliance with the principles and controllers' obligation under GDPR, including the responsibility to integrate these measures already at the design stage. Taking effective mitigation measures is also key to ensure that the risk of discrimination will not materialize, so when taken they can in fact reduce the likelihood of risks or the impact on protected groups (see Sect. 3.2). While discrimination in algorithmic systems can arise from a number of sources, as explained above, and there is no 'one size fits all' solution, the next section will present some of the good practices recommended by researchers and supervisory authorities to address the risk of discrimination at the different stages of the AI cycle and to contribute to 'equal and fair treatment by design'.

Design and Programming Stage. The design and programming stages are of key importance because at that moment the controller defines the purposes and means of the processing and the intended use of the AI system. Decisions made when defining categories, identifying fields and scope of application, and establishing relationships impact both the efficacy of the model, and what outputs will be generated. The following potential measures could be applied to prevent and mitigate algorithmic bias at this stage:

- Comply with **approved certification schemes or standards** for unbiased and accountable AI "by design" [3, 8] such as the British Standards Institute BS 8611 [37] as well as the upcoming IEEE P7003 [38], CEN/CENELEC and ISO initiatives on establishing such standards.
- Ensure **diversity of developers' teams** (ethnic, sex and different backgrounds) and close involvement in the design process of other important teams e.g. Data Protection Officer, security, legal & compliance, audit [2, 8];
- **Train developers for bias and discrimination awareness**, so that they are mindful about the importance of their classification, measurement and programming choices and the potential sources of discrimination as well as the state-of-the-art technical solutions to detect and correct them [4, 8];
- **Encode principles of equal treatment and non-discrimination** on all protected grounds (e.g. sex, age, ethnicity etc.), so that the algorithm is programmed explicitly not to consider or infer certain protected characteristics when making the predictions/automated decision (unless discrimination is objectively justified under point 3.1) [8]. Given that current **computational measurements of individual and group fairness** (e.g., through metrics such as individual fairness, equal opportunities, equalized odds, treatment equality etc. [20]) cannot be satisfied simultaneously unless under certain constraints, it is important to take into account the context and application in which fairness definitions need to be used and use them accordingly [4].
- Avoid bias and stereotypes in programming choices, e.g., in defining '**target variables**' and '**class labels**' (e.g. when defining new classes such as risky 'customer' or 'good employees') and use only **features** that are minimized, appropriate and properly weighted to what is intended to be measured as a target without using protected characteristics or highly correlated proxies, if not objectively justified under anti-discrimination law (e.g. sex or age is a genuine occupational requirement for the post) [15]. These rule-based decisions and assumptions should reflect the reality as a cause effect correlation and the programming choices made must be justified and documented.
- Consider if **special measures for vulnerable groups** (such as children, older, ethnic minorities, disabled, immigrants, poor) are necessary [1, 8], if their situation is not comparable to that of other groups because of objective differences (e.g. due to age or disability) or structural social discrimination beyond individuals' control. Such special design measures (e.g. introducing specific decision rules and/or obligatory human intervention, re-weighing targeted 'feature values' or calibrating computationally the similarity between groups [24]) could prevent indirect discrimination at the later application stage and provide additional safeguards for the rights of these vulnerable persons.
- Consider **if distinct AI models are necessary** for different contexts and subpopulations whose data are heterogenous and where generalized assumptions and/or aggregation may lead to false or biased conclusions for the whole population [20].
- Ensure **immutable auditable trails (logs)** of the data processing activities that can safeguard security and enable subsequent quality control and auditing [8, 16]. This is

highly relevant for the controller's accountability and obligation to take appropriate technical measures to monitor and audit the performance of the AI system and the decision-making process for errors and biases in the application stage.

- Ensure **interpretability and explainabilty of the AI model**, so that biases and errors can be easily detected by human operators managing the system [4, 5, 8]. Possible approaches are to provide a confidence score alongside each output or use 'local' explanations, using methods like Local Interpretable Model-agnostic Explanation (LIME), which summarizes the relationships between input and output pairs and can help detect errors [18].
- Develop and apply a robust framework for **Quality Assurance Control** with design requirements that support meaningful human review from the outset in all stages of the AI cycle [5], including design and programming, training, testing and validation and application.
- **Review the source code**, including by checking for 'redundant encodings' where membership in a protected class happens to be encoded in other proxy data and is highly correlated, which requires subsequent removal or re-calibration of the scoring factors contributing to the discriminatory effects [16, 18].
- Create **ethical review boards** to assess the potential harms and benefits of the AI system for the affected data subjects and the society at large. Such boards are recommended by both WP29 [2] and Council of Europe [9], in particular where the DPIA highlights a high impact of the use of AI on ethical and social values.
- Adopt **participatory approaches** [8] with obligatory involvement of the affected groups[12] and external stakeholders (e.g. research community, consumer protection and human rights organizations) to ensure that their points of views and concerns are taken on early in the design process and during the full AI cycle.

Training the AI. This is a crucial stage as AI 'learns' the rules and patterns by example based on troves of training data that help it improve. Hence, AI is only as effective as the quality of its training and the data used. Depending on what type of learning model is chosen (supervised, unsupervised or reinforced learning), the following prevention measures could be taken to mitigate the risk of bias:

- Respect **strict quality requirements for training datasets** (for supervised and unsupervised learning) to ensure the sampling is of sufficient quantity and quality for the larger dataset and complies with the following cumulative criteria:

  1. *Fit for Purpose:* The training data must be appropriate for the purpose of the AI application, which requires careful consideration if the input data is a good indicator for the output data as a correlation. Exclusion of irrelevant data will prevent the algorithms from identifying correlations that lack significance, or are coincidental [7]. While protected characteristics and sensitive data under Article 9 GDPR must be in general excluded (unless objectively justified where the model is designed

---

[12] See also article 35(9) GDPR which requires only facultative involvement of the affected data subjects.

to use it e.g., health apps), some researchers recommend to keep the protected attributes in the training dataset, so that the model becomes discrimination-aware [19]. Alternatively, differential privacy models could include randomness and encryption so that sensitive data are not considered in the learning process [22], but used only later for bias detection.

2. *Representative*: To avoid bias and ensure that the AI system reveals patterns that hold true for more than the particular sample under analysis, the training data must be balanced and sufficiently representative, thus covering poor and different economic status, people from different age groups, nationalities, sex, ethnic minorities, race, religion, cultures etc. [7]. All groups should have normally simple random sampling, i.e. every person in the total population should be covered in the application with an equal likelihood to be selected. If the training data is not sufficiently representative for the large population, other complementary data sources may need to be considered or new methods used to generate automatically prototypical representations in ways that guarantee statistical parity for any subgroup in the original data [26].

3. *Complete*: data must be complete and any parts that are missing for some people in the dataset identified. To assess data quality, information on missing data, and how it is being dealt with, is necessary as well [7].

4. *Accurate*: Controllers must ensure as much as possible accuracy of the data by considering the reliability of the data sources and carrying out prior checks for any errors, sources of noise, or redundancies in the dataset. The accuracy of the input data will define to a large extent also the accuracy of the AI predictions and the efficiency of the model [7].

5. *Up-to-date:* Timeliness of the training data is of crucial importance especially if AI is trained on data in real-time to predict behavior or occurrences. If historic data is used, it is advisable to assess if the time lapse would not lead to incorrect predictions, if the behavior has changed significantly meanwhile [7].

6. *Unbiased*: Training data must not represent in a biased way the different groups, e.g. choosing sampling where some minority groups' or women's performance are represented in a negative or stereotypical way [17] or data representing socially biased beliefs or behavior. Changing contexts when using different training datasets may also inject biases in the model [39]. A major source of risk is also the use of historic biased data (e.g. past admissions in schools or employment), for example, where racial minorities and women with credentials otherwise equal to other applicants have been consistently disfavored [15]. Controllers should de-bias the training data by balancing it and complementing it with data from other sources. Still, where more data are clearly not accessible or available, oversampling underrepresented communities may proactively compensate for some of the bias [7].

- Use **ML bias discovery methods** (e.g. regression) and **apply pre-processing strategies** to de-bias the training data and ensure its quality as per the criteria above by modifying the training input, the target variable or both [15]. When errors, gaps or other problems have been identified and the dataset pre-processed accordingly, final quality and representativeness should not vary in ways that correlate with class membership and should be sufficiently reliable. Another solution may be to generate synthetic training data to compensate for deficiencies in the existing training datasets or replace them altogether given the synthetic data are more privacy preserving and fair for individuals or subgroups [18].

- If necessary, introduce **in-processing approaches** to control the mapping from input to output data, thus safeguarding equality along the process and modifying the classification learning algorithm by integrating anti-discrimination criteria [15].
- Ensure strict quality control for **'labelling examples'** (in supervised learning only) where human bias and social prejudices are often induced through manually assigned class labels [15]. Human operators entrusted with this task must be properly trained for bias awareness and the risk of discrimination.
- Insert **randomness** in the training process to avoid overfitting the model and ensure generalization of the model predictions [16]. A related approach is to use a technique called regularization, which involves introducing new information to make trained models more generalizable [28].
- Create **AI models' cards and training datasheets** [29], including information on the dataset creation, composition, data collection process/methodologies and context, coverage, sampling procedures, preprocessing and distribution of the dataset, use and re-use of the data, maintenance. These datasheets and cards can highlight biases, assumptions and limitations of training datasets and the model and be provided to regulators and third parties in case of audits.

Testing and Validation. After the training and before the actual deployment, the model must be tested and validated to assess its *validity* and *reliability* in accordance with preliminary defined performance metrics and acceptable thresholds of errors and bias defined by the controller [4], taking into account the context, scale and the expected severity of the impacts.

- **Test the model for biases and errors with new (unseen) high quality test data** and test questions as "ground truth", thus checking the results of the AI system against the real world, where possible. To assess the risk of discrimination the new testing data should necessarily include also information about the protected characteristics, where the testing could be possibly done in cooperation with third trusted parties [4]. The accuracy of the predictions should be assessed for different groups in the population (ethic origin, race, sex, age etc.) and in different scenarios for false positives and false negatives by using different measurement techniques [14]. Bias can be detected through a number of statistical methods to show that groups or individuals are treated differently, for example the normalized difference of the mean group scores [19]. The datasets and AI outputs need to be analyzed in respect of the errors (error parity) and outcomes (outcome parity) [4] which must be preferably measured over time through temporal modeling [22]. If the analysis shows significant disproportionate impact across groups and/or significant accuracy disparity of predictions (false positives and false negatives), this shows bias that needs minimization of the difference in error rates between groups and/or bias correction strategies (see below).
- **Assess whether human or automated decision-making generates overall greater accuracy and minimize bias** [4]. This assessment should also play a key role in

deciding if the model should be deployed or envisaged as solely or partially automated that would require substantial and meaningful re-examination of the AI outcomes by a human reviewer before the output is applied to individuals.

- If bias is detected, **post-processing bias correction strategies** can be employed to modify the model to obey non-discrimination constraints, for instance, by changing the labels of some leaves in a decision tree, or removing selected rules from the set of discovered decision rules [15, 16].
- Allow a third **independent party to audit the AI model to** open the 'black box' and ensure it is working according to its programming [1]. The easiest way to detect discrimination is when full transparency and access is granted with the code and the training data made accessible to an external auditor or other stakeholders (e.g. research organizations, NGO). If these cannot be disclosed due to copyright, trade secrets, privacy concerns, methods to detect discrimination without having access to the training dataset need to be allowed (e.g. discrimination testing, sensitivity analysis [31, 33, 34]), or audit through a process that protects business secrets (e.g. by expert auditors).
- After successful testing and auditing, the model must be **validated** by a senior staff in compliance with the risk management framework, documenting also the chosen criteria for accuracy and computational fairness, the results from the testing and how the trade-offs between accuracy and fairness have been reconciled [4].

Application Stage (incl. continuous learning). Once the model has been successfully tested and validated, it can be applied to personal data of end users. If the AI system is obtained from a third party, the controller must first obtain contractual assurance that the model has been tested and validated, including by independent auditing for its accuracy and fairness and compliance 'by design' with the applicable data protection and equality law. The controller operating the system should also update the DPIA in light of the results of the testing, the final features of the AI model and the specifically envisaged data processing, using possibly also the product/service DPIA done by the designer/developer, if separate entities [1]. At the application stage, the following discrimination mitigation measure are suggested:

- Envisage a **trial period** when the AI system is intended to replace traditional decision-making systems and run concurrently the two systems for a period of time so as to investigate any significant difference in the type of decisions for protected groups between the two systems during the trial period [5].
- Ensure **transparency** of how the AI system works by providing data subjects with meaningful information about the logic involved, as well as the significance and the envisaged consequences of such processing. The description and assessment of the data used to train the algorithm is also arguably an essential component of the provision of meaningful information [7] given that without the history of the design and development of the model, it is not possible to truly understand how it works and the potential sources of bias. Such transparency of the automated decision-making process is obligatory not only under Articles 13 and 14 GDPR, but also under EU

anti-discrimination law[13]. While not obligatory, WP29 [1] has also recommended publication of a summary of the DPIA (excluding confidential information) as a measure to enhance controller's accountability and transparency.

- **Train human users/reviewers** how to use the AI system and what are the risks that may arise, including 'automation bias', so that they have a healthy level of skepticism about the accuracy and the limitations of the AI system and understand well how their own expertise is meant to compliment the AI system and use critically its outputs (correlation v. causation) [5, 38].

- **Use the AI system only for the purposes and the context for which it has been designed** and trained since changing them could lead to biased or wrong predictions [38]. Only personal data that are accurate, up to date and fit for purpose/minimized to what is necessary for the specific purpose of the AI system should be used as **input data** for the decision-making process [7]. Any necessary pre-processing should be carried out to remove irrelevant or incorrect data as well as protected characteristics or blatant proxies unless their use is explicitly justified under the EU equality law and the intended application of the AI system. Alternatively, sensitive characteristic (e.g. race or ethnic origin), if lawfully obtained on the basis of Article 9(2)a) or g) GDPR could be encrypted in order to be secured and excluded from the decision-making process, but used later for bias detection [30].

- In case of decision-making that is not solely automated, human reviewers should carry out **meaningful review** [2] and critically interpret the AI output data (correlation v. causation) to discover and, where necessary, correct any errors, unfair or discriminatory outcomes or arbitrarily generated profiles or automated decisions [5]. Arguably, such decisive influence of a human reviewer is indispensable in high-impact cases when *generalized predictive models* are applied, considering the high risk of stereotyping, statistical discrimination and 'discrimination by association' where individuals are no longer judged on the basis of their actual merits or behavior, but on the basis of characteristics or behavior they presumably share with members of their protected class group or newly formed statistically relevant group[14]. The reviewer should therefore take into account all relevant circumstances of the individual case, including by gathering additional information where necessary, and in line with the principle of accountability, remain accountable for the decision to accept, change or reject the AI outcome with clear internal escalating procedure [2, 5].

- Ensure **respect of data subjects' rights** (article 15-22 GDPR) by:

1. Providing them with **access** to their profiles, including the AI input and output data with an opportunity to **correct** them before decisions are taken so as to minimize the risks of errors and bias, including by providing any relevant additional information.
2. For solely automated decisions with legal and similarly significant effects, controllers must also arguably provide data subjects with understandable **explanations** about the decisions reached e.g., through counterfactual [32] or other appropriate types of 'local' explanations such as contrastive, reasoning etc. While not explicitly required

---

[13] CJEU, Case 109/88, *Danfoss*, EU:C:1989:383 para. 16.

[14] See in this sense also R. Binns [24] who argues that the 'human-in-the-loop' may be able to serve the aim of individual justice".

by art. 22 GDPR, such explanations are arguably necessary for compliance with the principles of accountability, transparency and fairness and essential to enable the affected data subjects to exercise their right to challenge the solely automated decision [2, 5].

3. Establish internal procedures to enable data subjects to request **human intervention and appeal solely automated individual decisions** [2, 5]. When the decision is contested as discriminatory, a human reviewer should thoroughly re-examine the individual case in the context of all relevant factors and check for unjustified direct or indirect discrimination which can result also from stereotyping or 'discrimination by association'. In this respect, a major challenge is that protected characteristics are often not observed in the input/output data, but this could be possibly compensated with sensitive analysis or new techniques which can compute exactly the sharpest possible bounds on disparity that could be learned from the data [18]. If a third party has certified the controller for algorithmic bias, this party could also possibly act as an external reviewer to carry out an independent investigation and review the decision, if challenged on grounds of discrimination.

4. Provide **remedy** to all data subjects already affected by the detected discrimination by granting them the same advantages as those enjoyed by persons within the favoured comparable category[15].

- If unjustified discriminatory effects are detected, the controller must update the DPIA accordingly as "high risk" and consider **post-processing bias correction measures**, which would amount to positive discrimination whereby the raw scores that exhibit disproportionate discriminatory impact can be calibrated into fairer scores by a parameter (θ) that allows continuous variation between a stronger focus on individual (equality) or group fairness (impact) [14]. Still, a careful proportionality assessment must ensure decision-maker's utility is maximized under the fairness constraints [14] and disadvantaged groups are not given absolute and unconditional priority at the expense of equal treatment, as required by case-law[16]. This will require **obligatory review by a human operator** of the different AI recommendations as proposed positive correction measure (the re-ranking) in view of all relevant facts of the case, given that this context-specific assessment cannot be fully automated [14].

- In an active learning environment, the output of algorithmic decision-making and the response to it often become part of the basis of future decisions. This means that **feedback loops need to be carefully assessed** to identify whether it is necessary to 'repair' the algorithms to avoid discrimination and, ultimately, to produce more accurate and representative results, for example by appropriately filtering the inputs fed to the system [34] or complementing them with additional more representative information. Biases injected into the AI model through popularity bias (e.g., due to presentation or ranking) and discriminatory users' behavior, beliefs or content should be also monitored and addressed [20].

- AI systems must be subject to **continuous monitoring and regularly tested and audited** for bias and re-calibrated for accuracy due to changing populations and

---

[15] CJEU, C–406/15 *Milkova*, EU:C:2017:198, para. 66.
[16] CJEU, Case C–450/93, *Kalanke*, EU:C:1995:322, para. 22.

subpopulations, new dynamics and impacts on affected groups [4]. In principle, the higher the impact on data subjects, the more frequently the AI system must be tested and audited [2]. This requires also review of the accuracy measures and change policy procedures to mitigate the risk of 'concept drift' so as to measure the estimated distance between model's classification errors over time [35]. Monitoring is also necessary to assess the effectiveness of the mitigation measures at place and their regular update. At least when there is a change of the risks represented by the processing, the DPIA must be reviewed and updated, thus highlighting the 'living' and systematic nature of this assessment all along the full AI cycle [1].

3.4 Consultation of the DPIA

In carrying out the DPIA, the controller must consult various stakeholders about the intended processing, the ensuing risks and the envisaged mitigation measures. While presented as a final step in the methodology, this consultation must be carried out along the different pre-deployment phases of the AI cycle and certainly before starting the processing.

First, Article 35(2) obliges the controller to seek the advice of the Data Protection Officer (DPO), where designated, who is also responsible for monitoring the performance of the DPIA and auditing the data processing operations for their compliance with the internal policies and the GDPR.

Where appropriate, the controller must also seek the views of the affected data subjects or their representatives (e.g. through a generic study [5]). If the data controller's final decision differs from their views, its reasons for going ahead or not should be documented. The controller should also document its justification for not seeking the views of data subjects, if not appropriate (e.g. due to confidentiality of companies' business plans, or disproportionate implications) [5].

Under Article 36 GDPR, the controller must also consult the DPA if the identified high risk of discrimination is not objectively justified and/or cannot be sufficiently minimized despite the bias mitigating measures. While the GDPR does not envisage any mechanisms for cooperation with the equality bodies enforcing the EU anti-discrimination law, this paper suggests that the DPA should cooperate with them in the assessment of the risks of discrimination and possibly in carrying out joint audits of potentially discriminating AI systems.

4   Conclusion

This paper has argued that GDPR can and should play an instrumental role in safe-guarding the fundamental rights to non-discrimination and equality. In this respect, the new controller's obligations for data protection 'by design' and Data Protection Impact Assessment have been examined as new powerful tools to prevent ex ante algorithmic discrimination, thus establishing a legal standard for 'duty of care' and holding the controller accountable to avoid discrimination at the outset when designing and using AI systems. In particular, the paper has proposed a methodological framework for assessing the risks of automated data processing to the right to non-discrimination, providing controllers with an indicative guidance about the main sources of risks and the potential measures to prevent and mitigate algorithmic discrimination.

While the coordinated approach in enforcing the GDPR and the EU equality law can bring significant benefits, it must be also recognized that there are still gaps in both frameworks. For example, individuals are not protected from the new and subtle forms of unfair and discriminatory treatment that AI systems enable, in particular when they differentiate on the basis of newly invented classes or groups different from the historically protected characteristics [17, 36, 40], considering the CJEU's rejection to forge new 'statuses' under Article 21 of the Charter despite this provision suggests only an open list of protected grounds[17]. Furthermore, the inherent discriminating nature of machine learning often generates groups of individuals who are no longer bound by explicit ties such as salient traits [17, 39, 40], so if no significant discriminatory impact can be proven on already protected groups, these newly formed grounds for differentiation will often escape the legal notion of 'status' if too narrowly interpreted[18]. The CJEU has also rejected compound forms of discrimination such as multiple and intersectional discrimination whereby several grounds co-exist or interact with each other in a way that produce specific types of discrimination that remain currently unprotected under EU law[19], while AI systems such as facial recognition may treat significantly adversely certain sub-groups, e.g. young black women [41].

Similarly, the protection under the GDPR is also incomplete given that many auto-mated processing operations would escape its scope when no individual is identified or singled out, but nonetheless sensitive information can be inferred and group profiles created that can still drive discriminatory actions [36, 39]. Albeit a useful tool with sig-nificant potential, the DPIA also suffers from a number of shortcomings such as lack of consistent methodology [10], disputable scope (e.g. types of risks and whether ethical impacts are also to be covered) [12], lack of publicity and built-in external stakeholder review, only facultative consultation of data subjects and no appeal procedure for public review [13].

All these gaps open the thorny policy debate, if there should be a specific regulatory framework for algorithmic fairness and accountability to effectively protect the rights to data protection and non-discrimination as well as other fundamental rights and values (e.g. rule of law, justice, democracy, equality). Considering that the newly formed Euro-pean Commission has committed to come up with such a proposal to respond to these challenges [42], the DPIA could be possibly upgraded into a fully-fledged algorithmic

---

[17] E.g. C-122/15, FOA (Kaltoft), EU:C:2016:391; C-354/13, EU:C:2014:2463; Betriu Montull, C-5/12, EU:C:2013:571.

[18] 'Status' has been defined by the ECtHR as *"identifiable, objective or personal characteristic by which persons or groups are distinguishable from one another"*, see Clift v The UK App no 7205/07 (ECtHR, 13 July 2010 para 55. While the ECtHR has ruled that the characteristic should not be personal in the sense that it must be "inherent and innate', in its past case-law it has excluded objective factors (e.g. location) not linked to a personal characteristic or personal choice (e.g. membership in trade union) as a potential protected 'status' under Article 14 ECHR, see for example *Magee v the United Kingdom* App no. 28135/95 (ECtHR, 20 June 2000) para 50. *Big Brother Watch and Others v The United Kingdom* App nos 58170/13, 62322/14 and 24960/15 (ECtHR 13 September 2018) para 516–518.

[19] CJEU, C-443/15, David L. Parris v. Trinity College Dublin and Others, 24 November 2016.

impact assessment by remedying the shortcomings, identified above, and safeguarding more effectively group privacy, substantive justice and the ethical values and interests of the society at large.

References

1. Article 29 Data Protection Working Party: Guidelines on Data Protection Impact Assessment (DPIA) and determining whether processing is "likely to result in a high risk" for the purposes of Regulation 2016/679, 4 October 2017, 17/EN WP 248 (2017)
2. Article 29 Data Protection Working Party: Guidelines on Automated Individual Decision-Making and Profiling for the Purposes of Regulation 2016/679, 17/EN WP 251, 03 October 2017
3. European Data Protection Board: Draft Guidelines 4/2019 on Article 25 Data Protection by Design and by Default, adopted on 13 November 2019
4. UK Information Commissioner's Office: Human Bias and Discrimination in AI systems, 25 June 2019. https://ai-auditingframework.blogspot.com/2019/06/human-bias-and-dis crimination-in-ai.html
5. UK Information Commissioner's Office: Automated Decision Making: The Role of Meaningful Human Reviews, 12 April 2019. https://ai-auditingframework.blogspot.com/2019/04/automated-decision-making-role-of.html
6. Norwegian Data Protection Authority: Artificial Intelligence and Privacy (2018)
7. EU Fundamental Rights Agency: Data Quality and Artificial Intelligence – Mitigating Bias and Error to Protect Fundamental Rights (2019)
8. High-Level Expert Group on AI established by the European Commission: Ethics Guidelines For Trustworthy Artificial Intelligence, 8 April 2019
9. Consultative Committee of the Convention for the Protection of Individuals with Regards to Automatic Processing of Personal Data (T-PD): Guidelines on the protection of individuals with regard to the processing of personal data in a world of Big Data, Strasbourg (2017). T-PD(2017)01
10. Kloza, D., Van Dijk, N., Casiraghi, S., Vazquez Maymir, S., Roda, S., Tanas, A. & Konstantinou, I. Towards a method for data protection impact assessment: Making sense of GDPR requirements, 5 Nov 2019, d.pia.lab Policy Brief, January 2019
11. Gellert, R.: We have always managed risks in data protection law. Understanding the similarities and differences between the rights-based and the risk-based approaches to data protection. Eur. Data Protect. Law Rev. 2(4), 481–492 (2016)
12. Mantelero, A: AI and Big data: a blueprint for a human rights, social and ethical impact assessment. Comput. Law Secur. Rev. 34(4), 754–772 (2018)
13. Kaminski, M.E., Malgieri, G.: Algorithmic Impact Assessments under the GDPR: Producing Multi-layered Explanations. University of Colorado Law Legal Studies Research Paper No. 19-28 (2019)
14. Hacker, P.: Teaching fairness to artificial intelligence: existing and novel strategies against algorithmic discrimination under EU law. Common Market Law Rev. 55, 1143–1186 (2018)
15. Barocas, S., Selbst, A.: Big data's disparate impact. Calif. Law Rev. 104, 671–732; 694–714 (2016)
16. Kroll, J.A., et al.: Accountable algorithms. Univ. Pennsylvania Law Rev. 165, 633 (2016)

17. Zarsky, T.: Understanding discrimination in the scored society. Washington Law Rev. **89**(4) (2014). SSRN: https://ssrn.com/abstract=2550248
18. Castelluccia, C., Le Métayer, D.: Understanding algorithmic decision-making: opportunities and challenges'. European Parliamentary Research Service, Scientific Foresight Unit (STOA) PE 624.261 (2019)
19. Žliobaitė, I.: Measuring discrimination in algorithmic decision making. In: 31 Data Mining & Knowledge Discovery, pp. 1060–1089 (2017)
20. Mehrabi, N., et al.: A Survey on Bias and Fairness in Machine Learning (2019)
21. Veale, E., Binns, R.: Fairer machine learning in the real world: mitigating discrimination without collecting sensitive data. Big Data Soc. **4**(2), 1–17 (2017)
22. Liu, L., Dean, S., Rolf, E., Simchowitz, M., Hardt, M.: Delayed impact of fair machine learning. In: Proceedings of the 35th International Conference on Machine Learning (2018)
23. Davis, J.: Design methods for ethical persuasive computing. In: 2009 Proceedings of the 4th International Conference on Persuasive Technology, p. 6. ACM (2009)
24. Binns, R.: On the apparent conflict between individual and group fairness. In: Proceedings of the Conference on Fairness, Accountability, and Transparency. ACM (2020)
25. Mittelstadt, B., Russell, C., Wachter, S.: Explaining explanations in AI. In: Proceedings of FAT* 2019: Conference on Fairness, Accountability, and Transparency (FAT* 2019) (2019). https://doi.org/10.1145/3287560.3287574. ISBN 978-1-4503-6125-5
26. Zemel, R., et al.: Learning fair representations. In: Proceedings of the 30th International Conference on Machine Learning, vol. 28, p. 325 (2013)
27. Kamiran, F., Calders, T.: Data preprocessing techniques for classification without discrimination. Knowl. Inf. Syst. **33**(1), 1–33 (2011)
28. Kamishima, T., et al.: Fairness-aware learning through regularization approach. In: Proceedings of the 3rd IEEE International Workshop on Privacy Aspects of Data Mining, p. 643 (2011)
29. Gebru, T., et al: Datasheets for Datasets (2018). arXiv:1803.09010 [cs.DB]
30. Kilbertus, N., Gascón, A., Kusner, M.J., Veale, M., Gummadi, K.P., Weller, A.: Blind justice: fairness with encrypted sensitive attributes. In: Proceedings of the 35th International Conference on Machine Learning, PMLR **80**, 2630–2639 (2018)
31. Sandvig, C., et al.: Auditing algorithms: research methods for detecting discrimination on internet platforms. Paper presented to "Data and Discrimination: Converting Critical Concerns into Productive Inquiry", Seattle, WA, USA, 22 May 2014
32. Wachter, S., Mittelstadt, B., Russell, C.: Counterfactual explanations without opening the black box: automated decisions and the GDPR. Harvard J. Law Technol. **31**(2) (2017)
33. Kallus, N., Mao, X., Zhou, A.: Assessing Algorithmic Fairness with Unobserved Protected Class Using Data Combination, 1 June 2019. https://arxiv.org/abs/1906.00285
34. Ensign, D., Friedler, S.A., Neville, S., Scheidegger, C., Venkatasubramanian, S.: Runaway feedback loops in predictive policing. In: Conference on Fairness, Accountability, and Transparency. Proceedings of Machine Learning Research **81,** 1–12 (2018)
35. Žliobaitė, I.: Learning under concept drift: an overview (2010)
36. Wachter, S.: Affinity profiling and discrimination by association in online behavioural advertising. Berkeley Technol. Law J. **35**(2) (forthcoming, 2020)
37. British Institute Standard 8611: Robots and robotic devices. Guide to the ethical design and application of robots and robotic systems (2016)
38. Institute of Electrical and Electronics Engineers: Standards P7003 - Algorithmic Bias Considerations (under development). https://standards.ieee.org/project/7003.html
39. Taylor, L., Floridi, L., van der Sloot, B.: Group Privacy: New Challenges of Data Technologies. Springer International Publishing, Cham (2019)

40. Naudts, L.: How machine learning generates unfair inequalities and how data protection instruments may help in mitigating them. In: Leenes, R., van Brakel, R., Gutwirth, S., De Hert, P. (eds.) Data Protection and Privacy: The Internet of Bodies (CPDP 2019) (2019)
41. Klare, B.F., Burge, M.J., Klontz, J.C., Bruegge, R.W., Jain, A.K.: Face recognition performance: role of demographic information. IEEE Trans. Inf. Forensics Secur. **7**(6), 1789–1801 (2012)
42. European Commission: White Paper On Artificial Intelligence - A European approach to excellence and trust COM, 65 final (2020)

Processing Operations 'Likely to Result in a High Risk to the Rights and Freedoms of Natural Persons'
Lessons to Be Learned from National Authorities' DPIA 'Blacklists'

Katerina Demetzou[(✉)]

Radboud Business Law Institute, Radboud University, Nijmegen, The Netherlands
K.Demetzou@cs.ru.nl

Abstract. The present paper presents five concepts that rest in the core of the reasoning of the European and national regulators behind the element of 'high risk' under the legal obligation to perform Data Protection Impact Assessments (Article 35 GDPR). These five concepts have been extracted from the national 'blacklists' published by 15 Data Protection Authorities and are the following: control, reasonable expectations, (negative) impact on rights and interests, scaling-up and identifiability. In cases where control over one's personal data is compromised or not guaranteed, where the reasonable expectations of the data subject over the processing of their personal data are not met, where processing operations have a negative impact on rights, freedoms, interests and the daily life activities of natural persons, where the processing scales-up and becomes broader and/or deeper and where the level of identifiability is high, then it is likely that a high risk to the rights and freedoms of natural persons is raised.

Keywords: High risk · DPIA · Control · Reasonable expectations · Identifiability · Nature · Scope · Context · Purpose

1 Introduction

Article 35 of the GDPR introduces a novel legal obligation, the performance of Data Protection Impact Assessments (DPIA) by the data controller in cases where 'a type of processing [...] is likely to result in a high risk to the rights and freedoms of natural persons'. It has been argued[1] that *risk* is a concept that comes with novelties in the legal field of data protection; these novelties mainly refer to the methodological approach[2] of risk and more specifically to the methodological approach of its two constitutive

---

[1] Van Dijk, N., Gellert, R., and Rommetveit, K. 'A Risk to a Right: Beyond Data Protection Impact Assessments' (2016) Volume 32, Issue 2, Computer Law & Security Review, 286–306.

[2] Gellert, R., 'Understanding the notion of risk in the General Data Protection Regulation (2018) Volume 34, Issue 2, Computer Law and Security Review, 2 *'ultimately the way risk is defined in the GDPR is somewhat irrelevant: what matters most is the methodology used and the type of risk at work therein'*. See also, Data Protection Commission, Guidance Note: Guide to Data Protection Impact Assessments (DPIAs), October 2019, 17 *'The key point is to ensure that a methodological*

© Springer Nature Switzerland AG 2020
L. Antunes et al. (Eds.): APF 2020, LNCS 12121, pp. 25–42, 2020.
https://doi.org/10.1007/978-3-030-55196-4_2

elements, i.e. likelihood and severity. Data controllers are legally obliged to identify, assess and mitigate risks to the rights and freedoms of natural persons following an 'objective' assessment.[3]

A processing operation can be legally characterised in various ways, for example, with regard to its legitimacy, lawfulness, necessity, proportionality, riskiness etc. The questions to be asked are, respectively, 'is the processing operation legitimate?', 'is it lawful?', 'is it necessary?', 'is it proportionate?', 'is it likely to result in a high risk to the rights and freedoms?'. In order to give an answer to each of these questions we need to turn to requirements that have been provided for by the legislature and further developed in case-law. To give an example, when examining the 'proportionality' of processing operations, there are specific steps that need to be taken (i.e. specific methodology), the same goes for 'lawfulness' (the legislature enumerates in Article 6 GDPR the lawful grounds for personal data processing). When the question 'is it likely that the processing operations will result in a high risk to the rights and freedoms of natural persons?' is asked, what are the criteria to be taken into account?

The answer is found in the wording of the GDPR. Article 35(1) reads that the criteria of 'nature, scope, context and purposes of the processing' are the ones that should be taken into account to determine whether it is likely that a processing operation results in a high risk to the rights and freedoms of natural persons. The same criteria are also found in Recitals and more specifically in Recital 76 which urges that the likelihood and severity of the risk to the rights and freedoms should be determined by reference to the nature, scope, context and purposes of the processing[4] as well as in Recital 90 which equally highlights that the assessment of the particular likelihood and severity of the high risk requires 'taking into account the nature, scope, context and purposes of the processing and the sources of the risk'. Last but not least, Recital 89 explains that the DPIA is an effective procedure because it focuses 'on those types of processing operations which are likely to result in a high risk to the rights and freedoms of natural persons by virtue of their nature, scope context and purposes'.

These four elements, 'nature, scope, context and purposes' appear in every processing operation, in that every operation is of a specific nature, has a certain scope, is taking place within a context and attains certain purposes. Understanding the content of the four elements is crucial. The reason is that, according to the legislature, on the basis of these four criteria (the quartet) we shall objectively assess the *riskiness* of a processing operation. It goes without saying that not every purpose of a processing operation is likely to raise high risk(s). To give an example, the use of tracking cookies for the purpose of targeted advertising could raise high risks in comparison to processing of the names

---

approach to identifying the data protection risks to the rights or freedoms of data subjects is adopted, and that records are kept of this process and of all the risks identified'.. https://www.dataprotection.ie/en/guidance-landing/guide-data-protection-impact-assessments, Accessed 12 Mar 2020.

[3] Recital 76 GDPR.

[4] These criteria are also mentioned and elaborated by the Norwegian Data Protection Authority (Datatilsynet), https://www.datatilsynet.no/rettigheter-og-plikter/virksomhetens-plikter/vurdere-personvernkonsekvenser/vurdering-av-personvernkonsekvenser/risikovurdering/, last accessed 2020/03/12.

of people who attended a conference with the purpose of sending them certifications of attendance. The same goes for the scope of processing operations; large scale processing taking place in an airport is likely to present higher risks than a smaller scale processing taking place in a bookshop through CCTV.

The scalability in risks identified in different processing operations relates to certain conditions that render certain types of processing operations more likely to raise high risks to the rights and freedoms than others. The legislature, the WP29[5] (now the EDPB) as well as the national data protection authorities (DPAs) have enumerated such conditions in the provisions of the GDPR, in the relevant guidelines and in the published national blacklists respectively. It is of major importance to understand what these conditions are for two reasons; first of all, having a comprehensive overview of the conditions facilitates the 'high level screening test'[6] of identifying whether a type of processing operation is 'likely to raise a high risk', and thus the legal obligation to perform a DPIA[7] is triggered. Secondly, this overview will help us reach valuable conclusions as to the reasoning of the regulators with regard to the concept of (high) risk in the GDPR. The research question that this paper aims to answer is the following:

'What are the conditions that qualify types of processing operations as "likely to raise a high risk to the rights and freedoms of natural persons" according to the European and national regulators? What conclusions can we draw from these conditions as to the reasoning of the regulators in qualifying types of processing operations as "likely to result in a high risk"?

To answer the research question, this paper is structured as follows. In Subsects. 1.1 and 1.2, the methodology as well as the relevance of answering the research question are explained. Section 2 will look into the criteria, the sub-criteria and the conditions for the high level screening test which have been extracted from the WP29/EDPB Guidelines and the DPAs' national blacklists. Section 3 will present the five basic concepts which constitute the core of the regulators' reasoning with regard to the concept of 'high risk' in data protection. Lastly, the Conclusion (Sect. 4) will briefly present the reasoning followed in the paper and will give an answer to the research question.

---

[5] The WP29 (Article 29 Working Party) was an advisory body which has now been replaced by the EDPB (European Data Protection Board). The EDPB is composed of representatives of the national supervisory authorities, and the European Data Protection Supervisor (EDPS). It is an independent EU body, which contributes to the consistent application of data protection rules throughout the European Union, and promotes cooperation between the EU's supervisory authorities. (https://edpb.europa.eu/about-edpb/ about-edpb_en).

[6] According to the ICO, this is a test that indicates processing operations which 'present a reasonable chance [they] may be high risk and so a DPIA is required to assess the level of risk in more detail'. See Information Commissioner's Office, 'When do we need to do a DPIA?', https://ico.org.uk/for-organisations/guide-to-data-protection/guide-to-the-general-data-protection-regulation-gdpr/data-protection-impact-assessments-dpias/when-do-we-need-to-do-a-dpia/, last accessed 2020/03/12.

[7] DPIA stands for Data Protection Impact Assessment.

1.1 Methodology

The end-goal of the paper is to extract conclusions as to the reasoning of the regulators behind characterizing types of processing operations as 'likely to result in a high risk'. To achieve that, Guidelines published by the WP29 and now endorsed by the EDPB, as well as the blacklists developed by 15 national DPAs have been consulted. In these documents the regulators (both the European and the national) describe the conditions which, when met, indicate that 'high risk' is likely to be raised and thus a DPIA is required.

In order to extract conclusions from these documents, the paper follows a deductive approach. The published blacklists provide many examples of types of processing operations as well as various requirements, many of which appear multiple times in these 15 documents. This is not unexpected given that the basis upon which the DPAs have built their reasoning is common, i.e. the guidelines adopted by the WP29.[8] It is also something that indicates the importance of certain requirements; the fact that, for example, processing of biometric data that leads to identification of natural persons has been included in multiple blacklists shows that the (high) level of identifiability (which is the case for biometric data) is a requirement that occupies an important position in the regulators' reasoning. However, for the aim of this paper, all repetitions shall be eliminated[9] and same or similar conditions of processing shall be grouped under an–as much as possible- inclusive and clear structure.

The grouping of the identified conditions requires certain labels under which they will fit. As explained in the Introduction, the quartet of 'nature, scope, context and purpose' constitutes the most appropriate framework for this grouping for the following reason; the legislature's wording explicitly mentions that these are the criteria to be taken into account in order to assess the likelihood of a high risk appearing.

The first step is therefore to examine the meaning of each one of these criteria so that the types of processing operations of the national blacklists are assigned under the most relevant criterion (for example, large scale processing operations to be grouped under the criterion of 'scope'). However, one important limitation is the lack of definitions for the notions of 'nature, scope, context' in the context of data protection. This does not apply for the criterion of 'purpose' which is a notion that has been extensively dealt with (important example being the WP29 Opinion on purpose limitation).[10] On the contrary, there is no straightforward answer to the questions 'what are the elements of a processing operation that need to be examined in order to characterize the nature/the scope/the

---

[8] Article 29 Data Protection Working Party 'Guidelines on Data Protection Impact Assessment (DPIA) and Determining Whether Processing Is "Likely to Result in a High Risk" for the Purposes of Regulation 2016/679' WP 248 rev 0.1, 4 April 2017.

[9] The elimination of repetitions does not in any way mean that this repetition has not been taken into consideration as to the importance of certain criteria. It is performed within the deductive approach.

[10] Article 29 Data Protection Working Party 'Opinion 03/2013 on purpose limitation' WP 203, Adopted on 2 April 2013.

context of the specific processing?'. Therefore, first and foremost, a concrete meaning has to be given to 'nature, scope, context'. For that, 25 interpretative guidelines, published by the WP29 which have now been endorsed by the EDPB, have been consulted. For reasons of consistency of this research, the criterion of 'purpose' has also been examined by looking into the same 25 interpretative guidelines.

After having identified what should be examined[11] when looking at the nature, the scope, the context and the purposes of processing operations, the next step is to group the conditions that render certain types of processing operations found in the published blacklists of 15 DPAs as likely to raise a high risk. The results of this grouping are presented in a Table.[12]

This Table shall in no way be considered an inclusive presentation of all types of processing operations which have been given a red flag by national DPAs. The aim is not to present an all-encompassing overview of operations likely to present a high risk, inter alia, because the developed lists are not exhaustive and could (although not substantially) change over time. They serve as a firm starting point in order to reach the final goal, meaning to draw broader conclusions as to the reasoning of the legislature behind the concept of high risk in the GDPR. Based on the Table of Subsect. 2.2, valuable conclusions can be drawn as to the pattern followed when assessing risks to the rights and freedoms.[13] These conclusions will bring us one step closer to understanding the meaning of *risk* under the GDPR.

1.2 Relevance

The research presented in this paper is relevant in two ways. First of all, the Table that offers an overview of the criteria and the sub-criteria adds to the existing literature in the sense that it provides for a consistent understanding of 'nature, scope, context, purpose' – four criteria of major importance in the data protection legal framework in general. A correct identification of the nature, the scope, the context and the purposes allows us to assess, not only the level of risk, but also other legal qualities of data processing operations such as lawfulness, legitimacy, proportionality etc. This overview may, therefore, serve as a basis upon which further work can be done. The structure and categorization presented in the Table of Subsect. 2.2, could also potentially prove useful to practitioners when performing DPIAs.

The second point of relevance has to do with the attempt to extract basic aspects in the reasoning of the regulators when qualifying certain types of processing operations as likely to result in a high risk to the rights and freedoms. The fact that this extraction is done on the basis of examples put forward both by the European (EDPB) and the national

---

[11] This paper calls them 'Sub-criterion/a'. They are presented in the second column of the Table in the form of questions/bullet points.

[12] This Table is the answer to the first part of the research question of this paper *'What are the conditions that qualify types of processing operations as "likely to raise high risks to the rights and freedoms of natural persons" according to the European and national regulators? [...]'.*

[13] The conclusions constitute the answer to the second part of the research question of this paper *'[...] What conclusions can we draw from these conditions as to the reasoning of the regulators in qualifying types of processing operations as "likely to result in a high risk?".*

regulators (DPAs) satisfies (at least partly) the quest for objectivity when assessing risks in data protection.[14] The added value of drawing broader conclusions is that it allows us to draft away from the case by case approach (mainly through examples of processing operations) which has been adopted by the legislature. We will be able to apply the same reasoning and reach results that guarantee equal level of protection of personal data to any type of processing operation that could appear in the future and has not (perhaps not yet) been captured by the legislature.

2   Overview of Criteria, Sub-criteria and Conditions for High Level Screening Test

This Section of the paper will closely examine the four criteria (or as elsewhere called 'conditions of implementation of data processing')[15] that the legislature has put forward for identifying and assessing risks to the rights and freedoms when data processing operations take place. This exercise will help the reader gain a more consistent understanding of the meaning of these four criteria. With regard to its structure, Sect. 2 is divided in two parts. The first part (2.1) is a brief textual overview of the criteria, the sub-criteria identified in the 25 interpretative documents by the WP29 and the conditions that qualify types of processing operations as likely to raise a high risk. The second part (2.2) is their visual presentation in a Table which is the result of the deductive approach taken towards the guidelines published by the WP29 (now EDPB) and the blacklists of the national DPAs.

2.1   Textual Overview

Nature of Processing
When talking about the 'nature' of processing operations one should look into the constitutive elements of the specific processing operation. According to the Norwegian DPA, '[t]o say something about the nature of data processing, the inherent characteristics of the processing must be described'.[16] Inherent characteristics, in the sense that without them such an operation would not have the meaning of a processing operation under the GDPR.[17] The nature of the processing operation is, thus, directly linked to the nature of the following (constitutive) elements: personal data, data subject, operation. These are

---

[14] According to Recital 76 GDPR '[...] Risk should be evaluated on the basis of an objective assessment'.

[15] Data Protection Commission (n 2), 11.

[16] Norwegian Data Protection Authority (Datatilsynet), https://www.datatilsynet.no/rettigheter-og-plikter/virksomhetens-plikter/vurdere-personvernkonsekvenser/vurdering-av-personver nkonsekvenser/nar-er-risiko-hoy/, last accessed 2020/03/12.

[17] Article 4 (2) GDPR, 'processing' means any operation or set of operations which is performed on personal data or on sets of personal data, whether or not by automated means, such as collection, recording, organisation, structuring, storage, adaptation or alteration, retrieval, consultation, use, disclosure by transmission, dissemination or otherwise making available, alignment or combination, restriction, erasure or destruction;'.

the elements that exist in every processing operation in order to fall under the material scope of the GDPR.[18]

Two clarifications need to be made at this point. With regard to 'data subject', it is not explicitly mentioned as a constitutive element of a processing operation that falls under the material scope of the GDPR. It is, however, constitutive of 'personal data'. According to Article 4(1) GDPR, 'personal data means any information relating to an identified or identifiable natural person ('data subject')'. It is therefore inconceivable to talk about personal data without talking about data subjects. This is the reason why 'data subject' is examined as part of the 'nature' of processing operations. The second point of clarification has to do with 'operation'. Although 'operation' is indeed a constitutive element of processing operations, I choose to attach it to the criterion of 'context'. The reason is that, as it will become clear later on, 'context' involves many sub-criteria that refer directly to the 'operation' (for example, the technology used for the processing operation). For reasons of inclusiveness and in order to avoid dividing 'operation' between two criteria (i.e. nature and context), 'operation' will be found under the criterion of 'context'. Thus, in order to characterize the nature of a processing operation, we need to look into two sub-criteria, the **nature of the personal data processed** and the **nature of the data subjects involved**. The analysis of the 25 WP29 interpretative guidelines offers more specific questions that should be raised for the two sub-criteria which are presented in the Table.

Scope of Processing
Coming to the criterion of 'scope' of processing operations, one should think of how broad or narrow the processing is, meaning the size, the width, the extent, the scale of the operations. The sub-criteria that will be hereby enumerated have been drawn out of various examples found in the WP29 guidelines. In order to characterize the scope of a processing operation, one has to look into the **number of actors** involved (not only data subjects but also data controllers, data processors, joint controllers, third parties etc.), the **volume and range of information** processed and the **extent (temporal and geographical)** of the processing. The most frequently used concept that relates to the 'scope' is the processing on 'large scale'. While the GDPR does not provide a definition of 'large scale'[19], the EDPB recommends[20] that specific factors be taken into account

---

[18] According to Article 2 (1) GDPR, 'This Regulation applies to the processing of personal data [...]'.

[19] Only Recital 91 provides some guidance.

[20] See for example, EDPB Opinion 7/2018 on the draft list of the competent supervisory authority of Greece regarding the processing operations subject to the requirement of a data protection impact assessment (Art. 35.4 GDPR), adopted on 25th September 2018, 7.

in deciding whether a processing is done on a large scale. More specifically the factors are:

a. The number of data subjects concerned, either as a specific number or as a proportion of the relevant population;
b. the volume of data and/or the range of different data items being processed;
c. the duration, or permanence, of the data processing activity;
d. the geographical extent of the processing activity.[21]

Context of Processing
The criterion of 'context' has proven to be the most inclusive criterion of all, in the sense that all sub-criteria could conceptually fit under 'context'. For categorization purposes, the sub-criteria that have been added are, first of all, those that do not directly fit under any other criterion and secondly those that have been explicitly mentioned by the European regulator in its guidelines. To give an example, the WP29 talks about the 'context of smart devices'[22], 'the context of cookies and related technologies'[23], 'the context of RFID applications'.[24] Based on the wording, the sub-criterion of 'technology' has been attached to 'context'. Having this in mind, in order to characterize the context of a processing operation, one has to look into multiple sub-criteria, namely: the **technique/technology** used for the processing, the **environment** within which the processing takes place, and the **relationship between the data controller and the data subject.** These sub-criteria were extracted from the WP29 guidelines. However, when looking into the blacklists published by the national DPAs, two additional sub-criteria can be extracted that are highly relevant when talking about the context of processing operations. These are the **origin/source of personal data** processed and the **security measures** adopted.

Purpose of Processing
The last criterion is 'purpose' which, put simply, is the *why* of the processing. It is the 'specific reason why the data are processed: the aim or intention of the data processing'[25] in other words 'what the personal data is intended to be used for'.[26] Before proceeding to enumerating the identified sub-criteria, it is important to make two terminological

---

[21] WP29 (n 8) and Article 29 Data Protection Working Party 'Guidelines on Data Protection Officer' 16/EN WP243.

[22] Article 29 Data Protection Working Party 'Opinion 02/2013 on apps on smart devices', 13/EN WP202, 14.

[23] Article 29 Data Protection Working Party 'Opinion 04/2012 on Cookie Consent Exemption', 12/EN WP194, 2.

[24] Article 29 Data Protection Working Party 'Opinion 5/2010 on the Industry Proposal for a Privacy and Data Protection Impact Assessment Framework for RFID Applications' 10/EN WP 175, 8.

[25] Article 29 Data Protection Working Party 'Opinion 06/2014 on the notion of legitimate interests of the data controller under Article 7 of Directive 95/46/EC', 14/EN WP217, 24.

[26] Norwegian DPA (n 16), Vurdering av personvernkonsekvenser (DPIA) *'For å ta stilling til graden av risiko, er det relevant å vektlegge hva personopplysningene, etter planen, skal brukes til'* https://www.datatilsynet.no/rettigheter-og-plikter/virksomhetens-plikter/vurdere-personvernkonsekvenser/vurdering-av-personvernkonsekvenser/nar-er-risiko-hoy/.

clarifications. Firstly, the purpose (or as elsewhere called the 'general objective')[27] is different from the 'interest'[28] which is a concept closely related to, but distinct from 'purpose'. It is the broader stake that a controller may have in the processing, or the benefit that the controller derives - or that society might derive - from the processing.[29] Secondly, the purpose should also be distinguished from the 'result/consequence' of processing. A result or a consequence might be, but might also not be in line with the intended 'purpose'. In Recital 75 of the GDPR the legislature enumerates types of damage (physical, material or non-material) that might result from processing operations.

In order to characterize the purpose of a processing operation, one has to look into the following sub-criteria that are formed into one-word questions: **What** (is the purpose)? **Whose** (is the purpose)? **How** (is the purpose achieved)? The sub-criterion '**How** is the purpose achieved' will be examined under the criterion of 'context' because the examination of the means of processing (the 'how') is mainly about the techniques and the technologies used (which both constitute sub-criteria of 'context').

2.2 Visual Overview

At this point it is of value to briefly explain the structure and the content of the following Table. The first column presents the four criteria (nature, scope, context, purpose) which have been chosen as the most appropriate framework based on which one shall decide whether (or not) processing operations shall be legally qualified as highly risky. The second column consists of the sub-criteria that have been attached to each criterion. The question answered is: 'what are the elements of a processing operation that need to be examined in order to characterize the nature/the scope/the context/the purpose of the specific processing?'. For each of the four criteria, the relevant sub-criteria have been extracted primarily by the WP29 guidelines but also (specifically in the case of 'context') by the national blacklists. Under each sub-criterion relevant questions or bullet points have been added to further clarify their meaning. The third column consists of those conditions that qualify processing operations as likely to present a high risk. These conditions have been extracted exclusively from the 15 national DPA blacklists as well

---

[27] EDPS, Guidelines on the concepts of controller, processor and joint controllership under Regulation (EU) 2018/1725, 7 November 2019, 24.

[28] Probably, the most important use of the concept of 'interest' in the GDPR is the case of 'legitimate interest' as a lawful ground under Article 6(f) GDPR.

[29] WP29 (n 25), 24.

as the relevant GDPR provisions and the guidelines of the WP29 specifically on DPIAs and the concept of *high risk*.[30]

Criterion	Sub-criterion/a	Conditions that qualify processing as 'highly' risk
NATURE	Personal data - Nature of information processed: objective information/subjective statements - Content of information processed - Level of identifiability - Degree of sensitivity Data subjects - Category/ies where the data subject potentially belongs (e.g. vulnerable categories)	Special categories of data *Eg. health data, criminal convictions and offences* Data of 'high significance or of highly personal nature' *Eg. data of electronic communications, data relating to financial situation* Data that allow personal information in relation to special categories of data to be determined or deduced *Eg. processing of data with the purpose of providing social support reveal information about financial/social status of the person* Unique identifiers *Eg. biometric, genetic data* Vulnerable data subjects *Eg. employees, minors, refugees, patients, victims of gender-related violence, those at risk of social exclusion*
SCOPE	Actors (i.e. data subject/controller/processor/joint controllers/third parties etc.) - Quantity: how many actors are involved? Information - Volume: how much information is processed? - Range: what type of data items are processed? (both personal and non-personal data, any type of information) Extent - Temporal: duration/permanence of data processing - Geographical: public space? International data transfers?	Large scale processing *Eg. profiling on large scale,* *e.g. electronic health records,* *e.g. systematic monitoring, tracking of individual's behavior,* *e.g. large scale data sharing between different controllers using telematics means,* *e.g. long data storage period,* *e.g. transfer of special categories of data to third countries*

(continued)

---

[30] WP29 (n 8).

(*continued*)

Criterion	Sub-criterion/a	Conditions that qualify processing as 'highly' risk
CONTEXT	Technique/technology Environment - Offline? Online? - What is the organisational and societal context at the time of processing? - What is the expected purpose of the processing in the specific context? - Is the actor that processes an individual/SME/major corporation? Relationship data controller – data subject - Is there an imbalance of power? Origin/Source of personal data - Where do the data come from? The data subject? Another source? - Is it primary data? Deduced data from matching/combination? - Are new (types of) data generated? Security measures	Innovative use of technology/New technology *Eg. algorithmic decision making,* *e.g. processing of personal data that is generated by devices connected to the internet and that can send or exchange data via the internet or otherwise (smart toys, smart cities etc.)* Power imbalance in relationship between data controller-data subject *Eg. employment context, mentally ill people, asylum seekers, consumers* Indirect collection of personal data *Eg. collection from third parties* Invisible processing *Eg. covert investigation* Matching/combination of data coming from multiple sources *Eg. processing involving the cross-referencing of digital goods data with payment data such as in mobile payments* Generation of new types of personal data *Eg. processing of answers to a psychometric test in order to generate a psychometric profile (new type of data)* Insufficient security measures. *Eg. insufficient protection against unauthorised reversal of pseudonimisation*
PURPOSE	What is the purpose? Whose is the purpose?	Function creep. *Eg. based on the availability of a new type of data new purposes are being developed* Specific types of purposes. *Eg. scoring, credit rating, profiling for predictive purposes, online behavioral advertising*

3 Five Concepts Behind the 'High Risk' Reasoning

In this Section, the second part of the research question raised in the Introduction of this paper will be answered, namely: *'[...] What conclusions can we draw from these conditions as to the reasoning of the regulators in qualifying types of processing operations as 'likely to result in a high risk?'* As already mentioned, the Table presented above is not an inclusive overview of all the processing operations presented by the national DPAs in their blacklists. It is instead an attempt to categorize the most important conditions that could trigger high risks to rights and freedoms. Section 3 proceeds to drawing some broader conclusions which will contribute to the discussion on the concept of *risk* under the GDPR. These conclusions stem from the conditions that qualify processing operations as likely to present a high risk. The reasoning of the legislature revolves around the following five concepts:

3.1 Control of the Individual Over Their Personal Data

The concept of control over one's personal data is pivotal. In cases where there is no control, loss of control or there is illusion of having control, the regulator appears to react by characterizing the relevant processing operations as likely to result in a high risk to rights and freedoms. Simply put, the less the control, the higher the likelihood of high risks.

Looking into the types of operations presented in the DPAs' blacklists, there are two main parameters which appear to be highly relevant when it comes to the concept of control: the first parameter is information. In cases where there is an information asymmetry between the data controller and the data subject or where no (adequate) information is provided to the data subject (e.g. in cases of 'invisible processing, where personal data have not been directly obtained by the data subject)[31] because it is either impossible or unfeasible to guarantee it, the degree of control over one's personal data becomes questionable.

A second parameter of control is vulnerability of data subjects. Three main cases are extracted from the blacklists whereby data subjects are considered vulnerable. First case is the case of minors (e.g. assessment of pupils and students).[32] Second case is where vulnerability emerges due to a power imbalance in the relationship between the data controller and the data subject such as in the employment context (e.g. use of GDPS on employees' vehicles).[33] Power imbalance can also manifest where 'processing of data concerns persons whose evaluation (and the services provided to them) depend on the entities or persons which have supervisory and/or evaluating powers'[34] such as 'systems

---

[31] Information Commissioner's Office, 'Examples of Processing "likely to result in high risk", https://ico.org.uk/for-organisations/guide-to-data-protection/guide-to-the-general-data-protec tion-regulation-gdpr/data-protection-impact-assessments-dpias/examples-of-processing-lik ely-to-result-in-high-risk/, last accessed 2020/03/12.

[32] Hungarian Data Protection Authority (Nemzeti Adatvédelmi és Információszabadság Hatóság), https://www.naih.hu/list-of-processing-operations-subject-to-dpia-35-4--gdpr.html, last accessed 2020/03/12.

[33] Office of the Commissioner for Personal Data Protection, 'Indicative list of processing operations subject to DPIA requirements under Article 35(4) of the GDPR', http://www.dataprotection. gov.cy/dataprotection/dataprotection.nsf/page2c_en/page2c_en?opendocument, last accessed 2020/03/12.

[34] Polish Data Protection Authority (Urząd Ochrony Danych Osobowych) 'List of types of processing operations requiring DPIA', https://uodo.gov.pl/en/558/939, last accessed 2020/03/12.

used for reporting irregularities (whistleblowing)'.[35] Third case is a de facto (contextual) vulnerability which appears due to constraints of various nature i.e. social constraints (e.g. asylum seekers)[36], physical constraints (e.g. people with disabilities)[37], mental constraints (e.g. people with a mental disability), financial constraints (e.g. people with low income), political constraints (e.g. political refugees). A case of de facto vulnerability which might not be very common, but which could raise high risks to the rights and freedoms of data subjects is the difficulty in detecting the data controller, meaning the actor who is primarily responsible for complying with the GDPR and for guaranteeing data subject rights (e.g. public non-permissioned blockchains).[38] Vulnerability could refer to aspects of the processing operation (e.g. elderly people who might not be able to understand what they are consenting to) but also to the possible outcomes of the processing, such as when the data subject is at risk of social exclusion,[39] at risk of being manipulated (e.g. minors) or of being discriminated against because they are member of a political or religious group, or a member of the LGBT community.

3.2 Reasonable Expectations of the Data Subject

A second concept prevalent in the examples put forward by the European and national regulators is the concept of 'reasonable expectations' of the data subject with regard to the fact that processing is taking place and/or with regard to various aspects of the processing operations (e.g. the purposes, the data storage period, the further processing etc.).

In cases where there is the element of unpredictability in the processing and therefore the reasonable expectations of the data subject are not met, there is greater likelihood of risks to be raised. Reasonable expectations relate, for example, to the context within which processing takes place. When there is clear expectation of confidentiality as is the case in the healthcare sector (e.g. processing of health data by using an active implantable medical device)[40] or where there is clear expectation of privacy (e.g. at home) and this expectation is not met (e.g. smart TVs, smart household appliances, Internet of Things)[41]

---

[35] Polish DPA (n 34).

[36] Italian Data Protection Authority (Garante per la protezione dei dati personali), 'List of types of treatments subject to the consistency mechanism to be subjected to impact assessment', https://www.garanteprivacy.it/web/guest/home/docweb/-/docweb-display/docweb/9059358, last accessed 2020/03/12.

[37] Spanish Data Protection Authority (Agencia Española de Protección de Datos) https://www.aepd.es/sites/default/files/2019-09/listas-dpia-en-35-4.pdf, last accessed 2020/03/12.

[38] This is not an example found in any of the 15 DPAs' blacklists. However, it is important to be included given that the likelihood of high risks being raised is very high, due to the position that the data controller has in the data protection ecosystem.

[39] Spanish DPA (n 37).

[40] Belgian Data Protection Authority (Autorité de protection des données). Recommandation d'initiative de la Commission de protection de la vie privée (CPVP) 01/2018 du 28 février 2018 concernant l'analyse d'impact à la protection des données et la consultation préalable, https://www.autoriteprotectiondonnees.be/publications/recommandation-n-01-2018.pdf, last accessed 2020/03/12.

then the risks are likely to be higher. The element of unpredictability can also arise due to the lack of knowledge with regard to new technologies, automated decision making etc. (e.g. innovative use or application of new technological or organisational solutions which can involve novel forms of data collection and usage).[42] Reasonable expectations could also relate to the scope of processing operations such as the geographical extent (e.g. transfers of special categories of data to third countries on the basis of the derogations provided for in article 49 GDPR)[43] or to the actors involved (e.g. large scale data sharing between different controllers using telematics means).

Reasonable expectations refer also to the possible uses of the personal data as well as to the content and nature of the information processed. In cases where assumptions are made, or there is deduction of information through matching, combination, (e.g. processing involving the cross-referencing of digital goods data with payment data, such as in mobile payments),[44] comparison of data, or where creation of profiles takes place or even identification of patterns (e.g. obtain and analyse data from various sources for the purpose of drawing conclusions)[45], then there is a high likelihood that the expectations of the data subject are exceeded and that high risks might be raised.

3.3 (Negative) Impact of Data Processing Operation on Rights and Freedoms

In cases where data processing operations might have a negative impact on other rights, freedoms, interests, activities and the daily life of natural persons, the likelihood that high risks are raised is higher. There are various ways in which data processing operations may interact with and have a negative impact on other rights, interests etc. Examples of these interactions are hereby presented, also backed up by types of processing operations that appear in the national blacklists.

(a) The misuse of personal data might have a serious impact on the daily life of the data subject (e.g. financial data which could be used to commit fraud in respect of payment).[46]
(b) The processing operations might affect the exercise of other fundamental rights (e.g. processing of location data, the collection of which jeopardises freedom of movement).[47]

---

[41] Norwegian Data Protection Authority (Datatilsynet), https://www.datatilsynet.no/rettigheter-og-plikter/virksomhetenes-plikter/vurdere-personvernkonsekvenser/vurdering-av-personvernkonsekvenser/nar-ma-man-gjennomfore-en-vurdering-av-personvernkonsekvenser/, last accessed 2020/03/12.

[42] See inter alia Hellenic Data Protection Authority 'List of the kind of processing operations which are subject to the requirement for a data protection impact assessment according to article 35 par. 4 of GDPR', https://www.dpa.gr/portal/page?_pageid=33,239286&_dad=portal&_schema=PORTAL, last accessed 2020/03/12.

[43] Cypriot DPA (n 33).

[44] Italian DPA (n 36).

[45] Polish DPA (n 34).

[46] Italian DPA (n 36).

[47] Italian DPA (n 36).

(c) The processing operations might deprive data subjects of their rights (e.g. indirect collection of personal data whereby the right to information cannot be guaranteed).[48]

(d) The processing operations might have legal or other significant effects (e.g. processing of employees personal data,[49] establishment of blacklists/warning lists).[50]

(e) The processing operations might expose the data subject to manipulation, physical threats etc. (e.g. monitor and influence behavior for online behavioral advertising purposes).[51]

One notices that the examples that clarify the various interactions presented above belong to all four criteria (i.e. nature, scope, context, purpose) of processing operations. We identify that the nature of the personal data processed (see cases (a), (b)), the nature of the data subject (see (d)), the context of the processing (see (c), (d)), as well as its purpose (see (e)) can all have a negative impact on various rights and freedoms, but also on aspects of a person's life.

3.4 Scaling up of Data Processing Operations

The concept of scale plays a major role in the reasoning of the regulators when it comes to risks in data protection. It seems to be the case that the higher the scale (the broader the scope), the more likely that high risks will be raised. It is of value to highlight that the scaling up can take place on two levels.

First and most obvious level is the level of society and natural persons at large.[52] On this first level, data processing takes place on a large scale with regard to how many actors are involved (e.g. profiling on large scale),[53] how much information is being processed (e.g. systematically monitoring, tracking or observing individuals' location or behavior)[54] or to what temporal or geographical extent this processing takes place (e.g. transfers of special categories of data to third country or international organisation).[55]

The second level is the level of the data subject herself. On this second level, data processing takes place on a large scale with regard to the volume and range of information processed for one data subject (e.g. social network,[56] systematic processing of

---

[48] Commission Nationale pour la protection des données Grand-Duché de Luxembourg, https://cnpd.public.lu/fr/professionnels/obligations/AIPD.html, last accessed 2020/03/12.

[49] Luxembourg DPA (n 48).

[50] Dutch Data Protection Authority (Autoriteit Persoonsgegevens), https://autoriteitpersoonsgegevens.nl/nl/zelf-doen/data-protection-impact-assessment-dpia, last accessed 2020/03/12.

[51] Dutch DPA (n 50).

[52] We shall not forget that the GDPR requires that risks are assessed with regard to 'natural persons' and not only data subjects.

[53] ICO (n 31).

[54] Data Protection Commission 'List of Types of Data Processing Operations which require a Data Protection Impact Assessment', https://www.dataprotection.ie/en/guidance-landing/data-processing-operations-require-data-protection-impact-assessment, last accessed 2020/03/12.

[55] Cypriot DPA (n 33).

[56] Polish DPA (n 34).

personal data concerning profiling for marketing purposes when data are combined with data collected from third parties)[57] or with regard to temporal extent of personal data processing of one data subject (e.g. systematic storage duration/systematic processing). The importance of identifying this second level lies in that it straightforwardly captures practices of systematic profiling/tracking etc. It also accentuates the fact that scaling up does not solely refer to the criterion of scope as one would assume. It emerges also from the 'context' (new technologies such as IoT, facilitate scaling up of processing), 'purposes' (more often than not, the purpose of processing is the scaling up itself – think for example profiling, online behavioral advertising), and 'nature' (for example, special categories of data that could reveal much more about the data subject, e.g. processing of data with the purpose of providing social housing to people,[58] could reveal information about the financial and social status of the data subject).

3.5 Identifiability of Individuals

Last but not least, the concept of identifiability. The higher the level of identifiability of data subjects, the more likely it is that a high risk will be raised. The level of identifiability primarily depends on the content of information. Looking at the types of processing operations that figure in the national 'blacklists', the vast majority of national DPAs have included the processing of genetic and biometric data for the purpose of 'uniquely identifying a natural person'[59] when it is combined with at least one more criterion.[60] Identifiability also emerges as a basic concept behind the 'high risk' reasoning, from the context of the processing operations. This becomes clear once we look into the technology used (for example tracking cookies and creation of profiles)[61] or once we look into the source and origin of the data that are being processed (such as combination, matching, comparing of data from various sources).[62] Identifiability also relates to the scope of processing operations in relation to the volume and range of information processed but also in relation to the actors involved in the processing.

4   Conclusion

In this paper the following research question is raised and answered:

'What are the conditions that qualify types of processing operations as "likely to raise a high risk to the rights and freedoms of natural persons" according to the European and national regulators? What conclusions can we draw from these conditions as to the reasoning of the regulators in qualifying types of processing operations as "likely to result in a high risk?"

To answer the question, the first step is to approach the meaning of the four criteria set forward by the legislature in the GDPR, namely 'nature, scope, context and purpose'.

---

[57] Hellenic DPA (n 42).

[58] French Data Protection Authority, CNIL https://www.cnil.fr/fr/listes-des-traitements-pour-les quels-une-aipd-est-requise-ou-non, last accessed 2020/03/12.

[59] See for example, Belgian DPA (n 40).

[60] ICO (n 31).

[61] See for example, Cypriot DPA (n 33).

[62] See for example, Hungarian DPA (n 32), ICO (n 31), Irish DPA (n 54).

These four criteria constitute the basis for categorizing the most important conditions that qualify processing operations as likely to raise a high risk to the rights and freedoms. For that, the national blacklists developed by 15 DPAs are consulted. These findings are presented in a Table in Subsect. 2.2. Having as a basis the types of processing operations presented by the DPAs' blacklists, Sect. 3 proceeds to broader conclusions as to the reasoning behind the qualification of types of processing operations as likely to raise high risks. There are five concepts upon which the reasoning behind high risks in data protection is built. These concepts are control, reasonable expectations, (negative) impact on rights and interests, scaling-up and identifiability. In cases where control over one's personal data is compromised or not guaranteed, where the reasonable expectations of the data subject over the processing of their personal data are not met, where processing operations have a negative impact on rights, freedoms, interests and the daily life activities of natural persons, where the processing scales-up and becomes broader and/or deeper and where the level of identifiability is high, then it is likely that a high risk to the rights and freedoms of natural persons is raised.

References

1. Van Dijk, N., Gellert, R., Rommetveit, K.: A risk to a right: beyond data protection impact assessments. Comput. Law Secur. Rev. **32**(2), 286–306 (2016)
2. Gellert, R.: Understanding the notion of risk in the General Data Protection Regulation. Comput. Law Secur. Rev. **34**(2), 279–288 (2018)
3. Data Protection Commission, Guidance Note: Guide to Data Protection Impact Assessments (DPIAs), October 2019. https://www.dataprotection.ie/en/guidance-landing/guide-data-protection-impact-assessments. Accessed 12 Mar 2020
4. Norwegian Data Protection Authority (Datatilsynet). https://www.datatilsynet.no/rettigheter-og-plikter/virksomhetenes-plikter/vurdere-personvernkonsekvenser/vurdering-av-personvernkonsekvenser/nar-ma-man-gjennomfore-en-vurdering-av-personvernkonsekvenser/. Accessed 12 Mar 2020
5. Norwegian Data Protection Authority (Datatilsynet). https://www.datatilsynet.no/rettigheter-og-plikter/virksomhetenes-plikter/vurdere-personvernkonsekvenser/vurdering-av-personvernkonsekvenser/risikovurdering/. Accessed 12 Mar 2020
6. Norwegian Data Protection Authority (Datatilsynet). https://www.datatilsynet.no/rettigheter-og-plikter/virksomhetenes-plikter/vurdere-personvernkonsekvenser/vurdering-av-personvernkonsekvenser/nar-er-risiko-hoy/. Accessed 12 Mar 2020
7. French Data Protection Authority, CNIL. https://www.cnil.fr/fr/listes-des-traitements-pour-lesquels-une-aipd-est-requise-ou-non. Accessed 12 Mar 2020
8. Information Commissioner's Office: Examples of Processing "likely to result in high risk. https://ico.org.uk/for-organisations/guide-to-data-protection/guide-to-the-general-data-protection-regulation-gdpr/data-protection-impact-assessments-dpias/examples-of-processing-likely-to-result-in-high-risk/. Accessed 12 Mar 2020
9. Information Commissioner's Office: When do we need to do a DPIA? https://ico.org.uk/for-organisations/guide-to-data-protection/guide-to-the-general-data-protection-regulation-gdpr/data-protection-impact-assessments-dpias/when-do-we-need-to-do-a-dpia/. Accessed 12 Mar 2020
10. Hungarian Data Protection Authority (Nemzeti Adatvédelmi és Információszabadság Hatóság). https://www.naih.hu/list-of-processing-operations-subject-to-dpia-35-4--gdpr.html. Accessed 12 Mar 2020

11. Office of the Commissioner for Personal Data Protection: Indicative list of processing operations subject to DPIA requirements under Article 35(4) of the GDPR. http://www.dataprotection.gov.cy/dataprotection/dataprotection.nsf/page2c_en/page2c_en?opendocument. Accessed 12 Mar 2020

12. Polish Data Protection Authority (Urząd Ochrony Danych Osobowych): List of types of processing operations requiring DPIA. https://uodo.gov.pl/en/558/939. Accessed 12 Mar 2020

13. Italian Data Protection Authority (Garante per la protezione dei dati personali): List of types of treatments subject to the consistency mechanism to be subjected to impact assessment. https://www.garanteprivacy.it/web/guest/home/docweb/-/docweb-display/docweb/9059358. Accessed 12 Mar 2020

14. Spanish Data Protection Authority (Agencia Española de Protección de Datos). https://www.aepd.es/sites/default/files/2019-09/listas-dpia-en-35-4.pdf. Accessed 12 Mar 2020

15. Data Protection Commission: List of Types of Data Processing Operations which require a Data Protection Impact Assessment. https://www.dataprotection.ie/en/guidance-landing/data-processing-operations-require-data-protection-impact-assessment. Accessed 12 Mar 2020

16. Belgian Data Protection Authority (Autorité de protection des données). Recommandation d'initiative de la Commission de protection de la vie privée (CPVP) 01/2018 du 28 février 2018 concernant l'analyse d'impact à la protection des données et la consulta-tion préalable. https://www.autoriteprotectiondonnees.be/publications/recommandation-n-01-2018.pdf. Accessed 12 Mar 2020

17. Hellenic Data Protection Authority: List of the kind of processing operations which are subject to the requirement for a data protection impact assessment according to article 35 par. 4 of GDPR. https://www.dpa.gr/portal/page?_pageid=33,239286&_dad=portal&_schema=PORTAL. Accessed 12 Mar 2020

18. Commission Nationale pour la protection des données Grand-Duché de Luxembourg. https://cnpd.public.lu/fr/professionnels/obligations/AIPD.html. Accessed 12 Mar 2020

19. Dutch Data Protection Authority (Autoriteit Persoonsgegevens). https://autoriteitpersoonsgegevens.nl/nl/zelf-doen/data-protection-impact-assessment-dpia, Accessed 12 Mar 2020

20. Article 29 Data Protection Working Party: Guidelines on Data Protection Impact Assessment (DPIA) and Determining Whether Processing Is "Likely to Result in a High Risk" for the Purposes of Regulation 2016/679, WP 248 rev 0.1, 4 April 2017

21. Article 29 Data Protection Working Party: Opinion 03/2013 on purpose limitation, WP 203, Adopted on 2 April 2013

22. Article 29 Data Protection Working Party: Guidelines on Data Protection Officer, 16/EN WP243

23. Article 29 Data Protection Working Party: Opinion 02/2013 on apps on smart devices, 13/EN WP202

24. Article 29 Data Protection Working Party: Opinion 04/2012 on Cookie Consent Exemption, 12/EN WP194

25. Article 29 Data Protection Working Party: Opinion 5/2010 on the Industry Proposal for a Privacy and Data Protection Impact Assessment Framework for RFID Applications, 10/EN WP 175

26. Article 29 Data Protection Working Party: Opinion 06/2014 on the notion of legitimate interests of the data controller under Article 7 of Directive 95/46/EC, 14/EN WP217

27. EDPS: Guidelines on the concepts of controller, processor and joint controllership under Regulation (EU) 2018/1725, 7 November 2019

28. EDPB Opinion 7/2018 on the draft list of the competent supervisory authority of Greece regarding the processing operations subject to the requirement of a data protection impact assessment (Art. 35.4 GDPR), adopted on 25 September 2018

Position Paper: Analyzing the Impacts of Facial Recognition

Claude Castelluccia[1] and Daniel Le Métayer[2(✉)]

[1] Univ. Grenoble Alpes, Inria, 38000 Grenoble, France
[2] Univ Lyon, Inria, INSA Lyon, CITI, 69621 Villeurbanne, France
`daniel.le-metayer@inria.fr`

Abstract. Considering the lack of consensus on the deployment of facial recognition technologies, many organizations, including public bodies, NGOs and private companies have alerted public opinion and called for a broad debate on facial recognition. We believe that such a debate is indeed necessary. However, in order to be really productive, it is essential to ensure that arguments can be expressed and confronted in a rigorous way. The main objective of this position paper is to help set the terms of this debate on a solid basis. To this aim, we present an incremental and comparative risk-analysis methodology for facial recognition systems. The methodology introduces, for a better separation of concerns, four levels of analysis: the purpose, the means, the use of facial recognition and its implementation. We discuss each of these levels and illustrate them with examples based on recent developments. Interested readers can find more details, in particular about the use of ethical matrices to facilitate the analysis, in an extended version of this position paper published as an Inria report [7].

Keywords: Facial recognition · Identification · Authentication · Surveillance · Ethics · Impact analysis

1 Introduction

Significant progress has been made in recent years in the field of image processing, particularly in facial recognition. The number of deployments and experiments of this type of system is rapidly increasing [1,3,13]. Most applications are motivated by security, safety or commercial considerations. However, there are diverging opinions on the use of these technologies, particularly in public spaces. For example, James O'Neill, New York Police Commissioner, highlights the usefulness of facial recognition to track suspects and concludes that "it would be an injustice to the people we serve if we policed our 21st century city without using

The authors would like to thank Clément Henin and Vincent Roca for their constructive comments on an earlier draft of this paper. This work is supported by the French National Research Agency in the framework of the "Investissements d'avenir" program (ANR-15-IDEX-02).

L. Antunes et al. (Eds.): APF 2020, LNCS 12121, pp. 43–57, 2020.
https://doi.org/10.1007/978-3-030-55196-4_3

21st century technology"[1]. On the other hand, several American cities have followed the example set by San Francisco and decided to ban the use of facial recognition by their municipal services, including their police forces. In the same spirit, Axon's ethics committee recommended that police body cameras should not be equipped with facial recognition functionality [2].

Considering the lack of consensus on a technology that can have a significant impact on society, many organizations[2], including public bodies, NGOs and private companies have alerted public opinion and called for a public debate on facial recognition. In its recent white paper on artificial intelligence, the European Commission also announces the launch of a debate on the use of "biometric data for remote identification" [9]. We believe that such a debate is indeed necessary. However, in order to be really productive, it is essential to ensure that arguments can be expressed and confronted in a rigorous way. In particular, it is critical to avoid, as much as possible, preconceptions and to distinguish established facts from assumptions or opinions. Indeed, arguments on this matter often mix different levels of discourse (e.g. some of them concern facial recognition in general, others application contexts or particular choices of implementation) and do not always make the distinction between objective facts and subjective statements or political positions.

As facial recognition applications are very diverse, it is necessary to precisely analyze the potential impacts of each system, taking into account all its features and the context of its deployment. For example, the use of facial recognition for a digital identity application, such as the ALICEM project in France[3], introduces risks that are, by nature, very different from those resulting from a system aimed at securing public space, such as the ones experimented in South Wales and the cities of London and Nice for example. These applications do not have the same purposes, do not use the same forms of facial recognition and their implementations are very different. Nevertheless, such case-by-case analysis should not overlook the more "systemic" risk related to a potential generalization of the reliance on facial recognition in our societies. This global risk must also be analyzed and debated because some believe that it may justify a total ban of facial recognition. Moreover, a facial recognition application should not be considered exclusively as a technical object but rather as a socio-technical system,

---

[1] How facial recognition makes you safer, James O'Neill, New York Times, 9 June 2019.

[2] For example, CNIL (Commission Nationale de l'Informatique et des Libertés), the French Data Protection Authority; ICO (Information Commissioner's Office), the UK Data Protection Authority; the AINow Institute; ACLU (American Civil Liberties Union); EFF (Electronic Frontier Foundation); Google; Microsoft, etc.

[3] ALICEM (acronym in French for "certified online authentication on mobile phones") allows a user to generate a secure digital identity remotely. Identification is carried out by presenting the passport. The system extracts the information from the passport (identity and a photograph of the holder) and asks the user to take a video of his face. The information is sent to a server that compares the person's face on the video and the passport photograph. If successful, the user is authenticated.

taking into account all its facets, including its economic, social and psychological dimensions.

The main objective of this position paper is to help set the terms of the debate on a solid basis. The aim is therefore not to take a position on facial recognition in general but to propose a methodology for the analysis of its impacts, illustrated by some examples. The examples selected here concern essentially the use of facial recognition in the context of public services, but the approach is general and can be applied equally to other types of applications.

We hope that the methodology proposed in this paper can be useful at two levels of discussion:

- First, for the general debate that should be launched about the deployment of facial recognition in our societies. This debate must consider all the potential impacts of this technology and must be conducted in an open manner, without excluding the possibility of a ban (e.g. in public places) or authorization under certain restrictions or conditions.
- Second, for the case-by-case analysis of each facial recognition project or system (in contexts where the previous debate would not lead to a ban).

We summarize in Sect. 2 the issues related to the deployment of facial recognition systems and present the four steps of our methodology in Sect. 3. We conclude with perspectives and some concrete proposals in Sect. 4.

2   Why Is Facial Recognition so Concerning?

Most facial recognition systems are composed of two main components: an image processing component and one or several databases containing pre-registered information (such as templates or images). The image processing component captures and processes images. The database usually consists of the face images of individuals that are used as a reference to compare with live images. This database can be either centralized or distributed. It can be controlled by a single or several entities[4]. As we will discuss in this paper, the risks associated with a facial recognition system depend on the choices made for both the image processing and the database components. It is therefore important to consider the whole system when analyzing a facial recognition system, and not to focus exclusively on the image processing component as it is often the case.

The concerns raised by the development of facial recognition stem from a combination of features that may lead to serious threats to civil liberties:

- It is a biometric technique, which uses features of the human body that cannot be changed, at least not easily, unlike digital attributes (mobile phone identifiers, cookies, etc.). The sensitive nature of biometric data is recognized by law. For example, the General Data Protection Regulation (GDPR) [11] prohibits the processing of biometric data for identification purposes unless one of the ten exceptions listed in Article 9(2) can be invoked.

---

[4] In some cases, the database can be distributed on devices, such as identity cards or mobile phones, and stay under the control of the users.

- Unlike other biometric features, such as fingerprints or genetic data, facial images can be captured without a person's knowledge, remotely, without contact, and in a very cost-effective way. The face is also the most visible part of the body, the most difficult to dissimulate.
- Unlike other biometric features, which require an enrollment phase, i.e. the initial capture of biometric information, facial images are already available on a large scale: many public or private actors may have a large volume of images that have been collected for other purposes or that are accessible via the Internet[5]. For example, half of the U.S. adult citizens have pictures of their faces included in databases (including driver's license databases) that are accessible by the FBI [13]. In France, any citizen applying for an identity card is now registered, with his or her photograph, in a database called TES.
- Consent, which is a common legal basis for the collection of personal data, is very difficult to implement for facial recognition in public spaces. Signs indicating of the presence of video surveillance cameras are not effective and do not allow for a really free and informed choice since the only alternative to consent is to remain outside the area covered by the cameras.
- Despite the great progress that has been made in recent years, particularly thanks to the development of deep learning and the possibility of exploiting large image databases, the performances of facial recognition systems are still limited. Depending on where they are deployed and the context of their use, they can have very high rates of false positives (people wrongly recognized) and/or false negatives (people wrongly not recognized) and theses rates may vary according to categories of population. Some systems have better results on people with white skin than on people with dark skin, on men than on women or on adults than on teenagers. These biases lead to different types of discrimination against certain populations [1,4,6].
- Facial recognition systems rely on databases that contain very sensitive information and require very rigorous management procedures. Many facial recognition risks are related to the management, integrity or confidentiality of these databases.

The increasing use of facial recognition devices for convenience also gives rise to the deeper fear of a progressive generalization of the reliance on this technology, which could become unavoidable and have major consequences for our societies. Such extensions can take place in many different ways, for example by using data collected on social networks[6], or databases originally set up for different purposes, as discussed above with the FBI, or by using a database beyond the allowed purpose. Extensions may also result from the introduction of new functionalities to an existing system, for example by extending facial recognition used for passport control to payments in an airport and then throughout the

---

[5] See for example: https://www.nytimes.com/interactive/2019/10/11/technology/flickr-facial-recognition.html or https://megapixels.cc/datasets/megaface/.

[6] Many cases have been revealed. See for example: https://www.nytimes.com/2020/01/18/technology/clearview-privacy-facial-recognition.html, https://www.nytimes.com/interactive/2019/10/11/technology/flickr-facial-recognition.html.

whole city, or by integrating the detection of suspicious behaviors into an existing video surveillance system[7]. It may be the case that some of these extensions will not be accepted by the populations, but experience shows that when they are carried out in a very progressive way and presented as natural evolutions, they do not encounter major opposition. Furthermore, in general, when humans have to balance immediate and identifiable benefits, however minor, against potentially serious but uncertain and vague harms, they generally tend to disregard the latter.

It is important to take also into account the fact that a large number of video surveillance cameras are already deployed in public spaces. At present, these images are either viewed live by supervisory agents or a posteriori by investigators[8]. The analysis of the impacts of facial recognition in this context must therefore compare the current situation (supervision and recognition by human agents) with an implementation based on automatic recognition. The advantages and disadvantages of each option must be weighed, considering the protective measures that can be put in place in both cases and without underestimating the risks associated with the current situation. Indeed, several studies have shown the serious abuses resulting from human supervision[9]. The replacement of certain tasks by automatic processing could make it possible to limit these deviations, or at least make them more traceable, if sufficient protective measures are implemented. Conversely, if the impact analysis leads to the conclusion that any use of these video surveillance images represents a disproportionate risk, whether the analyses are carried out by human operators or by a facial recognition system, then it is the use of video surveillance itself that should be challenged.

3 Incremental Impact Analysis

This section presents a risk-analysis methodology for facial recognition systems. The approach is incremental in the sense that it introduces four different levels of analysis, respectively the *purpose*, the *means*, the *use of facial recognition* and its *implementation,* which are pictured in Fig. 1. Another essential dimension of our method is the emphasis on the comparative nature of the analysis: both benefits and risks must be assessed in comparison with alternatives. The initial situation (before any deployment of the system) is generally used as an implicit benchmark, but other options should also be considered at each step: other means to achieve the purpose, other solutions than facial recognition, and other implementations of facial recognition. As an illustration, Fig. 2 shows examples of alternatives considered at each stage for a case study that will be used as a running example throughout the paper.

---

[7] See for example: https://www.aclu.org/blog/privacy-technology/surveillance-technologies/how-tsas-facial-recognition-plan-will-go-far.

[8] For example, to coordinate crews in the field or to monitor major events in real time in the case of the Nice urban supervision center.

[9] See for example: https://www.eff.org/wp/law-enforcement-use-face-recognition.

In the following sections, we present each level of analysis. We then conclude with a discussion of the connection of this analysis with GDPR Data Protection Impact Assessment (DPIA) (which corresponds to the fifth level in Fig. 1).

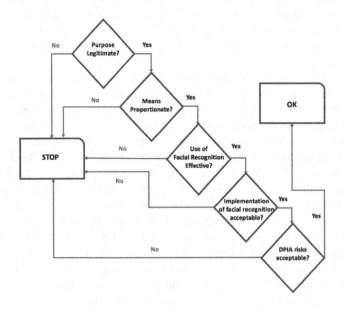

Fig. 1. Methodology to analyze the impact of facial recognition systems (4 steps + DPIA).

3.1   Level 1: Purpose of the System

The objective of this phase is to analyze the declared purpose of the system, independently of the means used to realize it (in particular through facial recognition). Examples of purposes could be "to prevent a terrorist from committing an attack on a train" or "to ensure that only authorized persons can enter a building". The purpose must be defined as precisely as possible in order to allow for the identification and analysis of all issues. For example, if we consider a secure digital identity solution, it is important to know whether its use will be mandatory to get access to certain websites and, if so, what those sites are. The stakes will be very different if the solution is an optional authentication solution to get access to specific government websites such as a tax authority website, or if it is intended to become mandatory for a large number of websites, public or private. In the second case, it would question the notion of anonymity on the Internet. Similarly, the legitimacy of a video surveillance image analysis system for the purpose of searching may depend on the precise characterization of the notion of "wanted person" (terrorist or criminal on the run, runaway child, missing adult, etc.). Some projects may also look questionable from the outset,

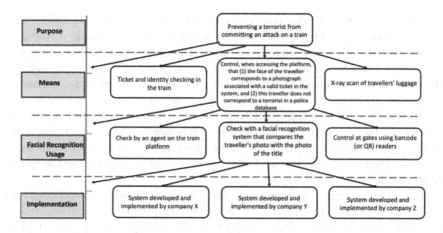

Fig. 2. Comparative analysis of an application.

politically or legally: this would be the case, for example, of an initiative to pre-vent certain people from participating in public demonstrations or to identify demonstrators. Moreover, even if a purpose is legitimate, it may be more or less critical and may have different impacts, in the short or long term, for different categories of population.

Examples of key questions to ask at this stage are:

- Is the declared purpose lawful?
- What are the expected benefits of the purpose and what interests does it serve (private or public, state, citizens, etc.)?
- Are the expected benefits of major or relative importance? Is the purpose really a priority?
- What are the possible impacts, positive or negative, in the short and long terms, of the purpose for all stakeholders[10], regardless of the means adopted to achieve it?
- Are the impacts of major or minor importance?
- On the basis of these elements, is the purpose legitimate?

3.2 Level 2: Means to Achieve the Purpose

The means describes the strategy adopted to achieve the purpose, independently of a particular implementation, by a computer system and/or human operators. For example, a hypothetical way to accomplish the purpose of "preventing a terrorist from committing an attack on a train" could be to "control, when accessing the platform, that (1) the face of the traveler corresponds to a pho-tograph associated with a valid ticket in the system, and (2) this photograph

---

[10] Stakeholders are defined as all entities, persons or groups of persons, who may be affected by a system, directly or indirectly, in an active (sponsor, developer, operator, user, etc.) or passive (citizen, passenger, etc.) manner.

or the identity of the traveler does not correspond to a terrorist contained in a police database". The first question to be asked is the effectiveness of the proposed means to achieve the purpose and the availability of any evidence (studies, experiments, etc.) to sustain it. For a better separation of issues, it is assumed at this stage that the means is perfectly implemented. In the example considered here, the proposed means can be challenged because it is ineffective to deal with internal attacks (from a malicious employee or subcontractor) or, in general, threats from persons who are unknown to the police services. Two options are possible at this stage of the analysis: either the means is not subject to revision, it is then considered ineffective and the project should be rejected; or the means can be modified and it then needs to be revised.

After analyzing the effectiveness of the proposed means, it is necessary to identify the possible impacts of this means on all stakeholders and on society as a whole (in particular on democracy). In the example of access control to station platforms, we can distinguish, for example, impacts on travelers, railway company employees, the company itself, citizens in general (or society), the State and also technology suppliers. If we consider, for example, travelers, we can identify as positive impact an increased sense of security (which may be justified or not) and as negative impacts, a restriction of the freedom to move anonymously and a feeling of surveillance. With regard to the possible risks, it is important to consider the number of persons included in the police database, the criteria used to include a person, and the type of authorisation, judicial or administrative, necessary to get access to this database.

With regard to possible alternatives to the proposed means, it is possible to imagine, for the train example, having luggage subject to X-Ray examination and using security gates for passengers (as in airports) without the need to check nominative tickets. It is then necessary to compare the two solutions, considering their positive and negative impacts. In this case, it could be argued that this alternative would better achieve the purpose while preserving the freedom to move anonymously. However, it could lead to longer waiting times at boarding. In a real analysis, these arguments should be supported by results or experimental studies which should enable a rigorous comparison of the options. Moreover, the legitimacy of the means and the relevance of the alternatives obviously depend on the purpose itself. Note that the above objection about the train platform access control system would not apply to a project whose purpose, for example, would be to control the access of a restricted area by a few authorized employees. In this case, the database would be limited to a small number of employees. Examples of key questions to ask at this stage are:

- Does the means effectively accomplish the purpose? What is the evidence to support this?
- What are the possible impacts, positive or negative, in the short and long term, of the means for all stakeholders, regardless of whether facial recognition is used to achieve this means?
- Are these impacts of major or minor importance?
- What could be alternative means of achieving the goal?

– On the basis of these elements, is the means proportionate to achieve the purpose?

3.3 Level 3: Use of Facial Recognition to Achieve the Means

The objective of this phase is to question the use of facial recognition to achieve the means (without reference to a particular implementation of the technology). In the example of the train mentioned above, facial recognition could take place in the gateways used by travelers to get access to the platforms. When the traveler arrives at a gateway, a photograph is automatically taken and a face is extracted. This extraction is then used to verify in a database that there is a reservation for a person corresponding to this face and this person does not appear in the police database.

It is assumed at this stage that facial recognition is implemented in a "perfect" way. In particular, it is assumed to be accurate, free of bias and secure. The associated databases are also assumed to be managed in a secure way. The issues addressed in this phase are therefore more theoretical than experimental by nature: they concern the inherent benefits and risks of facial recognition, independently of its actual implementation and current state-of the art.

As for the previous level, the first question to be asked is whether facial recognition is an effective solution to achieve the proposed means. With regard to risks, it is also important to consider the possible drifts or successive extensions to which the processing could give rise. This risk is often mentioned as a key issue by opponents of facial recognition. Such extensions may concern both the picture databases, the authorized purposes and the contexts in which the systems are used. The "slippery slope" argument must therefore be considered seriously, but it must be analyzed precisely and in concrete terms to avoid sophism. With regard to our example, it could be argued that there is a significant risk of generalization to all modes of transport (metro, tram, bus, etc.) that would lead to a total loss of the freedom to move anonymously. Beyond transport, we could also imagine a generalization to all closed places where people gather (cinemas, theaters, shopping centers, etc.): if these systems are considered effective, why would the protection that they offer be limited to public transports? If this generalization is not acceptable, where should the red line be set and what safeguards should be provided to ensure that this limit is enforced? In other cases, it is the databases themselves that could later be extended or cross-referenced with other databases. There is no shortage of examples in recent history to show that this kind of drift is not a fantasy[11]. This "systemic" risk and the consequences of mass surveillance on freedom of expression and democratic life have been widely documented and analyzed [15].

---

[11] The French national DNA database (FNAEG), already mentioned, provides a prime example: created in 1998 to centralize the fingerprints of persons convicted of extremely serious offenses (murder of a minor person preceded or associated with rape, torture or barbaric acts, etc.), it has been successively extended to include nearly three million DNA profiles in 2018.

It is also necessary to consider the necessity and proportionality of facial recognition. The answer to these questions may depend on many factors, including the scope of application: as mentioned by the ICO [14], a targeted facial recognition system, limited in time and space, to monitor known suspects is likely to be more justifiable than a large-scale, indiscriminate and permanent deployment.

Finally, it is important to consider existing alternatives to facial recognition. In the example of the train platform, one could imagine a solution relying on visual inspections by railway company employees. This control could involve a search for the person's photograph in the reservation database (based on his or her identity) and a direct comparison with photographs of wanted persons. We could also imagine reading a barcode or QR code that would give access to the photograph associated with the reservation. In any case, the main disadvantage would be longer boarding times, and probably a higher cost. The existence of less privacy-invasive alternatives may be a key factor in deciding whether the use of facial recognition is proportionate, as evidenced by the CNIL's opinion on experiments in high schools in Nice and Marseille, France. In this case, the CNIL held that "the objectives of securing and facilitating access to high schools can be achieved by means that are far less intrusive in terms of privacy and individual freedoms, such as badge control". In general, as suggested by the EDPS[12], the use of facial recognition for authentication purpose is more proportionate than its use for identification or tracking.

Examples of key questions to ask at this stage are:

- Is facial recognition an effective solution to achieve the means?
- Would its use require the creation or the reuse of a centralized database of images (as opposed to a distributed solution or the use of images remaining on local devices) and what entities would be in control of this database?
- Would it be used for authentication, identification or tracking?
- What are the possible impacts, positive or negative, in the short and long term, of facial recognition for all stakeholders? Are they of major or minor importance?
- Is this application of facial recognition likely to lead to extensions or generalizations? What would be their impacts? Can negative effects be prevented or reduced and positive effects promoted or amplified?
- What alternative technologies could be effective to achieve the means?
- Based on these elements, is the use of facial recognition proportionate to achieve the means?

3.4   Level 4: Implementation of Facial Recognition

The fourth level of our methodology takes into account the implementation of facial recognition technology. In particular, it analyzes the features (and weaknesses or limitations) of the technologies used, the configuration parameters,

---

[12] https://edps.europa.eu/node/5551.

data, parties involved, deployment environment, etc. At this stage, it is necessary to evaluate the system as a whole, including the image processing and database components, taking into account the countermeasures put in place, the control and transparency mechanisms, as well as the socio-economic conditions for its deployment.

The benefit of distinguishing risks related to the use of facial recognition from those related to a particular implementation is to separate the fundamental problems raised by the use of this technology from those related to the state of the art at a given time. For example, the conclusion of the analysis could be that the use of facial recognition would be acceptable (level 3) if it could meet a set of essential requirements (in terms of performance, reliability, safety, fairness, etc.) but that existing solutions are not yet mature enough or that the proposed one is not satisfactory (level 4).

This phase requires, first of all, to precisely define the system, i.e. its deployment context, the technical specifications of the solution, the configuration parameters, the data used, the parties involved and their roles, etc. It is then necessary to evaluate the implementation of the system, in particular:

– Its performance and reliability, by measuring, for example, false positive and false negative rates.
– Its security by analyzing the confidentiality, integrity and availability requirements. This phase requires assumptions about the potential adversaries (sources of risk), particularly in terms of objectives, capabilities and strategies.
– The guarantees on the data used, including the training data and the various databases used by the system, and the protection of users' privacy.
– The fairness or potential biases of the system, by assessing, for example, error rates for different groups (ethnic, demographic, etc.) of the population.
– Transparency and explainability: are the algorithms, models and data used by the system available (publicly or through restricted access by independent experts)? Are the system's behavior and results understandable and explainable to users, especially in the case of false positives or negatives?

Finally, it is necessary to analyze the technical, organizational and legal accountability mechanisms put in place. For example, the following questions should be asked: who are the actors involved and responsible for the system? How can these actors be "accountable" for their actions and to whom? What measures are planned to ensure the oversight of the processing? Do they involve independent third parties, stakeholder representatives, citizens?

More generally, a facial recognition system is not a technical object that can be analyzed in isolation, regardless of the socio-economic context of its deployment. Rather, it is an example of socio-technical system. The analysis of an implementation should therefore consider all its facets, including the sociological (actors concerned, roles and interests in the system, perception of the replacement of human activities by machines, impact on human relations, etc.), economic (development, deployment and maintenance costs, etc.) and strategic (dependence on certain industrial actors or foreign powers, risks of cyber-attacks, etc.) dimensions. These elements must then be evaluated in the light of the declared purpose and assessed in comparison with alternative solutions.

Examples of key questions to ask at this stage are:

- Are the technical specifications of the system known?
- Has the performance (reliability, security, fairness, etc.) of the system been rigorously assessed?
- Are accountability measures sufficient?
- What are the possible impacts, positive or negative, in the short and long term, of weaknesses in the implementation of the system for all stakeholders? Are they of major or minor importance?
- Can negative effects be prevented or reduced and positive effects promoted or amplified? Have sufficient countermeasures been put in place?
- What is the financial cost of the system (development, deployment, maintenance, etc.)? Is it acceptable in view of the purpose?
- Could other implementation options offer a better balance between risks and benefits (at an acceptable cost)?
- Based on these elements, is the solution acceptable?
- If not, could other options for implementing facial recognition be acceptable?

3.5 Connecting Our Analysis Framework with Data Protection Impact Assessments

In addition to the four levels of analysis presented in the previous section, Fig. 1 includes a fifth step, a Data Protection Impact Assessment (DPIA), which is required by the GDPR [11] and the Law Enforcement Directive [10] for applications processing biometric data. It should be noted that, even if this is not its primary objective, the approach proposed in this paper may be used to feed a DPIA. In particular, it includes, as required by Article 35 of the GDPR, "a systematic description of the envisaged processing operations and the purposes of the processing" and "an assessment of the necessity and proportionality of the processing operations in relation to the purposes". However, the objective of our method is different since it is not only about "an assessment of the risks to the rights and freedoms of data subjects" and its goal is not focused on the protection of personal data as provided for in the GDPR. Our analysis goes beyond personal data processing and covers ethical issues such as fairness or consequences in terms of well-being [7]. We also stress the fact that the impact analysis should, at each stage, question the proposed choices and consider alternative options. Conversely, we do not consider the legal dimension here, such as the legal basis for the processing, which should be part of the DPIA.

4   Conclusion

In this paper, we have presented an overview of our methodology and illustrated the approach with several examples. Interested readers can find more details about the practical use of the methodology in an extended version of this position paper published as an Inria report [7]. This report illustrates in particular the benefit of the use of ethical matrices [12] to facilitate the identification and analysis of issues, at each step of the analysis. Ethical matrices were initially proposed by Ben Mepham in the field of bioethics and they have then been used in other fields such as food or energy. They provide a way to represent concisely all issues for all stakeholders. As a result, they can serve as a basis for debate and argumentation when different points of view are expressed.

A key condition for the successful application of our methodology is the ability to provide evidence to support the arguments or assumptions put forward in the analysis. At least three types of arguments can be distinguished: (1) arguments already supported by experimental measures or results broadly accepted by the scientific community (such as those concerning the risks of bias in algorithms); (2) arguments that are not validated by sufficient studies but that could be tested (such as those concerning the benefits of facial recognition in the police field); and (3) arguments that are based on subjective or political positions (such as the argument that the development of facial recognition should not be too constrained so as not to harm innovation) and are not subject to experimental evaluation. In addition, when experiments are conducted to validate hypotheses, they must follow a precise protocol and should be validated by an independent third party. As the CNIL points out, experimentations "should not have the ethical purpose or effect of accustoming people to intrusive surveillance techniques, with the more or less explicit aim of preparing the ground for further deployment" [8].

We also believe that accountability [5] is key requirement for the deployment of any facial recognition system is. Indeed, it is not uncommon, even in democratic countries, that technologies initially deployed for the purpose of combating terrorism or crime are eventually extended to the surveillance of other categories of persons, such as journalists or activists. Facial recognition is not immune to this risk. Indeed, once images are captured, recorded and potentially analyzed, no technical solution can provide an absolute guarantee that the system will not be misused, prove to be less efficient than expected, or even erroneous. It is therefore essential to put in place measures requiring any entity to report on its use of a facial recognition system, including the implementation of precise rules for management of databases (procedure for entering a person into the database, cross-referencing with other databases, possibility of contestation, measures to enhance the security of the database, etc.), providing guarantees on the quality of the algorithms (performance, absence of bias, etc.), and recording in a secure manner all uses of the data, the purpose of these uses, the proof of their authorization, etc. To be effective, such measures should be overseen by a competent independent body capable of providing all stakeholders (including citizens or their organizations) with visibility and guarantees on the use of these systems. Last but not least, the sanctions imposed on entities that do not comply with their obligations should sufficiently deterrent.

It should be stressed that, although this paper is illustrated mainly with examples of facial recognition applications for public services, similar (or even more) attention should be paid to the uses of facial recognition by private actors. The associated risks can also be very high and the benefits less obvious. Failing to consider commercial applications would lead to the paradoxical situation, such as the one mentioned by Sidney Fussell about the city of San Francisco, where police forces cannot use facial recognition to look for a suspect after a shooting, while a shopkeeper in the city would be authorized to use the same technology to analyze the behavior of his customers[13].

Finally, we would like to emphasize that while the current focus on automated facial recognition is important and desirable (in particular because of the unique combination of features presented in Sect. 2), we should not forget that facial recognition is only one technology amongst many others to identify and profile users. Focusing on facial recognition should not distract us from other tracking and profiling technologies and from the structural question of whether governments or companies should be building massive databases of personal information in the first place. It is important to bear the broader picture in mind.

In conclusion, we would like to suggest several concrete actions that should be considered without delay:

- The definition of a reference framework for conducting impact analyzes of facial recognition systems. We hope that this paper can contribute to the development of such a reference framework, but it should be defined and issued by an official body. Previous examples of this approach in connected areas include the DPIA methodology and tool proposed by the CNIL[14] and the "algorithmic impact assessment" framework issued by the Canadian government[15].
- The definition of standards or methodologies for the testing, validation and certification of facial recognition systems. These standards should provide guarantees regarding the compliance of these systems with essential requirements, for example in terms of accuracy, absence of bias and database security. In addition, these guarantees should be verifiable by independent third parties. To this end, it is necessary to define standard evaluation schemes in the same spirit as existing information technology security or safety evaluation schemes.
- The definition of a protocol for the experimentation of facial recognition systems in real environments. As mentioned above, laboratory studies are sometimes insufficient and field testing may be necessary to validate certain assumptions. However, there is currently no reference protocol to organize these experimentations.

---

[13] https://www.theatlantic.com/technology/archive/2019/02/san-francisco-proposes-ban-government-face-recognition/581923/.

[14] https://www.cnil.fr/en/privacy-impact-assessment-pia.

[15] https://www.tbs-sct.gc.ca/pol/doc-fra.aspx?id=32592.

References

1. Angwin, J., Larson, J., Mattu, S., Kirchner, L.: Machine bias: There's software used across the country to predict future criminals. And it's biased against blacks. ProPublica (2016). https://www.propublica.org/article/machine-bias-risk-assessments-in-criminal-sentencing
2. Axon: First report of the Axon AI & Policing Technology Ethics Board (2019). https://www.policingproject.org/axon-fr
3. Big Brother Watch: Face off. The lawless growth of facial recognition in UK policing (2018). https://bigbrotherwatch.org.uk/wp-content/uploads/2018/05/Face-Off-final-digital-1.pdf
4. Buolamwini, J., Gebru, G.: Gender shades: intersectional accuracy disparities in commercial gender classification. Mach. Learn. Res. **81**, 77–91 (2018)
5. Butin, D., Chicote, M., Le Métayer, D.: Strong accountability: beyond vague promises. In: Gutwirth, S., Leenes, R., De Hert, P. (eds.) Reloading Data Protection, pp. 343–369. Springer, Dordrecht (2014). https://doi.org/10.1007/978-94-007-7540-4_16
6. Castelluccia, C., Le Métayer, D.: Understanding algorithmic decision-making: opportunities and challenges. Study for the European Parliament (STOA) (2019). https://www.europarl.europa.eu/stoa/en/document/EPRS_STU(2019)624261
7. Castelluccia, C., Le Métayer, D.: Impact analysis of facial recognition - towards a rigorous methodology. Inria Note (2020). https://hal.inria.fr/hal-02480647/document
8. CNIL: Facial recognition; for a debate living up to the challenges (2019). https://www.cnil.fr/sites/default/files/atoms/files/facial-recognition.pdf
9. European Commission: On Artificial Intelligence - A European approach to excellence and trust (2020). https://ec.europa.eu/info/sites/info/files/commission-white-paper-artificial-intelligence-feb2020-en.pdf
10. European Parliament: Directive 2016/680 of the European Parliament and of the Council of 27 April 2016 on the protection of natural persons with regard to the processing of personal data by competent authorities for the purposes of the prevention, investigation, detection or prosecution of criminal offences or the execution of criminal penalties, and on the free movement of such data (2016)
11. European Parliament: Regulation 2016/679 of the European Parliament and of the Council of 27 April 2016 on the protection of natural persons with regard to the processing of personal data and on the free movement of such data (General Data Protection Regulation) (2016)
12. Forsberg, E.-M.: The ethical matrix - a tool for ethical assessments for biotechnology. Golbal Bioeth. **17**, 167–172 (2004)
13. Georgetown Law Center on Privacy & Technology: The perpetual line-up. Unregulated police face recognition in America (2016). https://www.perpetuallineup.org/
14. ICO: The use of live facial recognition technology by law enforcement in public places (2019). https://ico.org.uk/media/about-the-ico/documents/2616184/live-frt-law-enforcement-opinion-20191031.pdf
15. Penney, J.: Chilling effects: online surveillance and wikipedia use. Berkeley Technol. Law J. **31**(1), 117–182 (2016)

Privacy by Design

Privacy Through Data Recolouring

Giuseppe D'Acquisto[1], Alessandro Mazzoccoli[3], Fabio Ciminelli[3],
and Maurizio Naldi[2,3](✉) (iD)

[1] Italian Data Protection Authority, Piazza Venezia 11, 00187 Rome, Italy
g.dacquisto@gpdp.it
[2] Department of Law, Economics, Politics and Modern Languages, LUMSA
University, Via Marcantonio Colonna 19, 00192 Rome, Italy
m.naldi@lumsa.it
[3] Department of Civil Engineering and Computer Science, University of Rome Tor
Vergata, Via del Politecnico 1, 00133 Rome, Italy

Abstract. Current anonymization techniques for statistical databases
exhibit significant limitations, related to the utility-privacy trade-off, the
introduction of artefacts, and the vulnerability to correlation. We propose an anonymization technique based on the whitening/recolouring
procedure that considers the database as an instance of a random population and applies statistical signal processing methods to it. In response
to a query, the technique estimates the covariance matrix of the true
data and builds a linear transformation of the data, producing an output that has the same statistical characteristics of the true data up to
the second order, but is not directly linked to single records. The technique is applied to a real database containing the location data of taxi
trips in New York. We show that the technique reduces the amount of
artefacts introduced by noise addition while preserving first- and second-
order statistical features of the true data (hence maintaining the utility
of the query output).

Keywords: Privacy · Anonymization · Differential privacy ·
Whitening · Recolouring

1 Introduction

Statistical databases have since long represented a major source of information
[24]. However, such databases may be queried to get accurate information on
smaller and smaller portions of the database. Such a focussed querying conflicts
with the need to protect the privacy of those subjects whose data are included
in the database. The related overall aim in managing the database is to protect
an individual's data (even obfuscating its presence), while providing a useful
response to the query.

The most prominent method to achieve that result is noise addition, which
consists of simply adding noise to the actual data. The technique has been tested
first by Spruill [25]. It has many variants (see the reviews by Brand in [4] and

© Springer Nature Switzerland AG 2020
L. Antunes et al. (Eds.): APF 2020, LNCS 12121, pp. 61–72, 2020.
https://doi.org/10.1007/978-3-030-55196-4_4

Domingo-Ferrer, Sebé, and Jordi Castellá-Roca in [6] as well as [20]), which differ
for the type of noise added (uncorrelated as in [27,28] vs correlated as in [5])
and for the operations performed on the data (just addition vs linear [14] or
nonlinear transformation [26]).

It has been shown that when the Laplace model is chosen to generate the
noise (rather than the straightforward Gaussian choice), we obtain what has
been named differential privacy, first defined in the introductory paper by Dwork
[7], later summarized in [8], and re-examined in 2011 [9]. Probably due to its
simplicity, the technique of adding noise suffers from several limitations, the most
severe of which is the inescapable trade-off between utility and privacy: the more
privacy protection we wish, the more noise we must add, the less useful is the
output data.

In this paper, we wish to redraw that trade-off, by proposing an alternative
technique that does not rely simply on the addition of noise but rather takes
into account the statistical characteristics of the true data to be protected. The
technique employs the whitening/recolouring method described first in [23] to
produce an output that has the same first- and second-order statistics of the true
data, yet does not show any direct link to the true individual records. In [23],
we stopped at the method formulation and some theoretical indistinguishability
properties. Here we show the application of our technique to a public database
containing the location data of taxi trips in New York and demonstrate the
applicability of the technique in a real instance as well as its properties.

The paper is organized as follows. After a brief outline of the differential
privacy technique and its limitations in Sect. 2, we survey the past attempts to
address those limitations in Sect. 3. Our recolouring technique is described in
Sect. 4, and the results of its application to the real instance of New York's taxi
trips are reported in Sect. 5.

2   Differential Privacy: Definition and Limitations

Our starting point in the development of privacy protection through whitening
and recolouring is differential privacy, which today represents the most established method to achieve privacy protection while exploiting the information
contained in statistical databases. In this section, we review the main concepts
involved in differential privacy and highlight its limitations.

In qualitative terms, we achieve differential privacy for a subject if its inclusion in the database of interest makes practically no difference in the query
results. In order to achieve differential privacy, we introduce uncertainty in the
query results through the addition of noise, so that any observer will get essentially the same information about any individual's private information through
querying the database, whether or not that individual is included in the database
itself. By adding noise to the query results, the outcome of the query becomes
a random variable (the resulting mechanism is often referred to as a randomized query response mechanism). Noise can be added either at the end of the
query process (the actual query output is the true outcome plus some noise) or

directly to the original data included in the dataset before the query is issued (which ensures that the outcome of the query is consequently randomized).

Actually, there exist two notions of differential privacy that have been defined and generally adopted in literature: ϵ-differential privacy and (ϵ, δ)-differential privacy (also called approximate differential privacy [19]).

First, a randomized query response mechanism $\mathcal{Q}$ is said to be ϵ-differentially private ($\epsilon > 0$) when, for each pair of neighbouring datasets D_1 and D_2 that differ on a single element (i.e., the data of one individual) and all subsets S of possible answers to that query, we have

$$\frac{\mathbb{P}[\mathcal{Q}(D_1) \in S]}{\mathbb{P}[\mathcal{Q}(D_2) \in S]} \leq e^\epsilon \qquad (1)$$

Instead, a query response mechanism $\mathcal{Q}$ is (ϵ, δ)-differentially private ($\epsilon > 0$ and $0 < \delta < 1$) when, for each pair of neighboring datasets D_1 and D_2 and all subsets S of possible answers to that query, we have

$$\mathbb{P}[\mathcal{Q}(D_1) \in S] \leq \mathbb{P}[\mathcal{Q}(D_2) \in S]e^\epsilon + \delta \qquad (2)$$

It is to be noted that the definition of ϵ-differential privacy is absolute: for any pair of neighbouring databases, the possible outputs of any query will appear with close probability. By contrast, (ϵ, δ)-differential privacy is less stringent, since it allows for queries with results that occur with $\delta > 0$ probability only if a specific individual is present in D_1 and not in D_2. Injecting Laplacian noise is a practical way to engineer an ϵ-differentially private query-response mechanism, while Gaussian noise can be applied to obtain an (ϵ, δ)-differentially private query-response mechanism.

Despite such desirable properties, differential privacy exhibits several serious limitations in practice.

First, differential privacy is defined for single database instances; that is, the neighbouring databases (D_1 and D_2) in the definitions are composed of constant (non-random) values. While differential privacy ensures that the query responses from these databases are probabilistically indistinguishable within some factor, there always exists a database instance that is more likely than others given the query response. Our recent research on this issue shows exactly how this database instance can be inferred via a Bayesian analysis of query responses [21].

Second, as with many data privacy measures (e.g., k-anonymity, l-diversity, and t-closeness), there is no universally accepted rule for the choice of the privacy controlling factor, which is ϵ in this case. Instead, setting this parameter is left to heuristics and open to interpretation. Also, it has been shown in [17] that the variance of the injected (Laplacian) noise must be proportional to the global sensitivity Δ of the query to maintain all the properties of differential privacy. That sensitivity (which, for brevity, we assumed to be scalar without loss of generality) is defined for two neighbouring databases D_1 and D_2 as [12]

$$\Delta = \max \| \mathcal{Q}(D_1) - \mathcal{Q}(D_2) \|. \qquad (3)$$

Sensitivity depends on the constants in D_1 and D_2: if the global sensitivity is large, so is the variance of the noise. The consequence is that either 1) the utility of the data for successive inquiries is drastically reduced or 2) the safeguards for the individuals to whom the data corresponds becomes more theoretical than factual.

This is confirmed by the mechanisms proposed in [22], where ϵ is set so that we have a p probability of finding the true value c within a $\pm w$ relative distance of the query output:

$$\epsilon = -\frac{\ln(1-p)}{wc}, \tag{4}$$

which leads to large noise injection whenever the desired probability is very low. Other choices proposed in the literature have been to let it be set by users [15]; linking it to a payment to users by the budget-constrained analyst [11]; relating it to the probability to detect the presence of the individual in the database [10].

Third, it has been shown in [23] that, when the probabilistic nature of the original data is taken into account, correlation within the data allows for potential re-identification. For instance, when a certain attribute for an individual is outlying with respect to its correlated attributes and is prominent in a sample database or - more formally - when, for a query $\mathcal{Q}$, there exists a region S of possible query outputs, such that

$$\mathbb{P}[\mathcal{Q}(D_1) \in S] \gg \mathbb{P}[\mathcal{Q}(D_2) \in S] \tag{5}$$

then the amount of noise that needs to be injected to make query responses to databases D_1 and D_2 probabilistically indistinguishable will be very high. However, in doing so, the original dataset will either 1) sustain a major utility hit, due to a loss of the correlation between the attributes or 2) fail to protect the individual in question. These deficiencies make it challenging for organizations to justify the adoption of differential privacy.

3   Related Literature

The limitations of differential privacy have been recognized in the literature, and some attempts have been made at removing them, in particularly by devising strategies to preserve higher-order statistics during the anonymization process. In this section, we review the most significant contributions.

For instance, in [18], it was recognized that the dependencies between the attributes of an individual could make individuals more vulnerable to privacy attacks. In order to address this vulnerability, a dependent perturbation mechanism was proposed that achieves differential privacy. More specifically, the amount of injected noise was made dependent on the values of specific attributes in the n-tuples (which can be viewed as the conditioning variables in a Bayesian setting). This requires the heavy computational burden of selecting a different noise distribution every time a query is submitted, depending on the state of the system.

An approach similar to ours was instead proposed in [16], under the name of spectral anonymization. In this technique, the anonymizer is not required to operate on the original basis of the data set. Rather, it projects the data onto a spectral basis, applies an anonymization method, and then projects the data back into the original basis. This approach did not, however, conform to differential privacy.

A neural network was proposed in [2] to generate synthetic data closely resembling those in the original dataset, through a generative adversarial network (GAN). In that approach, two separate neural networks are trained, a generator and a discriminator. The former is trained to generate individual records from a given distribution, while the latter takes in both real and synthetic data from the generator as input and is trained to classify a record as belonging to either set. As the classifier is trained, the generator learns to build datasets that fool the discriminator, which culminates in a situation where the discriminator can no longer differentiate between real and synthetic data. This approach achieves differential privacy but does not address the problem of how to add noise to the original data: without operational indications on the amount of noise to add when we wish a set level of differential privacy, we cannot achieve the desired balance between privacy and utility.

Finally, and more recently, a team at Amazon research has investigated how to improve the performance of differentially private Gaussian query response mechanisms (but not taking into account the issue of correlated data) [1]. In that paper, two privacy regimes are considered: 1) a high privacy regime (when $\epsilon \to 0$); and 2) a low privacy regime (when $\epsilon > 1$), each requiring a different noise variance calibration approach. This is specifically addressed through the exact cumulative Gaussian distribution function. An empirical evaluation with this approach was shown to be capable of achieving a 25% improvement in performance for (ϵ, δ)-differentially private mechanisms.

4   Recoloured Privacy

We have outlined the criticalities of differential privacy in Sect. 2 and the attempts to overcome its limitations in Sect. 3. In this section, we describe our proposal for a new anonymization scheme that does not suffer from the limitation of differential privacy. The resulting data processing scheme will be named recoloured privacy since it draws upon the use of a recolouring technique borrowed from signal processing.

We first introduce three novel significant features of our anonymization technique by contrasting them with the features of the current approach to differential privacy.

First, we shift the perspective from single database instances to a probabilistic approach. We model actual databases as samples drawn from a given probability distribution. When statistical patterns or characteristics (e.g., first- and second-order statistics, i.e. mean and covariance) of a population (e.g., consumers of goods or patients in a clinical trial) are known, this framing will enable us to assess the true effectiveness of differential privacy for a population as a whole, rather than just for the single instance.

Second, we will shift the perspective from global query sensitivity to local sensitivity. Our processing may be applied to each record separately. This will allow each database attribute to be amended independently to preserve data utility.

Third, we will address the correlation problem by introducing an additional layer to the process of data anonymization. Specifically, we propose to apply a linear transformation to the database records after the injection of noise, as suggested in [23]. In doing so, records will less prone to re-identification through outlying events. Moreover, this will allow for a larger portion of a population to benefit from privacy safeguards.

We can now describe the quantities of interest in a formal mathematical setting. We assume to have a sample database X, which is a collection of m independent records, each characterized by n attributes. The database can then be represented by an $m \times n$ matrix of independent n-tuples (each n-tuple representing the record of a specific individual). Each n-tuple can in turn be represented as a vector. The i-th tuple is the vector $\underline{x}_i = \{x_{i1}, x_{i2}, \dots, x_{in}\}$, $i = 1, 2, \dots, m$. For the time being, we consider each vectors x_i drawn from a zero-mean multivariate Gaussian distribution. We describe the generic Gaussian multivariate distribution with mean vector μ and covariance matrix Σ as $g(\mu, \Sigma)$, so that the distribution of $\underline{x}_i$ is $f_{\underline{x}_i} = g(\underline{0}, \Sigma)$. The noise injection stage is accomplished by adding i.i.d. zero-mean Gaussian noise $\underline{r}_i \sim g(\underline{0}, \sigma_i)$ to each vector, so that we have the noisy vector $z_i = \{x_{i1} + r_{i1}, x_{i2} + r_{i2}, \dots, x_{in} + r_{in}\}$. Since the injection of noise does not act on the mean value, but just on the covariance matrix, the resulting distribution after noise injection is $f_{z_i} = g(\underline{0}, \Sigma^*)$. The noisy version of the database is then indicated as Z. The resulting vector z is what is output in differential privacy, as shown in Fig. 1a. We recall that differential privacy is defined with reference to two databases differing for just one record, i.e. one row of the associated matrix.

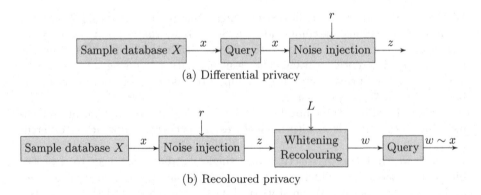

(a) Differential privacy

(b) Recoloured privacy

Fig. 1. Processing in differential privacy and recoloured privacy

Our proposal for anonymization, which we call recoloured privacy, is instead shown in Fig. 1b. Our scheme involves an additional processing stage (called Whitening/Recolouring) that outputs a modified database W. We aim to make the two databases (the original X and the modified W) probabilistically indistinguishable. We find that there exists a linear transformation L, such that two databases X and W have the same first- and second-order statistics (i.e., mean and covariance). If the sample database X is populated with Gaussian random variables, then the two databases are probabilistically undistinguishable: any query $\mathcal{Q}$ issued to X or W will yield the same probabilistic outcome. Probabilistic indistinguishability of databases is an absolute property and provide a much stronger guarantee than probabilistic indistinguishability of the query results.

The whitening/recolouring transformation L can be built on the eigenvalues and eigenvectors of the covariance matrices in the process. This will require a double layer of linear transformations, a technique that is well known in the field of digital signal processing [13], but not applied in the differential privacy domain. Specifically, this approach is carried out in two stages. The first is a whitening processing, namely a transformation of a random vector with given covariance matrix into another random vector whose covariance is the identity matrix. The second is a colouring processing (conceptually akin to the inverse of the whitening transform), where a multivariate variable whose components are i.i.d. with unit variance is transformed into a new random vector with some desired covariance matrix (in our case the same of the original process governing the database X).

For completeness, we report now that linear transformation; the details of the procedure can be read, e.g., in [13]. Let's consider the n-tuple representing the generic record $x \in \mathbb{R}^n$ be an n-dimensional Gaussian random vector with mean μ and covariance matrix Σ. We assume that the vector x has been reduced to zero mean by subtracting its mean value. After noise injection, we get the record z, whose covariance matrix Σ_z is assumed to be positive definite and can be represented as

$$\Sigma_z = \mathbb{E}[zz^T] = \Phi_z \Lambda_z \Phi_z^{-1} = \Phi_z \Lambda_z^{\frac{1}{2}} \Lambda_z^{\frac{1}{2}} \Phi_z^{-1}, \tag{6}$$

where Λ_z is the eigenvalues matrix of Σ_z (i.e., the diagonal matrix whose entries are the eigenvalues), its square root is the matrix $\Lambda_z^{\frac{1}{2}}$ such that $\Lambda_z = \Lambda_z^{\frac{1}{2}} \Lambda_z^{\frac{1}{2}}$, and Φ_z is the eigenvector matrix (i.e., the matrix whose columns are the eigenvectors), which exhibits the property that $\Phi_z^{-1} = \Phi_z^T$.

In order to accomplish the whitening stage, we need to transform the noisy record vector into a random vector whose covariance is the identity matrix, so that it possesses the statistical properties of white noise (total absence of correlation).

If we define an auxiliary vector $y = \Phi_z^T x$, we can show that its components are uncorrelated since its covariance is simply the diagonal matrix made of the eigenvalues of Σ_z:

$$\mathbb{E}[yy^T] = \mathbb{E}[\Phi_z^T zz^T \Phi_z] = \Phi_z^T \mathbb{E}[zz^T]\Phi_z = \Phi_z^T \Sigma_z \Phi_z = \Lambda_z. \tag{7}$$

If we now introduce the auxiliary vector $v = \Lambda_z^{-\frac{1}{2}} y = \Lambda_z^{-\frac{1}{2}} \Phi_z^T z$, we can prove that its covariance is the identity matrix

$$\Sigma_v = \mathbb{E}[vv^T] = \Lambda_z^{-\frac{1}{2}} \Phi_z^T \mathbb{E}[zz^T] \Phi_z \Lambda_z^{-\frac{1}{2}} = \Lambda_z^{-\frac{1}{2}} \Phi_z^T \Phi_z \Lambda_z^{\frac{1}{2}} \Lambda_z^{\frac{1}{2}} \Phi_z^{-1} \Phi_z \Lambda_z^{-\frac{1}{2}} = \mathbb{I}, \quad (8)$$

since $\Lambda_z^{\frac{1}{2}}$ is symmetric, so that v is statistically equivalent to white noise.

The linear transformation that whitens the input vector Z is therefore $v = \Lambda_z^{-\frac{1}{2}} \Phi_z^T z$ (see [3] for the computation of the square root of a matrix).

After whitening, we need to perform recolouring, i.e., return to the characteristics of the true population (i.e., a Gaussian random vector with covariance matrix Σ). Since the covariance matrix Σ of the true record x can be decomposed in the product of its eigenvalue and eigenvector matrices (respectively Λ and Φ) as

$$\Sigma = \Phi \Lambda \Phi^T = \Phi \Lambda^{\frac{1}{2}} \Lambda^{\frac{1}{2}} \Phi^T, \quad (9)$$

the linear transformation

$$u = \Lambda^{\frac{1}{2}} v \quad (10)$$

scales the samples, while the further transformation

$$w = \Phi u = \Phi \Lambda^{\frac{1}{2}} v \quad (11)$$

rotates the data to introduce the original correlation according to the desired covariance matrix. Equation (12) represents then the colouring transformation.

The overall linear transformation performing the whitening/recolouring stage is then obtained as the cascade of the transformations considered so far:

$$L = \Phi \Lambda^{\frac{1}{2}} \Lambda_z^{-\frac{1}{2}} \Phi_z^T. \quad (12)$$

5   Experimental Results

In order to demonstrate the applicability of our recolouring method, we consider a public dataset about the use of taxis in Manhattan. In this section, we report the main characteristic of that dataset and show the results of the application of the recolouring method.

Our dataset includes the pick-up and drop-off locations of taxis in Manhattan on January 15, 2003. It is made of roughly 240000 trips, though we extract just 750 of them for our purposes, limiting ourselves to trips starting and ending inside Manhattan. The full dataset is available at www.andresmh. com/nyctaxitrips/.

In Fig. 2a, we report the true location of pick-up locations on Manhattan's map. Similar plots can be obtained for drop-off locations; in the following, for space reasons, we will refer to the treatment of pick-up locations only.

We then see the effect of the two major steps in our anonymization procedure, i.e., the addition of noise and the whitening/recolouring process.

White Gaussian noise is added to true data with variance $\sigma_{add} = (1 + \alpha)\sigma^2$, where σ is the standard deviation of the true data, and α is a multiplying factor that represents the severity of the distortion. In Fig. 2b, c, we report the effect of noise injection with $\alpha = 0.2, 0.8$. We see that the addition of noise may introduce some artefacts, i.e., the output of locations outside valid areas. In the case of Manhattan map, this essentially means showing pick-up or drop-off points inside the green areas of Central Park and on the sea.

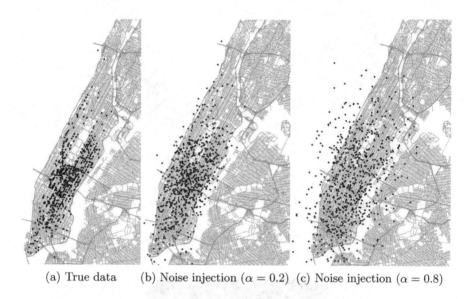

(a) True data   (b) Noise injection ($\alpha = 0.2$) (c) Noise injection ($\alpha = 0.8$)

Fig. 2. Pick-up points before and after noise injection

After injecting noise, we can manipulate the data through the application of our whitening/recolouring process with the linear transformation of Eq. 12. The results are shown in Fig. 3 for pick-up points. As can be seen, the data are much closer to the true data, though breaking the link with the true data for any single trip, and the presence of artefacts has been reduced. Most importantly, though not self-evident from the pictures, the first- and second-order statistics of the locations have been kept equal to the true data, as proven in [23].

We can get an additional view of the effect of recolouring by looking at the heatmaps, which allow us to see the concentration of taxis at any location; for pick-up points, black spots indicate the case of absence of trips starting at that location, while white spots correspond to the location of maximum concentration of starting points. In Fig. 4a, we see the heatmap of the true data, which shows two white spots (maximum concentration) in mid-Manhattan, very close to each other. The heatmaps in Figs. 4b and c show the effect of recolouring. As can be seen, the two white spots reappear, though being closer than in the true data, both when $\alpha = 0.2$ and when $\alpha = 0.8$. The presence of two white spots, though very close, can be inferred from the presence of two distinct red flames (especially visible in Fig. 4b). This means that recolouring allows getting the same statistics as the true data independently of the amount of noise that has been added.

(a) Recolouring ($\alpha = 0.2$)   (b) Recolouring ($\alpha = 0.8$)

Fig. 3. Pick-up points after recolouring

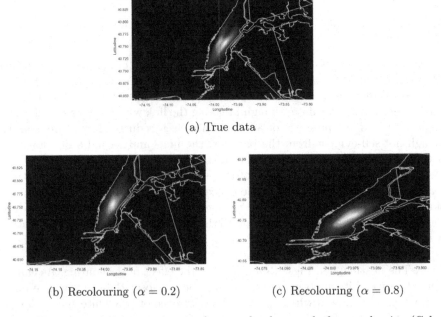

(a) True data

(b) Recolouring ($\alpha = 0.2$)   (c) Recolouring ($\alpha = 0.8$)

Fig. 4. Heatmaps of pick-up points in the true database and after recolouring (Color figure online)

6 Conclusions

Our transformation allows us to provide answers to queries that have the same first- and second-order statistics of the true data, hence are correct in a statistical sense. However, any link with the original data has been broken.

The transformation is linear, hence quite simple to implement, and relies just on the estimation of the covariance matrix of the original data.

In addition to the application to further databases to demonstrate the feasibility of the approach, we aim in our future work to quantify the performance, contrasting utility and privacy, and consider the accuracy of the estimation of the covariance matrix.

References

1. Balle, B., Wang, Y.X.: Improving the gaussian mechanism for differential privacy: Analytical calibration and optimal denoising. arXiv preprint arXiv:1805.06530 (2018)
2. Beaulieu-Jones, B.K., et al.: Privacy-preserving generative deep neural networks support clinical data sharing. Circ. Cardiovasc. Qual. Outcomes **12**(7), e005122 (2019)
3. Björck, Å., Hammarling, S.: A schur method for the square root of a matrix. Linear Algebra Appl. **52**, 127–140 (1983)
4. Brand, R.: Microdata protection through noise addition. In: Domingo-Ferrer, J. (ed.) Inference Control in Statistical Databases. LNCS, vol. 2316, pp. 97–116. Springer, Heidelberg (2002). https://doi.org/10.1007/3-540-47804-3_8
5. Ciriani, V., Capitani di Vimercati, S., Foresti, S., Samarati, P.: Microdata protection. In: Yu, T., Jajodia, S. (eds.) Secure Data Management in Decentralized Systems. Advances in Information Security, vol 33, pp. 291–321. Springer, Boston (2007). https://doi.org/10.1007/978-0-387-27696-0_9
6. Domingo-Ferrer, J., Sebé, F., Castellà-Roca, J.: On the security of noise addition for privacy in statistical databases. In: Domingo-Ferrer, J., Torra, V. (eds.) PSD 2004. LNCS, vol. 3050, pp. 149–161. Springer, Heidelberg (2004). https://doi.org/10.1007/978-3-540-25955-8_12
7. Dwork, C.: Differential privacy. In: Bugliesi, M., Preneel, B., Sassone, V., Wegener, I. (eds.) ICALP 2006. LNCS, vol. 4052, pp. 1–12. Springer, Heidelberg (2006). https://doi.org/10.1007/11787006_1
8. Dwork, C.: Differential privacy: a survey of results. In: Agrawal, M., Du, D., Duan, Z., Li, A. (eds.) TAMC 2008. LNCS, vol. 4978, pp. 1–19. Springer, Heidelberg (2008). https://doi.org/10.1007/978-3-540-79228-4_1
9. Dwork, C.: A firm foundation for private data analysis. Commun. ACM **54**(1), 86–95 (2011)
10. He, X., Yuan, H., Chen, Y.: Exploring the privacy bound for differential privacy: from theory to practice. EAI Endorsed Trans. Secur. Saf. **5**(18) (2019)
11. Hsu, J., et al.: Differential privacy: an economic method for choosing epsilon. In: 2014 IEEE 27th Computer Security Foundations Symposium (CSF), pp. 398–410. IEEE (2014)
12. Johnson, N., Near, J.P., Song, D.: Towards practical differential privacy for SQL queries. Proc. VLDB Endow. **11**(5), 526–539 (2018)

13. Kessy, A., Lewin, A., Strimmer, K.: Optimal whitening and decorrelation. Am. Statist. **72**(4), 309–314 (2018)
14. Kim, J.J.: A method for limiting disclosure in microdata based on random noise and transformation. In: Proceedings of the Section on Survey Research Methods, pp. 303–308. American Statistical Association (1986)
15. Kohli, N., Laskowski, P.: Epsilon voting: Mechanism design for parameter selection in differential privacy. In: 2018 IEEE Symposium on Privacy-Aware Computing (PAC), pp. 19–30. IEEE (2018)
16. Lasko, T.A., Vinterbo, S.A.: Spectral anonymization of data. IEEE Trans. Knowl. Data Eng. **22**(3), 437–446 (2009)
17. Lee, J., Clifton, C.: How much is enough? Choosing ε for differential privacy. In: Lai, X., Zhou, J., Li, H. (eds.) ISC 2011. LNCS, vol. 7001, pp. 325–340. Springer, Heidelberg (2011). https://doi.org/10.1007/978-3-642-24861-0_22
18. Liu, C., Chakraborty, S., Mittal, P.: Dependence makes you vulnerable: differential privacy under dependent tuples. In: Proceedings Network and Distributed System Security Symposium (NDSS 2016) (2016)
19. Meiser, S.: Approximate and probabilistic differential privacy definitions. IACR Cryptology ePrint Archive **2018**, 277 (2018)
20. Mivule, K.: Utilizing noise addition for data privacy, an overview. arXiv preprint arXiv:1309.3958 (2013)
21. Naldi, M., D'Acquisto, G.: Differential privacy for counting queries: can Bayes estimation help uncover the true value? arXiv preprint arXiv:1407.0116 (2014)
22. Naldi, M., D'Acquisto, G.: Differential privacy: an estimation theory-based method for choosing epsilon. CoRR, arXiv Preprint Series abs/1510.00917 (2015). http://arxiv.org/abs/1510.00917
23. Naldi, M., Mazzoccoli, A., D'Acquisto, G.: Hiding alice in wonderland: a case for the use of signal processing techniques in differential privacy. In: Medina, M., Mitrakas, A., Rannenberg, K., Schweighofer, E., Tsouroulas, N. (eds.) APF 2018. LNCS, vol. 11079, pp. 77–90. Springer, Cham (2018). https://doi.org/10.1007/978-3-030-02547-2_5
24. Shoshani, A.: Statistical databases: characteristics, problems, and some solutions. In: Proceedings of the 8th International Conference on Very Large Data Bases, pp. 208–222. Morgan Kaufmann Publishers Inc., Burlington (1982)
25. Spruill, N.L.: The confidentiality and analytic usefulness of masked business microdata. Rev. Public Data Use **12**(4), 307–314 (1984)
26. Sullivan, G.R.: The use of added error to avoid disclosure in microdata releases. Ph.D. thesis, Iowa State University (1989)
27. Tendick, P.: Optimal noise addition for preserving confidentiality in multivariate data. J. Statist. Plan. Infer. **27**(3), 341–353 (1991)
28. Tendick, P., Matloff, N.: A modified random perturbation method for database security. ACM Trans. Database Syst. (TODS) **19**(1), 47–63 (1994)

Privacy by Design Identity Architecture Using Agents and Digital Identities

Kalman C. Toth[1]($\boxtimes$) (iD), Ann Cavoukian[2], and Alan Anderson-Priddy[3]

[1] Sovereign Image, Portland Oregon, USA
kalmanctoth@gmail.com
[2] Global Privacy and Security by Design Centre, Toronto, Canada
ann.cavoukian@gpsbydesign.com
[3] Portland State University, Portland Oregon, USA
andersonpriddy@protonmail.com

Abstract. Today's web is comprised of a patchwork of identity solutions because neither identity nor privacy were designed-in when it was created. This paper proposes an integrative identity architecture that satisfies the principles of privacy by design from inception. Comprised of identity agents and digital identities that are tightly held by their owners, the architecture decentralizes control over identity from providers to users. Owners can manage their digital identities and private data such that liability risks are reduced for service providers without compromising ease-of-use. Identity agents and digital identities enable owners to prove who they are when required, protect their private and identifying data, and securely collaborate. Digital identities are virtualized to look and behave like credentials found in one's wallet thereby facilitating technology adoption and reducing dependency on remote access passwords. A gestalt privacy by design process has been used to discover and validate the architecture's privacy requirements and design elements, systematically reasoning about how the design satisfies the requirements. The process can be applied to organically improve the architecture and create a reference model for open source development. This paper also relates the architecture to W3C's models for verifiable credentials and decentralized identifiers, summarizes the architecture's features, capabilities and benefits, and suggests areas for further study.

Keywords: Privacy by design · Identity · Authentication · Verification · Security

1 Introduction

The integrative identity architecture described herein addresses the alarming growth in lost privacy, identity theft, impersonation and fraud due to breaches and identity theft over the web. The identity architecture has been motivated by the numerous identity and privacy challenges Internet stakeholders are grappling with every day. The work has also been stimulated by the European Union's General Data Protection Regulation (eugdpr.org) which addresses these and other serious privacy problems.

© Springer Nature Switzerland AG 2020
L. Antunes et al. (Eds.): APF 2020, LNCS 12121, pp. 73–94, 2020.
https://doi.org/10.1007/978-3-030-55196-4_5

The described architecture deploys *identity agents* that work on behalf of Internet device owners to tightly control and manage *digital identities* encapsulated therein. Identity agents enable consumers and providers to prove their identities, verify digital identities of other owners, and protect their private data and identifying information. Synthesized from prior art, the proposed architecture elaborates the principles of *Privacy by Design* as articulated by Ann Cavoukian [1] wherein she describes the goals of minimizing the disclosure of private information and data collection; protecting private information; securing transactions end-to-end; enabling express consent to access owner data; and establishing privacy as the system default setting. Our architecture also addresses anonymous and pseudo-anonymous forms of digital identity, ease-of-use, usability, and interoperability. We acknowledge Europe's related legal tradition in the field of data protection by design.

2 Challenges Addressed

The Internet's problems with identity, privacy and security have been revealed in recent years by large-scale breaches such as those of Capital One, the Marriott, Sony, Target, JP Morgan, Home Depot, Yahoo, Equifax, Facebook, and Google. Critical root causes include latent vulnerabilities in web services and browsers, and the huge volume of private data collected by providers to sustain their business models and password provisioning. Many providers are honeypots for hacking and malware.

Online web access suffers from many weaknesses. Widely acknowledged, the Internet is far too dependent on passwords. Users create and reuse weakly specified passwords that are easy to crack while validating questions are easy to guess. Identifying information is routinely used to name online accounts thereby helping unscrupulous actors create bogus accounts and impersonate. Biometrics, geo-location schemes and behavioral analytics have marginally elevated identity assurances.

A critical area lacking attention is third-party identity proofing. Banks, license bureaus, passport issuers and enterprises routinely proof the identity of their customers, citizens and employees before issuing attested credentials. To date, little has been written about incorporating proofing and attestation into web-based identity solutions.

Sir Timothy Berners-Lee, inventor of the world-wide-web, has expressed serious concern about privacy, especially as it relates to the Facebook scandal which allowed the private data of millions of users to be misused by political operatives. He has resolved to take back power from the big Internet players by giving users control over their private and identifying information [2].

3 Relevant Background

In 2005, Kim Cameron [3] said that the web is comprised of a patchwork of identity schemes. This suggests that inadequately and inconsistently deployed identity provisioning is a critical root cause of many of the Internet's privacy issues.

To tackle the web's privacy problems, Ann Cavoukian [1, 4] advocates Privacy by Design (PbD) where, among other things, privacy is proactive, preventative and embedded in the design; disclosure and data collection are minimized; privacy and security are simultaneously enhanced; end-to-end security thwarts surveillance; consent to access private data is expressly delegated; visibility, transparency and accountability are paramount; people control their privacy; and privacy is a system's default setting.

George Tomko and Cavoukian [5] propose applying artificial intelligence (AI) and machine learning (ML) to create cognitive agents to secure private data, control disclosure, delegate consent, and de-identify collected information.

Various writers have advocated moving away from server-controlled identity provisioning to single sign-on, federated, and decentralized (user controlled) identity schemes. Christopher Allen [6] and the Sovrin Foundation [7] have proposed leveraging blockchain technology to enable *self-sovereign digital identities* where users control their identities and central authorities have no control over them.

The World Wide Web Consortium (W3C) has been developing [8] an identity data model for specifying "verifiable credentials" (VCs) that can be deployed such that verifiable credentials are cryptographically secure, privacy respecting, and machine verifiable. The model enables multiple methods including digital signatures and zero-knowledge-proofs to verify the integrity and authenticity of verifiable credentials.

The W3C has also been developing a model for decentralized identifiers (DIDs) [9] which are independent of centralized registries, identity providers and certificate authorities. Using distributed ledger (blockchain) technology or other forms of decentralized networks, discrete entities (people, organizations, things) can register and thereby control one or more distinct DIDs across given contexts. Each DID is associated with a DID Document specifying cryptographic material, verification methods (e.g. digital signature), and endpoints used to prove that the entity controls the DID.

In the 2015 timeframe our founders began to develop the identity architecture described herein. Our original design concept was comprised of collaborating identity engines (identity agents) managing e-credentials (self-sovereign digital identities) on behalf of their owners (people and things). The architecture's identity agents decentralize control from central authorities to individual persons by tightly binding them to their digital identities and public/private keys thereby elevating non-repudiation strength and identity assurances associated with their digital identities.

4 Decentralizing Digital Identity: Shifting Control to Users

A critical vulnerability of server-centric identity schemes is that service provider repositories become honeypots for identity theft because of the enormous volume of private and identifying information such systems collect. The identity architecture described in this paper addresses this problem by shifting control over digital identity from service providers to users, that is, decentralizing identity.

Decentralization is realized by deploying identity agents that strongly bind owners to digital identities used to identify the owner, interoperate with other identity agents and applications, and proof and attest the identities of other owners.

Rather than agreeing to service provider requests for more private data than necessary, decentralization enables users to create and control digital identities that specify elements of their private and identifying information that they can subsequently use instead of passwords to prove who they are. This reduces how much information providers need to safeguard mitigating breach risk. Decentralizing identity disperses the attack surface across many users and devices reducing hacking and malware risks.

5   The Identity Landscape

Figure 1 positions popular identity solutions across the identity landscape in terms of:

A. What one knows - e.g. passwords and PINs,
B. What one holds - a device,
C. What one is - biometric authenticators,
D. What one asserts - attributes, claims, images, and
E. What others attest - in response to identity proofing and knowledge.

Group **A** includes online web services, single sign-on (SSO) systems and federated identity schemes that use remote access passwords and/or PINS to authenticate users. Group **B** depicts messaging solutions where peers use software apps installed on their personal platforms to collaborate securely. Group **C** shows authenticators leveraging biometrics and other schemes to authenticate holders and secure channels between users and web services. Group **D** depicts the World Wide Web Consortium's emerging Verifiable Claims model (W3C VC) [8] for specifying machine-readable digital identities, and the W3C DID model for specifying decentralized identifiers [9]. Group **E** includes

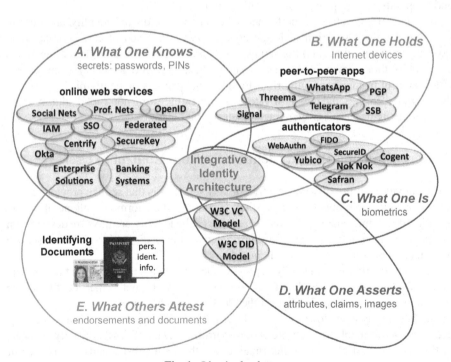

Fig. 1. Identity landscape

web-based systems where the identities of online users are proofed and attested by third parties using physical documents and web resources. The W3C VC and W3C DID models are covered by both **E** and **D** because third parties can elect to proof and attest verifiable credentials and decentralized identifiers.

None of the solutions depicted in Fig. 1 cover all five dimensions. They leave gaps in the identity landscape and exhibit certain operational shortcomings.

5.1 Covering the Gaps in the Identity Landscape

The following scenarios describe how the architecture addresses certain of these gaps:

a. Most users today specify distinct online user profiles and passwords for the web services they use - manually updating them as circumstances and needs demand. This represents a serious pain-point for most users. The identity agents of the proposed identity architecture addresses this by enabling users to explicitly control, assert, maintain, register and share digital identities that are subsequently employed to prove who they are and secure their private data and transactions. Since digital identities supported by the proposed identity architecture are virtualized physical credentials, maintaining them will be a relatively intuitive task for most users.

b. Messaging applications such as PGP, Signal and WhatsApp use distinct cryptographic methods and protocols to secure messages. The identity agents of the proposed identity architecture implement an application programming interface (API) that such apps can use to secure messages exchanged between collaborating users.

c. Selected enterprise systems today reduce or eliminate password usage by deploying personally held authenticators (e.g. FIDO, WebAuthn) employing biometrics and/or other such schemes to cryptographically bind users to designated web services. The proposed architecture leverages native and tethered authenticators to deploy digital identities that can be intuitively selected and used to cryptographically bind the owner to such web services - potentially across multiple sites.

d. Certain web applications, including social networks, deploy dissimilar password provisioning and reset procedures; implement liberal data collection and information sharing policies; and collect significant volumes of private and identifying data. The proposed architecture deploys identity agents and digital identities on personally held devices that enable owners to assert and control how much identifying and private data they disclose thereby minimizing how much is collected.

e. Web identities today are typically issued by centralized authorities. In the case of financial institutions, such as the banks, identity proofing is primarily conducted in-person. Online identity proofing and attestation has received little or no attention to date. Identity agents will enable identity proofing and attestation of owners' digital identities by ordinary users as well as designated identity providers.

f. The World Wide Web Consortium's emerging models for verifiable credentials [8] and decentralized identifiers [9] propose applying digital signature and zero-knowledge proofs to verify credentials and identifiers. However, they do not describe how bindings between users and their VCs or DIDs can be verified. In contrast, identity agents proposed herein are tightly controlled by their owners; encapsulate the owner's digital identities and integrated public/private key-pairs; and can crypto-graphically bind an owner's identity and attestation to digital identities, consent tokens and other such digital artifacts. Relying parties can cryptographically verify that the attested artifact is controlled by the identified owner (see Sect. 7.1).

6 The System Concept

The proposed identity architecture is comprised of *identity agents* and *digital identities* installed on the Internet devices of consumers and providers [11–13]. Identity agents encapsulate the owner's digital identities and work on behalf of their owners. Each identity agent leverages strong authentication mechanisms, possibly using multiple factors. The owner's digital identities specify characterizing attributes of the owner and have multiple public/private encryption key-pairs. These keys can be used by the identity agent to encrypt private information of the owner stored outside the context of her identity agent. An identity agent thereby binds the owner to selected private and identifying information specified by the owner's digital identities as well as private and identifying information stored outside her device or remotely.

Figure 2 illustrates the system concept. Depicted is a user having an identity agent that encapsulates the owner's authentication data thereby tightly binding the owner to her digital identities, her collaborators' digital identities, her consent tokens, and other artifacts - possibly by means of multiple authenticators. The owner's identity agent is

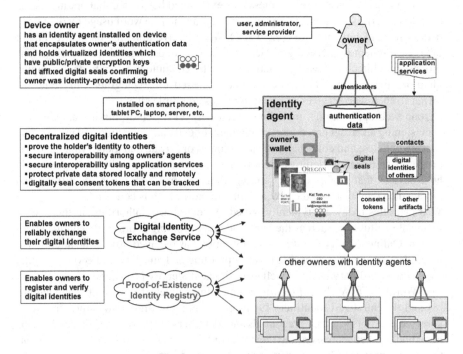

Fig. 2. System concept diagram

the integrative glue giving life to her digital identities, virtualizing them for intuitive ease-of-use such that they mimic physical credentials in her wallet.

An identity agent tightly binds the owner to his/her digital identities; protects each owner's private and identifying information; integrates with locally installed application services; and reliably interoperates with the identity agents of collaborating owners. Identity agents can use a web service to securely exchange digital identities with other parties as well as a proof-of-existence web service to safely register their digital identities such that collaborating owners can verify them.

The identity architecture is designed to encapsulate essential complexity within identity agents including the management of digital identities; protecting "secrets" (PINS, passwords, private keys); supporting local application interfaces; and implementing agent-to-agent protocols. This approach will enable the development[1] of well-behaved identity agents that consistently and correctly handle digital identities while protecting private information. Deploying such identity agents across the web will considerably improve upon the current patchwork of identity solutions and will off-load web applications and services from critical identity and privacy-related tasks.

7   Systematized Prior Art

The following prior art has been systematized to implement the identity architecture:

1. Symmetric and public key encryption methods;
2. Digital signature adapted to create digital seals;
3. Proof-of-existence using hashing adapted with digital seals;
4. Diffie-Hellman key agreement method adapted to exchange digital identities, and
5. Proof-of-possession combined with proof-of-custody to verify collaborators.

Three patents and one patent-pending provide additional details regarding items 2-5.[2]

7.1   Encryption Keys, Digital Sealing and Non-repudiation

The identity architecture[3] deploys digital identities with integrated private/public keys[4] including embossing/inspecting, signing/verifying, and decrypting/encrypting keys. Identity agents use embossing and inspecting keys to create, affix and verify digital seals[5] and attestations to digital identities, consent tokens, and other artifacts. Digital sealing elevates non-repudiation strength over traditional digital signature because owners tightly control their identity agents, digital identities and private keys used to cryptographically bind their identities and attestations to such digital artifacts.

---

[1] The founding team has created proof-of-concept and experimental prototypes validating the principle privacy requirements and design elements of the proposed identity architecture.

[2] Founding team intents to issue a license to open source developers similar to RedHat's patent promise to discourage patent aggression https://www.redhat.com/en/about/patent-promise.

[3] "Electronic Identity and Credentialing System", US Patent 9,646,150 B2, May 9, 2017.

[4] PGP (Pretty Good Privacy) uses signing/verifying and decrypting/encrypting key-pairs.

[5] "Methods for Using Digital Seals for Non-Repudiation of Attestations", US Patent 9,990,309B2, 2-20-2018; note: "sealing images" are used to render (virtualize) digital seals.

8 Methodology: Privacy by Design Process and Validation

Early in the development of critical systems, systems engineers often apply a "gestalt" process to discover requirements and design options, iterating until they converge on a suitable design satisfying the requirements. Figure 3 depicts the gestalt privacy by design process conducted to discover the identity architecture's privacy requirements and design elements. Privacy Requirements (R) specifies that the system is to enable users to prove who they are, protect their private and identifying information, and collaborate securely. System Design (D) specifies that owners' have devices with identity agents deploying digital identities used to meet the privacy requirements.

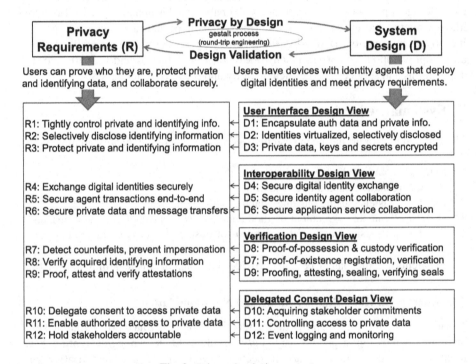

Fig. 3. Privacy by design process

Upon thoroughly iterating over all the requirements and design features, this privacy by design process has yielded mutually validated privacy requirements R1, R2 … R12 and design elements D1, D2 … D12 broken down by four design views as shown in Fig. 3. Each iteration organically contributed to the goal of showing that privacy by design principles have been met including minimizing the disclosure and collection of private and identifying information; securing transactions end-to-end; expressly delegating consent for specified purposes; capturing events for accountability purposes; and establishing privacy as the default setting. The privacy by design process can be applied to improve these privacy requirements and design elements.

9 Identity Architecture Validation

This section summarizes the results of our gestalt validation process. The annex reasons about how the design elements satisfy the privacy requirements.

9.1 User Interface Design View

This design view includes design elements D1 (encapsulate authentication data and private information), D2 (identities virtualized and selectively disclosed), and D3 (private data, keys and secrets encrypted). Figure 4 illustrates this view showing the owner, her device, identity agent, authentication data, digital identities stored in her wallet, and digital identities of others (collaborators) maintained in her contacts list.

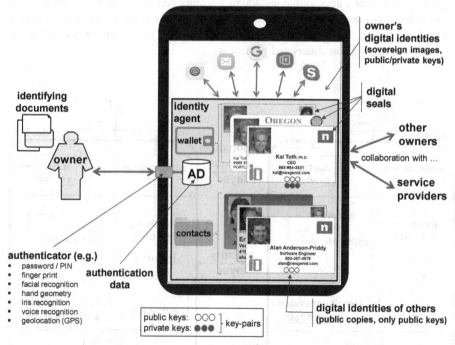

Fig. 4. User interface design view

Design element D1 (encapsulate authentication data and private information) satisfies privacy requirement R1 (tightly control private and identifying information). To protect against loss, theft and enable custody verification, the identity agent integrates with the device's authenticator(s) via an application programming interface (API) to encapsulate enrolled authentication data and identifying information of the owner.

Design element D2 (identities virtualized and selectively disclosed) satisfies privacy requirement R2 (selectively disclose identifying information). Owners manage digital identities mimicking the look and behavior of real-world credentials in their physical wallets. Identity agents leverage a common identity data model (e.g. [8]).

Design element D3 (private data, keys and secrets encrypted) satisfies privacy requirement R3 (protect private and identifying information). Digital identities have public/private keys that can be used by the owner's identity agent to protect private data and secrets including authentication data, passwords, PINs and digital identities.

Privacy by Design Default Settings. When the identity of a remote party is uncertain, the identity agent should use anonymous and pseudo-anonymous identities.

9.2 Interoperability Design View

This design view implements design elements D4 (secure digital identity exchange), D5 (secure identity agent collaboration) and D6 (secure application service collaboration). Figure 5 depicts two devices having identity agents capable of interoperating. Each agent offers a common user interface; exposes an API to applications; and leverages the transport layer. Interoperating identity agents thereby implement an identity layer among collaborating consumers and providers.

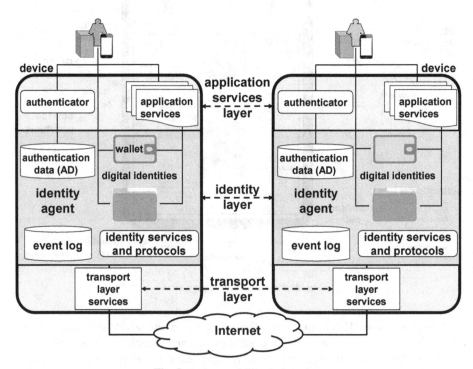

Fig. 5. Interoperability design view

Design element D4 (secure digital identity exchange) satisfies privacy requirement R4 (exchange digital identities securely). Options include exchanging digital identities in the clear; using one-time passwords; using HTTPS; and transferring them wirelessly. To mitigate risks, the Diffie-Hellman (DH) key agreement method [14] has been adapted[6]. Figure 6 depicts the protocol sequence where identifiers id1 and id2 are hashed and used to store and retrieve the public keys of each owner's digital identity, and the DH key agreement method is employed to calculate a shared symmetric key subsequently used to securely transfer the owners' digital identities. Figure 7 (1) depicts two owners using this exchange service.

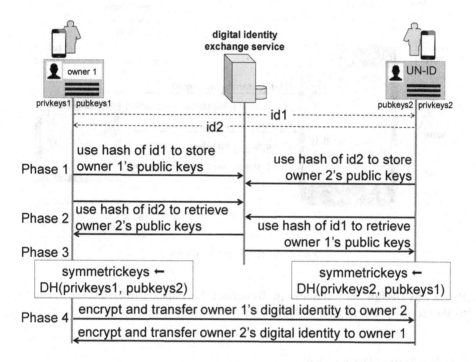

Fig. 6. Digital identity exchange service

Design element D5 (secure identity agent collaboration) satisfies privacy requirement R5 (secure agent transactions end-to-end). Once identity agents have reliably transferred digital identities, they can use them to bilaterally secure transactions end-to-end. The sender's signing key and the recipient's encrypting key are used when sending, and the recipient's decrypting and sender's verifying key when receiving.

Design element D6 (secure application service collaboration) uses identity agent APIs to satisfy privacy requirement R6 (secure private data and message transfers). Under the control of the sender, the application service acquires the sender's and recipient's digital identities, calculates a fingerprint[7], and then signs, encrypts and sends the message. The receiving application service receives, decrypts, verifies the signature and verifies the fingerprint of the incoming message.

---

[6] "Architecture and Methods for Self-Sovereign Digital Identity", US Patent (pending), provisional filed Oct. 8, 2018, utility application filed Nov. 12, 2018.

[7] Digital fingerprints are computed by hashing selected public encryption keys.

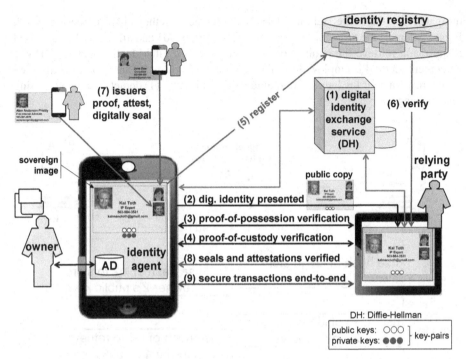

Fig. 7. Verification design view

Privacy by Design Default Settings. By default, the adapted Diffie-Hellman should be used to securely exchange digital identities before using them.

9.3 Verification Design View

The Verification Design View implements design elements D7 (proof-of-possession and proof-of-custody verification), D8 (proof-of-existence registration and verification), and D9 (proofing, attesting, sealing and verifying seals). Figure 7 depicts synchronous verification (2-4); asynchronous registration and verification (5, 6); issuing and verifying digitally sealed attestations (7, 8), and securing transactions (9).

Design element D7 (proof-of-possession and proof-of-custody verification) satisfies privacy requirement R7 (detect counterfeits and prevent impersonation). Figure 7 (2–4) shows two parties collaborating synchronously (online). The owner's identity agent presents a public copy of her digital identity (2) to the relying party's identity agent which verifies the digital identity by launching a proof-of-possession challenge (3) that only the originator can satisfy using a designated private key of her digital identity [10]. The relying party's identity agent then sends a proof-of-custody (4) demand to the originator's identity agent to authenticate the holder. Executed bilaterally, this protocol ensures that digital identities have been securely exchanged enabling subsequent transactions to be secured end-to-end (9).

Design element D8 (proof-of-existence registration and verification)[8] satisfies privacy requirement R8 (verify acquired identifying information) by combining digital sealing with proof-of-existence popularized by blockchain [15]. Figure 7 (5, 6) shows an owner registering a digital identity and a relying party verifying it. When registering a digital identity (5), the identity registry conducts proof-of-possession and proof-of-custody (D7) challenges to verify the registrant. If verified, the owner's agent hashes, seals and stores the hashed and sealed identity into the registry. A relying party acquiring a digital identity can hash it and inspect the seal (6) to verify it exists.

Design element D9 (proofing, attesting, sealing and verifying seals) satisfies privacy requirement R9 (proof, attest, and verify attestations) by proofing [16] and affixing attestations using digital seals. Figure 7 depicts two issuers having proofed, attested and digitally sealed the owner's digital identity (7) and a relying party verifying the affixed digital seals and attestations (8). Multiple parties can proof and fix attestations that cannot be repudiated using digital seals (see Sect. 7.1).

Privacy by Design Default Settings. Default settings should routinely register digital identities whenever they are created and updated and verify proof-of-existence, proof-of-possession and proof-of-custody whenever handling value transactions.

9.4 Delegated Consent Design View

This design view includes design elements D10 (acquiring stakeholder commitments), D11 (controlling access to private data) and D12 (event logging and monitoring). In contrast to server-centric consent models, our consent model enables stakeholders to use their digital identities to create digital seals that cryptographically bind their commitments to consent tokens which they cannot repudiate (see Sect. 7.1). Events are logged to enable mutual accountability.

Design element D10 (acquiring stakeholder commitments) satisfies privacy requirement R10 (delegate consent to access private data). Figure 8 shows a collaboration sequence wherein the requester, the owner, and the custodian use their identity agents to digitally seal a circulated consent token. These commitments include requesting (1), clearing/approving (2, 3), and granting access (4) to the resources of the owner. The requestor uses the finalized consent token to submit access requests (5) to the custodian to access the owner's resources (6) until expired or revoked.

Design element D11 (controlling access to private data) satisfies privacy requirement R11 (enable authorized access to private data). Finalized consent tokens control requester access to the resources of the owner managed by the resource custodian.

Design element D12 (event logging and monitoring) satisfies privacy requirement R12 (hold stakeholders accountable). Commitments and access events, traceable to stakeholders by way of digital seals and consent tokens, are tracked and reported.

Privacy by Design Default Settings. By default, stakeholders should be required to register digital identities and consent tokens in a proof-of-existence registry.

---

[8] "Systems and Methods for Registering and Acquiring E-Credentials using Proof-of-Existence and Digital Seals", US Pat 10,127,378 B2, issued Nov. 13, 2018.

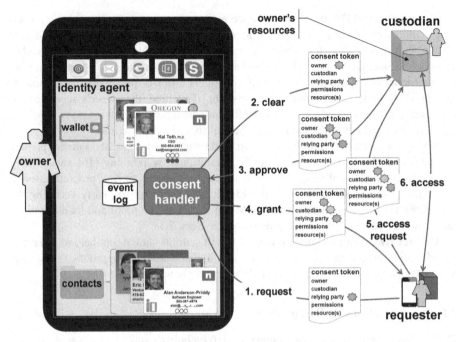

Fig. 8. Delegated consent design view

10 Closing Remarks

A privacy by design architecture leveraging software-based agents to decentralize identity has been proposed. The architecture has been validated by applying a gestalt process that can be used to create a reference model for development going forward.

The described architecture uniquely integrates authentication data, cryptographic mechanisms, and virtualization to create identity agents that deliver unanticipated identity and privacy enhancing capabilities. Identity agents enable owners to control what they disclose, protect their private information and transactions, and reliably delegate consent. Shifting control over identity from service providers to users mitigates breach risk because providers need not collect as much private information. Decentralization thwarts hacking and mitigates impersonation risk because the attack surface is more widely dispersed. Meanwhile, broad-based identity proofing and attestation elevates identity assurances and reduces impersonation risks. Combined, these capabilities will significantly reduce dependency on remote access passwords and facilitate technology adoption.

11 Areas for Further Study

Quantitative assessment of the risks, liabilities, and trade-offs posed by centralizing identity over decentralizing them; using formal verification methods, trusted platform modules, and trusted execution environments; exploiting artificial intelligence and machine learning; leveraging W3C's verifiable credentials and decentralized identifier [DID] models; and adopting elements of Signal's messaging protocol [17].

Annex: Identity Architecture Validation

A gestalt privacy by design process has been used to iteratively identify and validate the privacy requirements and design elements of the identity architecture. This annex explains how each design element satisfies the privacy requirements thereby mutually validating the design elements and the privacy requirements. The paragraphs below reference Fig. 4, Fig. 5, Fig. 6, Fig. 7 and Fig. 8 in the body of this paper.

A. User Interface Design View

The User Interface Design View shown in Fig. 4 encompasses design elements D1, D2 and D3 implementing privacy requirements R1, R2 and R3. The proposed privacy by design default settings for the User Interface Design View are also identified.

R1: Tightly Control Private and Identifying Information.
D1: Encapsulate Authentication Data and Private Information.

Design element D1 combined with physical custody of the owner's Internet device satisfies R1 by providing strong assurances that the owner, whether an end-user or a system administrator, controls her Internet device, installed identity agent, and encapsulated digital identities.

Although physical custody of her device enables the owner to maintain control over her identity agent, this is not enough to guarantee that her device has not been stolen or lost. Relying parties need objective proof that the owner of a remotely held device has control over it. This design element satisfies this need by exploiting native mechanisms built into Internet devices (smart phones, tablet PCs, laptops) including password, PIN, biometric, and geo-location authentication mechanisms.

Design element D1 significantly reduces the risk of theft and loss of the owner's device by encapsulating the owner's authentication data while providing the device's authenticator(s) access to this data by way of an application programming interface (API). When the owner's device is first used, her native authenticator enrolls her authentication data by writing this data via the API to the identity agent. Subsequently, the authentication data can be accessed via the API to support the authenticator's mechanisms for verifying the device owner. Once a positive authentication indication is detected, the identity agent's digital identities, interfaces and other data are made available for use. The authentication data is not revealed by the identity agent.

Design element D1 thereby provides strong assurances that the owner tightly controls his/her digital identities including private and identifying information, secrets and crypto keys. When digital identities are created, the identity agent of an owner allocates public/private encryption key-pairs to each and vaults its so-called *sovereign image*. The private keys of the digital identity are not disclosed by the identity agent. However, the identity agent can distribute public copies[9] to other parties.

R2: Selectively Disclose Identifying Information.
D2: Identities Virtualized and Selectively Disclosed.

Identity agents use an identity data model (e.g. [8]) to support the specification of digital identities that characterize the owner (e.g. claims, attributes and images). Design element D2 satisfies R2 by addressing usability and ease-of-use thereby enabling owners to create and select digital identities that have the appearance and behavior ("look and feel") of identity credentials used in the real world.

Figure 4 depicts the owner holding multiple digital identities in her wallet such as a digital business card, digital driver's license, e-health card, digital credit card, and/or electronic membership card. Instead of using remote access passwords, owners intuitively select digital identities that disclose only the private and identifying information necessary to satisfy the needs and purposes of the collaborating service provider or consumer. To facilitate disclosure, design element D2 enables owners to specify "anonymous identities" where the attributes are known only to the owner; "pseudo-anonymous identities" where the attributes are disclosed only to trusted collaborators; and "civil identities" where identifiers and attributes partially or fully elaborate identifying information.

R3: Protect Private and Identifying Information.
D3: Private Data, Keys and Secrets Encrypted.

Digital identities have multiple public/private encryption key-pairs that can be used to protect private data and secrets of the identity agent owner. Design element D3 satisfies R3 by applying these encryption keys to prevent hackers and malware from maliciously accessing such data including authentication data, digital identities, encryption keys, passwords, and PINs encapsulated by the identity agent. A designated public key of a digital identity of the owner can be used to encrypt her private data and secrets. Only the owner can decrypt the data using the paired private key.

Privacy by Design Default Settings of User Interface Design View
When the identity of an originating party is unknown or uncertain, the identity agent should not use digital identities that include identifying, private or secret information. Anonymous and pseudo-anonymous identities could be used as defaults when first establishing an online session or when exchanging digital identities with newly introduced or unvetted parties at meetings or public gatherings. Wireless mechanisms like QR codes, NFC, WiFi and Bluetooth could be used to securely transfer digital identities and private data when collaborators meet in-person.

B. Interoperability Design View

The Interoperability Design View shown in Fig. 5 encompasses design elements D4, D5 and D6 implementing privacy requirements R4, R5 and R6. Figure 6 supports the

---

[9] Public copies of a digital identity disclose only the public keys (private keys not revealed).

reasoning behind how design element D4 satisfies privacy requirement R4. The proposed privacy by design default settings for this design view are also identified.

R4: Exchange Digital Identities Securely.
D4: Secure Digital Identity Exchange.

Design element D4 satisfies R4 by enabling digital identities to be reliably and securely exchanged, the aim being to prevent man-in-the-middle attacks akin to robocalls and wiretaps on telephone networks. Options for exchanging digital identities include exchanging them in the clear; exchanging one-time passwords (OTPs) out-of-band; transferring them over HTTPS once logged in using an online password; and meeting in-person to transfer digital identities wirelessly.

Although the above methods carry various risks, they are safe enough to use in many contexts. One risk is that of digital identities being highjacked. Such risks can be mitigated by using an online service and combining hashing with Diffie-Hellman's key agreement method (DH) [14]. Our adapted Diffie-Hellman protocol[10] is depicted in Fig. 6 as well as in Fig. 7 (1) where it is shown in the context of verification.

Figure 6 illustrates how two owners can securely exchange public copies of their digital identities. Owners 1 and 2 have digital identities they wish to exchange respectively using identifiers id1 and id2. They first use their identity agents to store the public keys of their digital identities in the exchange service's repository at locations computed by respectively hashing id1 and id2 (e.g. using SHA256). Subsequently exchanging id1 and id2 by alternate means (e.g. physical transfer or out-of-band), they use their identity agents to hash the opposite owner's identifier to locate and retrieve the public keys of the other owner. The DH key agreement method is then applied by both owner's identity agents to combine the private keys of the owner with the retrieved public keys of the other owner thereby generating the same symmetric encryption key (or keys) for both owners. Finally, the symmetric keys are applied to encrypt and thereby securely exchange public copies of their digital identities.

To overtake the owners' digital identities, a malicious high-jacker would be obliged to successfully intercept id1 and id2, breach the digital identity exchange service, and discover the private keys from the captured public keys. Alternatively, the high-jacker could attempt to breach both owners' devices and identity agents.

R5: Secure Agent Transactions End-to-End.
D5: Secure Identity Agent Collaboration.

Design element D5 satisfies R5 by enabling collaborating identity agents to secure transactions end-to-end in order to thwart surveillance and tampering. Once identity agents have reliably transferred digital identities, they can use them to securely collaborate bilaterally by selecting designated keys bound to their digital identities. When sending a payload, the sender's private signing key and the recipient's public encrypting

---

[10] "Architecture and Methods for Self-Sovereign Digital Identity", US Patent (pending), provisional filed Oct. 8, 2018, utility application filed Nov. 12, 2018.

key are applied. When receiving, the recipient's private decrypting key and the sender's public verifying key are applied.

R6: Secure Private Data and Message Transfers.
D6: Secure Application Service Collaboration.

Design element D6 enables collaborative services (e.g. web messaging apps) to implement R6 by leveraging already exchanged digital identities held in owners' wallets and contact lists to secure messages end-to-end. The owners' identity agents expose an API to the service at each endpoint. By means of these APIs, the sending owner directs the service to select a digital identity from her wallet and a digital identity of the recipient from her contacts list. The sender's identity agent uses the private signing key of her digital identity and the public encrypting key of the recipient's digital identity to respectively sign and encrypt the message and send this message together with digital fingerprints[11] of the sender's and recipient's digital identities to the recipient. The service at the recipient's endpoint uses the identity agent's API to select the digital identities from the recipient's wallet and contacts list, verify the received digital fingerprints, decrypt the message, and verify the digital signature.

Privacy by Design Default Settings of Interoperability Design View
By default the interoperability design view could be configured to invoke the adapted Diffie-Hellman exchange protocol to reliably transfer collaborators' digital identities. Identity agents and applications could default to using digital identities to secure all transactions end-to-end. Owners should be warned of the risks of choosing to exchange digital identities and transactions when using less reliable transfer methods.

C. Verification Design View

The Verification Design View shown in Fig. 7 encompasses design elements D7, D8 and D9 implementing privacy requirements R7, R8 and R9. The proposed privacy by design default settings for the Verification Design View are also identified.

R7: Detect Counterfeits and Prevent Impersonation.
D7: Proof-of-Possession and Proof-of-Custody Verification.

Design element D7 combines prior art proof-of-possession [10] with proof-of-custody (remote authentication-on-demand) to satisfy R7 by verifying that a remotely located owner controls her digital identities and device. This adaptation relies on the identity agent encapsulating the owner's authentication data and digital identities.

Figure 7 (2, 3, 4) shows two parties synchronously collaborating online. The identity agent of the depicted owner presents a public copy of her digital identity to the identity agent of the relying party (2). The identity agent of the relying party verifies the presented identity and obtains proof that the originator controls the associated digital identity. To accomplish this, the relying party's identity agent uses a public key of the presented

---

[11] Digital fingerprints are computed by hashing selected public encryption keys.

digital identity to launch a proof-of-possession challenge (3) to verify the presented digital identity. Such challenges can only be satisfied by using the paired private key of the digital identity controlled by the originator's identity agent. Executed bilaterally, both parties can determine whether the identity agent of the collaborator controls the presented digital identity thereby detecting counterfeits.

Once possession of the private key has been verified, the identity agent of a relying party can send a proof-of-custody demand (4) to the originating identity agent to verify custody by the enrolled holder using design element D1. An affirmative proof-of-custody indication is returned if the originator is successfully authenticated. This element of the protocol can also be conducted bilaterally.

Used together, collaborating identity agents can execute proof-of-possession and proof-of-custody challenges to prove that the corresponding party controls the presented digital identity thereby detecting impersonation and ensuring that subsequent transactions can be secured end-to-end (9).

R8: Verify Acquired Identifying Information.
D8: Proof-of-Existence Registration and Verification.

To satisfy R8, design element D8 has adapted[12] a "proof-of-existence" hashing method popularized by blockchain [15] with our digital sealing method. This method enables owners to verify each other's digital identities when collaborating asynchronously (e.g. email and messaging). Figure 7 illustrates the owner registering a digital identity (5) in a proof-of-existence identity registry and a relying party verifying it (6).

When registering a digital identity in the proof-of-existence identity registry (5), the registry's identity agent first uses design element D7 to execute proof-of-possession and proof-of-custody challenges to verify the identity of the registrant. If successfully verified, the owner's identity agent hashes the digital identity, digitally seals the hashed digital identity, and uses the registry's identity agent to store the hash and digital seal in the registry. A relying party, having acquired a registered digital identity from the owner, verifies the acquired digital (6) by having her identity agent hash the digital identity, use the hash to verify that the record exists in the identity registry, retrieve the digital seal, and use a designated public key of the acquired digital identity to verify the affixed digital seal. These steps enable a relying party to determine whether an acquired digital identity exists and was registered by the originating owner. A breach of the registry will not reveal private data of registered digital identities (attributes, images, keys, etc.) because they are hashed.

R9: Proof, Attest and Verify Attestations.
D9: Proofing, Attesting, Sealing and Verifying Seals.

Design element D9 satisfies R9 by implementing procedures and methods for proofing, attesting, creating and verifying digital seals and attestations affixed to digital identities. NIST provides identity proofing guidance [16].

---

[12] "Systems and Methods for Registering and Acquiring E-Credentials using Proof-of-Existence and Digital Seals", US Pat 10,127,378 B2, issued Nov. 13, 2018.

Figure 7 depicts two issuers having proofed, attested and affixed digital seals to the owner's digital identity. The process begins with an issuing owner meeting the requesting owner to validate her identity by inspecting presented identifying information. If successfully identity-proofed, the issuer uses his identity agent to affix an attestation (e.g. "proofed") to her digital identity using a digital seal (7). A digital seal is created by using a pre-determined sealing image and the private embossing key of a selected digital identity of the issuer (see 7.1). A relying party can verify such digital seals and attestations (8) by using the public inspection key of the public copy of issuer's digital identity.

As illustrated, multiple parties (users and providers) can proof, attest and digitally seal a given digital identity. Digital identities affixed with multiple digital seals arguably elevate identity assurances over digital identities having a single digital seal or no seals at all. Digital seals can be used to affix attestations to other electronic documents including consent tokens as discussed below.

Privacy by Design Default Settings of Verification Design View
Default settings could include routinely registering digital identities whenever they are created and updated. Proof-of-existence, proof-of-possession and proof-of-custody methods should be employed by default whenever executing high risk or high value transactions (e.g. for banking and critical infrastructures).

D. Delegated Consent Design View

The Delegated Consent Design View shown in Fig. 8 encompasses design elements D10, D11 and D12 implementing privacy requirements R10, R11 and R12. The privacy by design default settings for this design view are identified below.

Today's consent models are managed by service providers. For example, OpenID Connect (openid.net) is a server-centric consent model where user authentication and access tokens are wholly controlled by service providers. In contrast, the model described herein decentralizes consent by using digital seals to cryptographically bind stakeholder commitments and identities to consent tokens which can be expired, revoked, registered and tracked. Since commitments are affixed using digital seals, they cannot be repudiated (see Sect.7.1). Figure 8 depicts the consent delegation process. Each consent token identifies the resource owner, resource custodian, requester, the owner's private resources, access permissions including purposes, and expiry date/time. Given digital seals have sealing images, consent tokens rendered by identity agents visualize commitments for users. The event logger enables accountability.

R10: Delegate Consent to Access Private Data.
D10: Acquiring Stakeholder Commitments.

Design element D10 satisfies R10 by enabling resource owners to use their identity agents to delegate consent to other parties requesting access to their private resources. Stakeholders use their identity agents to digitally seal a circulated consent token.

Figure 8 shows a consent token collaboration sequence (1–6) among stakeholders. They use their identity agents and selected digital identities to create digital seals affixing their commitments to the consent token. The resource owner first requires the requesting owner to affix requested permissions and intended purpose to the consent token with a digital seal, and then the resource custodian's approval to provide access by affixing a digital seal. Once satisfied, the resource owner grants access by digitally sealing the access token and issuing it to the requester who can present the token to the resource custodian whenever requesting access.

R11: Enable Authorized Access to Private Data.
D11: Controlling Access to Private Data.

Design element D11 satisfies R11 by using finalized consent tokens to provide authorized access to owner resources controlled by resource custodians according to commitments and approvals affixed to the consent token by stakeholders.

R12: Hold Stakeholders Accountable.
D12: Event Logging and Monitoring.

Design element D12 implements R12 by tracking and reporting digitally sealed stakeholder commitments as well as access, expiry and revocation events.

Privacy by Design Default Settings of Delegated Consent Design View
Identity agents should register consent tokens when digitally sealed into a proof-of-existence registry to enable expiry and revocation checking by stakeholders.

E. Summary

Our privacy by design validation process has confirmed that the proposed identity architecture is capable of reliably and securely supporting the following:

- Identity agents will be able to control owners' authentication data and deploy digital identities thereby enabling them to control what they disclose;
- Digital identities managed by identity agents will enable owners to secure their transactions end-to-end and protect their private data stored locally or remotely;
- Owners will be able to use their identity agents to proof and attest the digital identities of other parties thereby elevating identity assurances and privacy protection;
- Owners will be able to use their identity agents and digital identities to create digital seals enabling express delegated consent among stakeholders;
- The identified privacy default settings will minimize how much private and identifying information is disclosed by owners, and how much is collected by service providers and collaborating peers.
- Visibility and transparency into the design by way of the privacy by design process will enable third-party validation and improvement benefiting users and providers.

References

1. Cavoukian, A.: Privacy by Design, The 7 Foundational Principles. https://www.ipc.on.ca/wp-content/uploads/Resources/7foundationalprinciples.pdf
2. Brooker, K.: Tim Berners-Lee tells us his radical new plan to upend the World Wide Web, FastCompany, 29 September 2018
3. Cameron, K.: The Laws of Identity, May 2005. http://myinstantid.com/laws.pdf
4. Cavoukian, A.: Consumers bear the cost of their privacy protection, Globe and Mail, 7 September 2018
5. Jones, H.: Accelerating the future of privacy through smartdata agents, Cognitive World, AI & Big Data, 3 November 2018
6. Allen, C.: The path to self-sovereign identity, 27 April 2016. http://coindesk.com
7. Sovrin Foundation, Sovrin: A Protocol and Token for Self-Sovereign Identity and Decentralized Trust, Version 1, January 2018. https://sovrin.org
8. World Wide Web Consortium (W3C), verifiable credentials data model 1.0: expressing verifiable information on the Web, W3C recommendation, 19 November 2019
9. World Wide Web Consortium (W3C), Decentralized Identifiers (DIDs) v1.0: Core Data Model and Syntaxes, WC3 Working Draft 09 December 2019
10. Asokan, N., Niemi, V., Laitinen, P.: On the usefulness of proof of possession. In: 2nd Annual PKI Workshop, 28–29 April 2003, pp. 136–141 (2003)
11. Toth, K.C., Anderson-Priddy, A.: Architecture for self-sovereign digital identity. Computer Applications for Industry and Engineering, New Orleans, LA, 8–10 October 2018
12. Toth, K.C., Anderson-Priddy, A.: Self-sovereign digital identity: a paradigm shift for identity. IEEE Secur. Priv. **17**(3), 17–27 (2019)
13. Toth, K.C., Anderson-Priddy, A.: Privacy by design using agents and sovereign identities. In: Information Security and Privacy Protection Conference (IFIP-SEC), Work in Progress and Emerging Technology Track, Lisbon, Portugal, 25–27 June 2019 (2019)
14. Rescorla, E.: Diffie-Hellman key agreement method, RTFM Inc., June 1999
15. Robles, K.: BlockchainMe, tool for creating verifiable IDs on the blockchain, 2 December 2016. https://github.com/kiarafrobles/blockchainMe
16. NIST Special Publication 800–63A, Digital Identity Guidelines, Enrollment and Identity Proofing, January 2017. https://doi.org/10.6028/NIST.SP.800-63a
17. Cohn-Gordon, K., et al.: A formal analysis of the signal messaging protocol, November 2017. https://eprint.iacr.org/2016/1013.pdf

Preliminary Remarks and Practical Insights on How the Whistleblower Protection Directive Adopts the GDPR Principles

Rita de Sousa Costa[1](✉) [iD] and Inês de Castro Ruivo[2](✉) [iD]

[1] PLMJ Advogados, Lisbon, Portugal
rita.desousacosta@plmj.pt
[2] Banco Santander, Lisbon, Portugal
ines.ruivo@santander.pt

Abstract. Major scandals have evidenced that whistleblowers face vulnerability, and that corruption, wrongdoing and malpractice have caused serious harm to the public interest. It was therefore no surprise that the EU legislature approved a legal framework intended to protect the reporting persons. Indeed, on 23 October 2019, Directive (EU) 2019/1937 of the European Parliament and of the Council on the protection of persons who report breaches of European Union law was finally published. However, the Directive cannot be seen in isolation but must rather be considered in relation to different fundamental rights and societal values. Accordingly, the purpose of this paper is to address a few remarks from a data protection standpoint that could possibly affect the implementation of the new Whistleblower Protection Directive. The principles enshrined in the GDPR are the starting points for the discussion. Furthermore, the paper also seeks to provide more guidance for data controllers to implement reporting channels that comply with the GDPR. Finally, it is drawn up a three-tier model to give effect to a set of obligations deriving from the transparency principle.

Keywords: Whistleblowing · Internal reporting channels · Data protection · Transparency

1 Introduction

Major scandals such as, among others, "LuxLeaks" or "Panama Papers" [2] have evidenced that whistleblowers, as stressed by MEPs [3], face enormous vulnerability, and that corruption, malpractice and negligence cause serious harm to the public interest [4]. For instance, Margrethe Vestager, the EU Commissioner for Competition and current Executive Vice-President of the European Commission, stated, in an interview given to Euractiv, that "LuxLeaks could not have happened if it was not for the whistleblower, and the team of investigative journalists" [1].

In the aftermath of these events, the European Commission formed an intent to increase the protection of whistleblowers with the ultimate purpose of supplying

© Springer Nature Switzerland AG 2020
L. Antunes et al. (Eds.): APF 2020, LNCS 12121, pp. 95–109, 2020.
https://doi.org/10.1007/978-3-030-55196-4_6

national and Union enforcement systems with information, leading to effective detection, investigation and prosecution of breaches of Union law [7].

Whistleblowers take centre stage in the prevention and discovery of breaches. The protection of whistleblowers against retaliation is considered to be essential for them to feel safe to report the information they possess. In the words of Commissioner Věra Jourová, Vice President of the European Commission, "Whistleblowers should not be punished for doing the right thing" [9].

On 7 October 2019, the EU Council approved the Whistleblower Protection Directive [10]. It was published in the Official Journal on 23 October 2019 and is intended to protect the persons who report breaches of European Union Law, either to private and public entities or to competent authorities. The adoption of the Whistleblower Protection Directive was motivated by the lack of legal protection for whistleblowers in the European Union. In fact, until the adoption of this Directive, only ten Member States had passed laws protecting whistleblowers [8]. Nevertheless, this type of laws is not new in certain Member and former Member States, such as France or the United Kingdom, and, of course, outside of Europe in countries such as the USA [5, 6].

At the core of the Directive is the prohibition of retaliation against whistleblowers and the creation of measures to ensure their protection [11]. The Directive starts by defining its scope, i.e., the areas where infringement presents a higher risk. This includes, inter alia, public procurement, financial services, product safety and compliance, transport safety or protection of the environment. The personal scope of the Directive is deliberately broad. It includes all persons that may have information on infringements of the law through work-related activities, and was probably influenced by Council of Europe Recommendation CM/Rec(2014)7 [12].

The Directive then provides that legal entities in the private and public sectors must establish appropriate internal reporting channels and procedures in order to receive and pursue reports. This obligation is also incumbent upon competent authorities, which are required to set up external reporting channels. The Directive promotes the use of internal channels first.[1] In this regard, scholars have pointed out that the organizations do prefer internal rather than external whistleblowing schemes, because it allows them to address their problems and to avoid the exposure related to external whistleblowing. In what regards to the whistleblowers, it really depends on their own context [13].

Whistleblowers are protected provided that the conditions established in Chap. IV of the Directive are met. In short, the whistleblowers must have reasonable grounds to believe that the information was true at the time of the reporting and that the breach falls within the scope of the Directive.

This paper explores, in the next sections, the processing of data in connection to reports and the applicable data protection principles and obligations. The connection between the EU Whistleblower Protection Directive and the General Data Protection Regulation ("GDPR") [14] is twofold. Firstly, the GDPR is applicable to the processing of data in the context of handling reports in order to ensure the protection of whistleblowers, in particular their identity.[2] Secondly, the infringement of laws on protection of privacy

---

[1] Recital 47 and Article 7(2) of the Directive.
[2] Recital 84, and Articles 13(d) and 17 of the Directive.

and personal data falls within the scope of the Directive, since a whistleblower may report breaches that relate to data protection law. This means that persons who report these types of breaches will be subject to protection.[3] The infringement of laws that guarantee the protection of privacy and personal data is, therefore, equated to breaches, inter alia, in the areas of prevention of money laundering and terrorist financing, protection of the environment or consumer protection.

In a nutshell, the purpose of this paper is to address several issues on the implementation of the new Whistleblower Protection Directive from a data protection standpoint. The GDPR is a complementary instrument for the protection of whistleblowers and other persons involved.[4] The principles enshrined in the GDPR are the starting points for the discussion. Furthermore, the paper seeks to provide more guidance for data controllers to implement reporting channels that comply with the GDPR. It is also drawn up a prospective three-tier model to give effect to a set of obligations deriving from the transparency principle.

2   The Whistleblowing Principles Vis-à-Vis the Personal Data Protection Principles

The Directive clearly states that any processing of data carried out under it must respect the GDPR.[5] There are references to the main GDPR principles – lawfulness, fairness and transparency, purpose limitation, data minimisation, accuracy, storage limitation, integrity and confidentiality (security), and accountability – and two legal requirements: to provide information to the data subjects and to implement data protection by design and by default [16–19].[6] Given the importance of implementing the data protection principles and rights by design, the scope of Sect. 6 is to propose the adoption of practical measures to enhance transparency towards the data subjects.

On the one hand, the GDPR lays down the rules relating to the protection of natural persons and, on the other, the Whistleblower Protection Directive recognises that infringement of these fundamental rights may also cause serious harm to the public interest and create risks for the welfare of society.[7] The Whistleblower Protection Directive, therefore, strengthens the message that data protection has a clear EU dimension and that the enforcement of the GDPR remains a priority.

---

[3] Article 2(1)(a)(x) of the Directive.

[4] Along with the GDPR, the "soft law" adopted either by the national Data Protection Supervisory Authorities (DPA) or the European Data Protection Board (EDPB) has an important role in addressing the matter at stake. Indeed, for years the guidance provided by these entities has been key to handle the data protection concerns that permeate the whistleblowing issue. Even scholars have noted that this guidance is useful. See, for example, the conclusions of the author referenced in [15]. We will reference some of this "soft law" along the paper too.

[5] Article 17 of the Directive.

[6] Recital 83 and Article 13(d) of the Directive, and Article 25 of the GDPR.

[7] Recital 3 of the Directive.

In the light of the GDPR, the private and public sector entities and competent authorities that are obliged to adopt reporting channels act as data controllers[8] [20, 21]. As
to the data subjects, these are the reporting persons[9], the persons concerned, and third
persons, for example, witnesses or colleagues.

It is common for entities to engage external reporting platform providers to operate
reporting channels, who then act as data processors. The Whistleblower Protection Directive recognises that these third parties can be authorised to receive reports of breaches
on behalf of controllers, provided they offer appropriate guarantees of respect for inde-
pendence, confidentiality, data protection and secrecy.[10] This contractual relationship
must meet the requirements of Articles 28 and 32 of the GDPR. Article 28 states that
controllers need to assess whether the processor provides sufficient guarantees in terms
of technical and organisational measures to ensure the protection of the rights of the data
subjects. In addition, the parties are required to enter into a contract that sets out details
of the processing including those established in Article 28(3)(a) [22]. Finally, since the
processing is likely to result in a high risk to the rights of the persons concerned, data
controllers must undertake a data protection impact assessment, pursuant to Article 35
of the GDPR [23, 24].

The purpose of the next sections is to provide a critical perspective on how the
Whistleblower Protection Directive has incorporated GDPR principles and to offer further guidance to data controllers and data processors when implementing reporting
channels.

3   The Lawfulness of the Processing

The core principle of the EU data protection law provides that data can only be processed
in a lawful manner in respect to the data subject.[11] This means that data cannot be processed if the reasons behind that processing activity do not rely on one of the conditions
set out in Article 6(1) of the GDPR [25].

Before the approval of the Whistleblower Protection Directive, when implementing
an internal reporting channel, it was widely accepted that the lawfulness of the processing
of personal data could rest on compliance with a legal obligation[12] (e.g., preventing

---

[8] The GDPR defines "controller" in Article 4(7). On the notion of data controllers, see
the CJEU's case-law: C-131/12 *Google Spain e Google*, ECLI:EU:C:2014:317; C-212716
Wirtschaftsakademie Schleswig–Holstein, ECLI:EU:C:2018:388; C-25/17 *Jehovan todistajat*,
ECLI:EU:C:2018:551; C-40/17 *FashionID*, ECLI:EU:C:2019:629.

[9] The terms "reporting person(s)" and "whistleblower(s)" are used interchangeably in the text.

[10] Recital 25 of the Directive.

[11] Article 5(1)(a) of the GDPR.

[12] Article 6(1)(c) of the GDPR.

wrongdoing or even crime in the financial sector such as money laundering) [26, 27][13] or, more frequently, on the purpose of legitimate interests pursued by the controller[14] (e.g., compliance with internal corporate ethical codes) [28] or, in case of public authorities, on the performance of a task carried out in the public interest or in the exercise of official authority vested in the controller[15] (e.g., the ICO's whistleblowing scheme) [29]. The consequences of this approach on the lawfulness of the processing is that when there is no legal obligation to comply with, companies or other legal entities are not obliged to implement internal reporting channels, but if they want to, they have a ground because they are pursuing their legitimate interests. Nevertheless, in the recent past, certain DPA have adopted a very restrictive interpretation of the possibilities given to the private parties to implement internal reporting channels.[16]

Thus, with the publication of the Whistleblower Protection Directive, a few questions arise: can compliance with the Directive constitute the lawfulness of the data processing according to Article 6(1)(c) of the GDPR? Is the response the same regardless of whether it is given as of today or after the deadline for implementation into national law? And what about the further national implementation acts? (Fig. 1).

First of all, it seems quite clear that the Directive's national implementation acts will constitute grounds for lawful processing. The Directive establishes the obligation on Member States to create the mechanisms intended to oblige certain public and private parties to implement reporting channels, so they must process personal data whether they want to or not.

Secondly, until the deadline for Member States to implement the Directive into national law, the Directive clearly does not constitute a legal obligation to comply with in accordance with Article 6(1)(c) of the GDPR. In this period, one cannot even envisage the possibility of triggering the direct effect theory.[17]

---

[13] For example, see Article 71 of Directive 2013/36/EU of the European Parliament and of the Council of 26 June 2013, on access to the activity of credit institutions and the prudential supervision of credit institutions and investment firms, and the obligation it establishes on Member States to ensure "that competent authorities establish effective and reliable mechanisms to encourage reporting of potential or actual breaches of national provisions". In another field, see Article 32 of Regulation (EU) 596/2014 of the European Parliament and of the Council of 16 April 2014 (market abuse regulation).

[14] Article 6(1)(f) of the GDPR.

[15] Article 6(1)(e) of the GDPR.

[16] See, for instance, the Portuguese DPA's restricted opinion on the issue, which for years precluded the possibility to implement internal reporting channels on matters other than "accounting, internal accounting controls, auditing, and the fight against corruption and banking and financial crime" [30].

[17] See the historical case C-148/78 *Ratti*, ECLI:EU:C:1979:110, where the CJEU held, in para. 46, that "since a directive by its nature imposes obligations only on Member States, it is not possible for an individual to plead the principle of 'legitimate expectation' before the expiry of the period prescribed for its implementation".

Finally, questions may be brought as to whether the Directive can constitute the legal basis of the processing activity – considered to be "compliance with a legal obligation" – if Member States fail to meet the deadline for its implementation. That would be one of the fields of application of the "direct effect" of the directives. The question is not easy to answer for a couple of reasons: (i) the Directive must be analysed provision-by-provision to assess whether an actual provision has direct effect; (ii) certain provisions of the Directive may have vertical direct effect, thus being directly applicable. However, there are also certain provisions set out in the Directive that address the relationship between private parties, which likely precludes their "direct effect".[18]

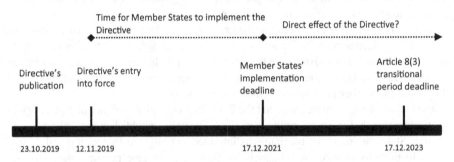

Fig. 1. Timeline of the Whistleblower Protection Directive

4   Purpose and Storage Limitation

Another core principle of the GDPR is purpose limitation.[19] Accordingly, personal data must not be further processed in a way incompatible with the original legitimate purpose.[20] This is key to properly implement the whistleblowing framework. It means

---

[18] As is widely known, the direct effect was firstly recognised by the CJEU in the seminal C-26/62 *Van Gend en Loos*, ECLI:EU:C:1963:1. In short, the theory of the direct effect states that, with certain conditions being met, individuals can invoke the EU law (e.g., treaties, regulations, directives, decisions) before courts, regardless of the provisions of the national law. It is a very useful tool to address the Member States' failure to comply with EU law, which includes, inter alia, failure to implement directives into national law in due time. Direct effect can either be "vertical" or "horizontal". It is vertical when individuals invoke an EU law provision against a public entity such as Member States. It is horizontal when individuals invoke an EU law provision against other private parties (e.g. an individual vis-à-vis other individual or a company). When it comes to directives, since they require a national implementing act, horizontal direct effect is highly controversial. The established doctrine, based on several CJEU's case law, states that horizontal direct effect of a directive cannot be invoked. However, some legal scholars have argued that, in a few cases, the Court has indirectly open up the door for other ways of addressing the protection of individuals, thus indirectly admitting a blurred form of directives' horizontal direct effect [31].

[19] Article 5(1)(b) of the GDPR.

[20] Acknowledging that, regardless of the purpose limitation principle, further processing is important for many data controllers in practice, Seinen, W., et al. [32] developed a sound analysis on the possible ways to legitimate it.

that one cannot use the whistleblowing material for purposes other than the ones stated in the rules of the reporting channel.[21] Indeed, failure to comply with this principle is a serious infringement of the GDPR.[22]

Furthermore, Article 5(e) of the GDPR establishes the storage limitation principle. Accordingly, personal data must be kept in a way that "permits identification of data subjects for no longer than is necessary for the purposes for which the personal data are processed". The Whistleblower Protection Directive reinforces this principle by stating that personal data which are accidentally collected must be deleted without undue delay.[23] On the other hand, for the information that is relevant to handling a report, data controllers need to "ensure that there is adequate record-keeping, that every report is retrievable and that information received through reports can be used as evidence in enforcement actions where appropriate".[24] This Recital calls for interpretation in light of the GDPR, meaning that data controllers need to include in their policies retention periods for reports presented through these channels, in line with documentation obligations.

While defining the data retention periods, data controllers should take into consideration both legal obligations and limitation periods. Information contained in reporting channels can have a significant impact on individuals, both the reporting persons and the persons concerned. For this reason, controllers should also review the retention of this personal data routinely. It is up to the controller to decide them according to the storage limitation principle along with the accountability principle [34]. In case of disciplinary or judicial proceedings against the persons concerned, it is defensible that the data controller is allowed to keep the data until the end of those proceedings.[25] However, attention must be paid to the further Member States' implementation acts in case they establish retention periods.

5 The Transparency Principle

The GDPR has elevated transparency to the highest level of importance. Article 5(1)(a) establishes that personal data must be "processed lawfully, fairly and in a transparent manner in relation to the data subject". Anyway, transparency is not new in EU data protection law. According to WP29, the word "transparency" was referenced in Recital 38 of the Directive, although no other allusion could be found [35]. It is also a broad obligation [36, 37] that applies to three central areas, as declared by WP29:

"(1) the provision of information to data subjects related to fair processing; (2) how data controllers communicate with data subjects in relation to their rights under the GDPR; and (3) how data controllers facilitate the exercise by data subjects and their rights" [35].

---

[21] As stated by the French DPA (CNIL), *"Le traitement mis en œuvre doit répondre à un objectif précis et être justifié au regard des missions et des activités de l'organisme"* [33].

[22] Article 83(5)(a) of the GDPR. In certain jurisdictions, the use of data in a way incompatible with the purpose of the processing can even be a crime. See, for instance, Article 46 of the Portuguese Data Protection Act – Law no. 58/2019, of 8 August.

[23] Article 17, 2nd indent, of the Directive.

[24] Recital 86 of the Directive.

[25] See, for example, the Portuguese DPA's Opinion already referenced in [30].

Even if the word is not present, transparency is embedded in the Whistleblower Protection Directive. On a more general level, the Directive is an instrument of transparency, similarly to the GDPR. It recognises that reports are essential in order to detect, investigate and prosecute breaches of Union Law, enhancing transparency as a consequence. Moreover, the Directive incorporates the transparency obligations set out in the GDPR, in particular the provision of information to the whistleblowers by competent authorities. Article 13(d) of the Directive provides that competent authorities must publish on their websites information regarding the confidentiality rules applicable to reports, and, in particular, the information in relation to the processing of personal data in accordance with Articles 5 and 13 of the GDPR. It is not clear why this obligation is not included in Chap. II (Internal Reporting and Follow up). Nevertheless, it follows from the GDPR that private and public sector entities – and not only authorities – are obliged to apply the GDPR principles and to inform the data subjects pursuant to Article 13.

In order to make informed decisions on whether, how and when to report, the reporting persons should be provided information in a "transparent, easily understandable and reliable"[26] manner. Even the wording is very close to that of Article 12 of the GDPR, which states that controllers must provide information relating to the processing to the data subject "in a concise, transparent, intelligible and easily accessible form".

As the WP29 has stated, transparency is a user-centric concept [35] and, in the context of whistleblowing, the correct application of this principle can be decisive to promote, and not to deter, reporting. If it is absolutely clear, for the reporting persons, that their identity must remain confidential, they would be much more inclined to report the breach of their knowledge. However, it should also be noted that, in certain circumstances, disclosure of the reporting persons' identity may result from the law in the context of investigations led by the competent authorities or of judicial proceedings.[27]

Moreover, although the reporting persons' identity must be kept confidential by the data controller, this does not mean that they are kept in the shadow during the analysis of the report. It is only fair and transparent that the reporting person is informed on the investigation and actions being taken by the data controller. Transparency towards the reporting persons enables them to assess if the data controller is acting upon the report and if a communication to external competent authorities might be justifiable. Therefore, after receiving the report, data controllers shall acknowledge its receipt to the reporting person within seven days.[28] The data controller must also provide feedback to the reporting person within a reasonable timeframe, which must not exceed "three months from the acknowledgement of receipt or, if no acknowledgement was sent to the reporting person, three months from the expiry of the seven-day period after the report was made".[29]

On the other side, under Article 14 of the GDPR, the persons concerned, which are the data subjects of the data collected from a third party (the reporting person), have the right to be informed of the processing of their data. In an old Opinion issued by the WP29, it recommended informing the persons concerned of the following information:

---

[26] Recital 75 of the Directive.

[27] Article 16 of the Directive.

[28] Article 9(1)(b) of the Directive.

[29] Article 9(1)(f) of the Directive.

(i) the facts of which they are accused; (ii) the department of the company that received the report; (iii) how they can exercise their rights of access and rectification [38]. In addition, Article 14 of the GDPR establishes, as a general principle, informing the data subjects about the processing activity as soon as possible and, at the latest, within one month of the collection of their data.

However, it emerges from Article 23(1)(e) and (i), and Article 23(2) of the GDPR that Member States may restrict, by way of a legislative measure, the scope of the rights of the data subject. The effectiveness of the Whistleblower Protection Directive depends on the completion of these legislative measures, where required.[30] As one would expect, informing the person concerned may compromise the investigation. Alongside the Whistleblower Protection Directive, Article 14 of the GDPR itself sets out exception to its general rule, precisely when informing the data subject could compromise the purpose of the processing. Therefore, it is allowed not to inform the person concerned immediately. The question then arises as to when the right to information of the person concerned should be granted. First, it must be noted that the analysis at issue must be done on a case-by-case basis [39]. In any case, broadly speaking, it may make sense to comply with the right to information of the person concerned either (i) at the end of the investigation procedure after the internal investigations and possible collection of additional evidence – but before taking any disciplinary measure, for example – or (ii) immediately after the report is submitted if the circumstances of the case indicate that the knowledge of the person concerned will not frustrate the investigation. It is important to note that after the one-month deadline set out in Article 14(3)(a), the legal entity is recommended, in respect to the principle of accountability, to document the grounds to the triggering of the exception established in Article 14(5)(b). Examples of grounds could be, among others, the difficulty in gathering the evidence or the risk of the investigation being compromised [39].

It is clear that the rights of the person concerned are necessarily restricted, since this is a matter of collision of rights. The right of access can be one of these restricted rights. The legal entities must ensure all technical and organisational measures to enable the removal of all the reporting persons' data contained in the report. This includes not only the identification data that the reporting persons may include in a form – which is, in principle, easier to separate – but also increased attention should be paid to the facts of the report that may lead to their identification.

Regarding the right to rectification of the persons concerned, it should be noted that, as the data subjects, they have the right to check the accuracy of their data and to add any data they wish.[31] However, the right to rectification cannot be a way for the persons concerned to abusively amend, in their own interests, the information contained in the report. This is, of course, an obvious conclusion, which is also endorsed by DPA, such as the CNIL [33]. Thus, the legal entities should carefully assess the way in which they exercise their right to rectification.

Finally, the rights to erasure, limitation and opposition of the person concerned will necessarily be conditioned until the end of the procedure initiated by the legal entities. Otherwise the purpose of the processing will be frustrated. This must be stated

---

[30] Recital 84 of the Directive.

[31] C-434/16 *Nowak*, ECLI:EU:C:2017:994.

in the privacy policy. The grounds are clear and may be, inter alia, the possibility of compromising the evidence.

When it comes to third persons, such as witnesses and colleagues, it emerges from the GDPR that the legal entities are also obliged to inform them in accordance with Article 14, that is, as soon as possible and, at the latest, within one month of the collection of their data. In order to protect the reporting person and the internal investigations, it is also justified that the abovementioned restrictions to the rights to rectification, erasure, limitation and opposition are applicable to third persons.

6 A New Framework to Enable Transparency

There are arguably quite a few layers of transparency to comply with. In the next paragraphs, we develop a possible model of enhancing transparency: the three-tier transparency model (Fig. 2). Complying with the three tiers is not legally mandatory, since enabling transparency is not a legal formula. The tiers do not even need to be implemented together. In any case, what we propose is a possible beacon to implement a good standard of transparency compliance regarding the reporting internal channels. Along with the transparency tiers, it is also worth noting that providing training to employees on how to handle internal whistleblowing mechanisms is key to properly implement the reporting channels.

The three proposed tiers encourage the legal entities to enhance transparency by combining several channels of communication. The adoption of this model embodies implementing data protection by design, as it increases "the probability for the information to effectively reach the data subject", as stressed by the European Data Protection Board [40].

— *Tier one: privacy policy(ies)/notice(s) to implement in the company adapted to the internal reporting channel.*

There are two possible ways to address the "tier one". There can be one main policy/notice devoted to the reporting channel, where compliance with Article 13 of the GDPR and the Whistleblower Protection Directive – the information rights of the reporting person – and compliance with Article 14 of the GDPR – the information rights of the person concerned – must be achieved, in one single standalone text (option 1). Or there can be more than one policies/notices devoted to the channel, where compliance with either Article 13 or Article 14 of the GDPR together with the Whistleblower Protection Directive must be achieved in a separately manner (option 2).

When adopting option 1, it is advisable for the entity to publish the information – the privacy policy/notice – on its websites in a separate, easily identifiable and accessible section.[32] This is key for the reporting persons external to the company. Additionally, the policy/note can also be made available in the intranet, cloud, email or smartphone applications (if applicable). One option is to make the acceptance of the policy/notice a compulsory step of the reporting process, when this is made through an online platform.

---

[32] Recital 59 of the Directive.

When adopting option 2, the reporting person privacy policy/notice should be made available on the data controller's websites in a separate, easily identifiable and accessible section. Additionally, it can be made available in the channels referred in the above section. One the other hand, the person concerned privacy policy/notice – when is not available online together with the reporting policy/note – must, however, be made available in the above internal channels such as the intranet, the cloud, the data controller's smartphone application (if applicable) or the email (however, the email should be seen more as a confirmatory tool used together with one of the others than a primary way to provide the information, because it is not as searchable, and the information is not as easily to further reach).

Furthermore, when reporting breaches by telephone, it might be impractical to provide all the information by the same means. In these cases, the controller should inform the reporting person where to find the complete information and the data subject should be aware at least of the identity of the controller and the purposes of the processing for which the personal data are intended.

— Tier two: acknowledgment tools within the data controller's environment.

Following the procedures proposed in the tier one section, it is also recommended to ensure that the message was received and acknowledged. Employees are frequently provided with information on an array of new procedures and updates and, therefore, we consider that it is important to bring this specific topic to their attention. This applies to the obligations of transparency towards the persons concerned, who are the data controller's employees. It could be done, for instance, (i) by sending an email to the employees; (ii) by sending a chat message; or (iii) by sending a notification to the company's smartphone application (if applicable).

— Tier three: contractual regulation.

A third possible tier of transparency is adding a new section in the template of the standard employment agreement. Amending the employment agreements in force could be a possibility, but it seems, nevertheless, disproportionate. This is the third tier of transparency because, although extremely rigorous and plain, a contract is not the simplest, best remembered or friendliest way to deliver these policies. Finally, of course, the third-tier method is only applicable to the transparency of reporting persons and persons concerned who are also employees of the company. It is not applicable to possible external reporters. This would also force the data controller to review or amend agreements already in force.

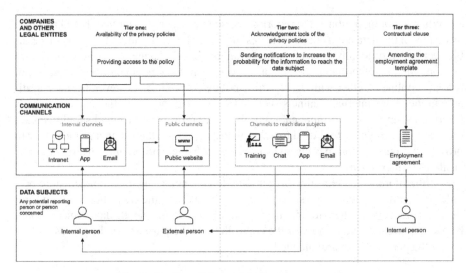

Fig. 2. Outline of the model of transparency tiers

7 Concluding Remarks

Mishandling the personal data of a whistleblower or of any person involved in a potential infringement of the law is apt to give rise serious consequences that legal remedies and compensation may not avoid.

The effective safeguarding of whistleblowers depends on the joint enforcement of both the new Whistleblower Protection Directive and the GDPR. The Whistleblower Protection Directive makes an express reference to some of the most important principles and legal requirements laid down by the GDPR.

The first aim of the paper was to analyse how these data protection principles should be applied in order to serve the purposes of the Whistleblower Protection Directive. The entities that are bound to establish internal reporting channels need to address not only those main principles and obligations, but also the whole data protection framework.

The second goal of the paper was intended to provide practical guidance to companies and other legal entities on how to duly inform the data subjects involved, notably reporting persons and persons concerned, about the processing of data in the context of whistleblowing channels. The proposed model combines several channels of communication and takes advantage of the multiple means by which employers communicate with their employees. Compliance with all three tiers is probably not considered necessary to accomplish the transparency obligations set out in the GDPR with the derogations from the Whistleblower Protection Directive. However, it is certainly difficult to argue that an entity adopting a method of this kind is not complying with these obligations established in the data protection law.

Given the direction followed by the EU legislature, we are confident that future whistleblowers will feel safer to do what the public interest commands. This is because the Member States must implement into national law the Directive's obligations, and the majority of those obligations must be addressed together with the GDPR.

In short, the combined application of Directive alongside the GDPR undoubtedly provides a strong framework capable of protecting the whistleblowers' right to data protection.

Acknowledgements. The authors gratefully acknowledge comments received by Mr. Simon Gillibrand, Mr. Cedric Lauradoux, and the two anonymous reviewers.
Disclaimer: The views and opinions expressed in the text are the authors own and do not necessarily represent the views and opinions of the authors' employers.

References

1. Valero, J.: Vestager: we should thank the Luxleaks whistleblowers. Euractiv (2016). https://www.euractiv.com/section/digital/interview/vestager-we-should-thank-the-luxleaks-whistleblowers/. Accessed 15 Jan 2020
2. Fitzgibbon, F.: Panama Papers FAQ: all you need to know about the 2016 investigation. International Consortium of Investigative Journalists (2019). https://www.icij.org/investigations/panama-papers/panama-papers-faq-all-you-need-to-know-about-the-2016-investigation/. Accessed 15 Jan 2020
3. European Parliament: Protecting whistle-blowers: new EU-wide rules approved (2019). https://www.europarl.europa.eu/news/en/press-room/20190410IPR37529/protecting-whistle-blowers-new-eu-wide-rules-approved. Accessed 15 Jan 2020
4. European Commission: Whistleblowers protection – European Commission initiatives on the protection of persons reporting on breaches of Union law. https://ec.europa.eu/info/aid-development-cooperation-fundamental-rights/your-rights-eu/whistleblowers-protection_pt. Accessed 15 Jan 2020
5. Stolowy, S., Paugam, L., Londero, A.: The whistle-blower: an important person in corporate life? An answer from comparative law. J. Bus. Law **3**, 167–184 (2019)
6. Chalouat, I., Carrión-Crespo, C., Licata, M.: Law and practice on protecting whistle-blowers in the public and financial services sectors. WP 328. International Labour Organization, Genova (2019). https://www.ilo.org/wcmsp5/groups/public/—ed_dialogue/—sector/documents/publication/wcms_718048.pdf. Accessed 15 Jan 2020
7. Explanatory Memorandum of the Proposal of Whistleblower Protection Directive COM(2018) 218 final, 2018/0106(COD) (2018). https://www.europarl.europa.eu/RegData/docs_autres_institutions/commission_europeenne/com/2018/0218/COM_COM(2018)0218_EN.pdf. Accessed 15 Jan 2020
8. Council: Better protection of whistle-blowers: new EU-wide rules to kick in 2021 (2019). https://www.consilium.europa.eu/en/press/press-releases/2019/10/07/better-protection-of-whistle-blowers-new-eu-wide-rules-to-kick-in-in-2021/. Accessed 15 Jan 2020
9. Whistleblower protection in the EU: Commission welcomes adoption by the Council (2019). https://ec.europa.eu/commission/presscorner/detail/en/MEX_19_6032. Accessed 15 Jan 2020
10. Directive (EU) 2019/1937 of the European Parliament and of the Council of 23 October 2019 on the protection of persons who report breaches of Union law. https://eur-lex.europa.eu/legal-content/en/TXT/?uri=CELEX%3A32019L1937. Accessed 15 Jan 2020
11. Abazi, V.: Whistleblowing in Europe: a new era of legal protections. In: Czech, P., Heschl, L., Lukas, K., Nowak, M., Oberleitner, G. (eds.) European Yearbook on Human Rights, pp. 91–110. Intersentia, Cambridge (2019)

12. Council of Europe Recommendation CM/Rec(2014)7 of the Committee of Ministers to member States on the protection of whistleblowers. https://search.coe.int/cm/Pages/result_details. aspx?ObjectId=09000016805c5ea5. Accessed 15 Jan 2020
13. Jeon, H.: Where to report wrongdoings? Exploring the determinants of internal versus external whistleblowing. Int. Rev. Public Adm. **22**(2), 153–171 (2017). https://doi.org/10.1080/122 94659.2017.1315235
14. Regulation (EU) 2016/679 of the European Parliament and of the Council of 27 April 2016 on the protection of natural persons with regard to the processing of personal data and on the free movement of such data, and repealing Directive 95/46/EC (General Data Protection Regulation). https://eur-lex.europa.eu/legal-content/EN/TXT/PDF/?uri=CELEX:32016R0679& from=en. Accessed 15 Jan 2020
15. Lewis, D.B.: Whistleblowing and data protection principles: is the road to reconciliation really that rocky? Eur. J. Law Technol. **2**, 1 (2011)
16. Cavoukian, A.: Privacy by Design. The 7 Foundational Principles (2009). https://www.ipc. on.ca/wp-content/uploads/resources/7foundationalprinciples.pdf. Accessed 15 Jan 2020
17. ENISA: Privacy and Data Protection by Design – from policy to engineering (2014). https://www.enisa.europa.eu/publications/privacy-and-data-protection-by-design/at_ download/fullReport. Accessed 15 Jan 2020
18. Rubinstein, I.S., Good, N.: The trouble with Article 25 (and how to fix it): the future of data protection by design and default. Int. Data Priv. Law (2019). https://doi.org/10.1093/idpl/ ipz019
19. Spagnuelo, D., Ferreira, A., Lenzini, G.: Accomplishing transparency within the general data protection regulation. In: Proceedings of the 5th International Conference on Information Systems Security and Privacy, vol. 1. pp. 114–125. ICISSP, Prague (2019)
20. WP29: Opinion 1/2010 on the concepts of "controller" and "processor". WP 169 (2010). https://ec.europa.eu/justice/article-29/documentation/opinion-recommendation/files/ 2010/wp169_en.pdf. Accessed 15 Jan 2020
21. EDPS: EDPS Guidelines on the concepts of controller, processor and joint controllership under Regulation (EU) 2018/1725 (2019). https://edps.europa.eu/sites/edp/files/public ation/19-11-07_edps_guidelines_on_controller_processor_and_jc_reg_2018_1725_en.pdf. Accessed 15 Jan 2020
22. Weiss, J.B. (ed.): Data Processing Agreements: Coordination, Drafting, and Negotiation. IAPP, Portsmouth (2019)
23. ICO: Examples of processing 'likely to result in high risk'. https://ico.org.uk/for-organi sations/guide-to-data-protection/guide-to-the-general-data-protection-regulation-gdpr/data-protection-impact-assessments-dpias/examples-of-processing-likely-to-result-in-high-risk/. Accessed 15 Jan 2020
24. WP29: Guidelines on Data Protection Impact Assessment (DPIA) and determining whether processing is "likely to result in a high risk" for the purposes of Regulation 2016/679. WP 248 rev.01 (2017). http://ec.europa.eu/newsroom/document.cfm?doc_id=47711. Accessed 15 Jan 2020
25. Voigt, P., von dem Bussche, A.: The EU General Data Protection Regulation (GDPR) A Practical Guide. Springer, Cham (2017). https://doi.org/10.1007/978-3-319-57959-7
26. European Banking Authority: Guidelines on internal governance under Directive 2013/36/EU, EBA/GL/2017/11, pp. 39–41 (2017). https://eba.europa.eu/sites/default/documents/files/doc uments/10180/1972987/eb859955-614a-4afb-bdcd-aaa664994889/Final%20Guidelines% 20on%20Internal%20Governance%20%28EBA-GL-2017-11%29.pdf?retry=1. Accessed 15 Jan 2020
27. Fleischer, H., Schmolke, K.U.: Financial incentives for whistleblowers in European capital markets law. Eur. Company Law **9**, 250 (2012)

28. Szabó, D.G., Sørensen, K.E.: Integrating Corporate Social Responsibility in Corporate Governance Codes in the EU. Eur. Bus. Law Rev. **24**, 6 (2013)
29. ICO: Report bad practices as a whistleblower, Information Commissioner's Office. https://ico.org.uk/global/privacy-notice/report-bad-practices-as-a-whistleblower/. Accessed 15 Jan 2020
30. CNPD: Deliberação n.° 765/2009 Princípios Aplicáveis aos Tratamentos de Dados Pessoais com a finalidade de Comunicação Interna de Actos de Gestão Financeira Irregular (Linhas de Ética) (2009). https://www.cnpd.pt/bin/orientacoes/DEL765-2009_LINHAS_ETICA.pdf. Accessed 15 Jan 2020. (in Portuguese)
31. Craig, P., De Burca, G.: EU Law: Texts, Cases and Materials, pp. 206–222. Oxford University Press, Oxford (2015)
32. Seinen, W., Walter, A., van Grondelle, S.: Compatibility as a mechanism for responsible further processing of personal data. In: Medina, M., Mitrakas, A., Rannenberg, K., Schweighofer, E., Tsouroulas, N. (eds.) APF 2018. LNCS, vol. 11079, pp. 153–171. Springer, Cham (2018). https://doi.org/10.1007/978-3-030-02547-2_9
33. CNIL: Délibération n° 2019-139 du 18 juillet 2019 portant adoption d'un référentiel relatif aux traitements de données à caractère personnel destinés à la mise en œuvre d'un dispositif d'alertes professionnelles. NOR: CNIL1935146X (2019). https://www.legifrance.gouv.fr/affichCnil.do?oldAction=rechExpCnil&id=CNILTEXT000039470506&fastReqId=2024022847&fastPos=4. Accessed 15 Jan 2020 (in French)
34. WP29: Opinion 3/2010 on the principle of accountability, WP173 (2010). https://ec.europa.eu/justice/article-29/documentation/opinion-recommendation/files/2010/wp173_en.pdf. Accessed 15 Jan 2020
35. WP29: Guidelines on transparency under Regulation 2016/679, WP260 rev.01 (2018). https://ec.europa.eu/newsroom/article29/document.cfm?action=display&doc_id=51025. Accessed 15 Jan 2020
36. Ausloos, J.: GDPR transparency as a research method (2019). https://ssrn.com/abstract=3465680. Accessed 15 Jan 2020
37. Clifford, D., Ausloos, J.: Data Protection and the Role of Fairness. Yearb. Eur. Law (2018). https://doi.org/10.1093/yel/yey004
38. WP29: Opinion 1/2006 on the application of EU data protection rules to internal whistleblowing schemes in the fields of accounting, internal accounting controls, auditing matters, fight against bribery, banking and financial crime, WP117 (2006). https://ec.europa.eu/justice/article-29/documentation/opinion-recommendation/files/2006/wp117_en.pdf. Accessed 15 Jan 2020
39. EDPS: Guidelines on processing personal information within a whistleblowing procedure (2019). https://edps.europa.eu/sites/edp/files/publication/19-12-17_whisteblowing_guidelines_en.pdf. Accessed 15 Jan 2020
40. EDPB: Guidelines 4/2019 on Article 25 Data Protection by Design and by Default (2019). https://edpb.europa.eu/sites/edpb/files/consultation/edpb_guidelines_201904_dataprotection_by_design_and_by_default.pdf. Accessed 15 Jan 2020

Data Protection and Security

Webs of Trust: Choosing Who to Trust on the Internet

Matteo Dell'Amico$^{(\boxtimes)}$ [ID]

NortonLifeLock Research Group, Biot, France
della@linux.it
https://www.nortonlifelock.com/about/corporate-profile/
research-labs/matteo-dellamico

Abstract. How to decide whether to engage in transactions with strangers? Whether we're offering a ride, renting a room or apartment, buying or selling items, or even lending money, we need a degree of trust that the others will behave as they should. Systems like Airbnb, Uber, Blablacar, eBay and others handle this by creating systems where people initially start as untrusted, and they gain reputation over time by behaving well. Unfortunately, these systems are proprietary and siloed, meaning that all information about transactions becomes property of the company managing the systems, and that there are two types of barriers to entry: first, whenever new users enter a new system they will need to restart from scratch as untrusted, without the possibility of exploiting the reputation they gained elsewhere; second, new applications have a similar cold-start problem: young systems, where nobody has reputation yet, are difficult to kickstart.

We propose a solution based on a *web of trust*: a decentralized repository of data about past interactions between users, without any trusted third party. We think this approach can solve the aforementioned issue, establishing a notion of trust that can be used across applications while protecting user privacy. Several problems require consideration, such as scalability and robustness, as well as the trade-off between privacy and accountability.

In this paper, we provide an overview of issues and solutions available in the literature, and we discuss the directions to take to pursue this project.

Keywords: Reputation · Decentralization · Social networks · Trust · Privacy · Security · Scalability · Network embeddings · Sybil attack · Whitewashing · Distributed ledgers · Smart contracts

1 Introduction

The Internet enables decentralized point-to-point communication between billions of users, and this has unlocked an enormous potential for interactions between them. The so-called *sharing economy*, represented by companies such

L. Antunes et al. (Eds.): APF 2020, LNCS 12121, pp. 113–126, 2020.
https://doi.org/10.1007/978-3-030-55196-4_7

as Airbnb, Uber, Blablacar, etc., exploits this, by putting in contact users that would otherwise not know each other, and letting them engage in transactions (e.g., share the cost for a ride, rent a room, etc.) that often make use of resources that would otherwise be wasted. Crucially, these services provide *reputation systems* that allow us to predict whether somebody will behave in the way they should.

These services are certainly both useful and successful, but they have a couple of shortcomings that we're interested in tackling. First, they are *proprietary*: all the data about user interactions is kept and monetized by the companies handling those services, with little control by users themselves about their own data, and the company is effectively monopolistic in its market, with the possibility of requiring high transaction fees; second, they are *siloed*, meaning that a user's information—and reputation—remains confined in that particular platform. This creates two different types of barriers to entry: first, users that enter a platform will be considered as totally unknown to the world, without the possibility of leveraging the trust they may have earned in the past, for example thanks to social connections and/or past interactions in a similar platform; second, new applications have a similar cold-start problem: if nobody has reputation, fewer people will be confident enough to start interacting, creating unnecessary friction until, if ever, enough users obtain a reputation that is positive enough.

A solution where a single entity, whether a corporation or a nation state, manages the reputation of people from all points of view is obviously criticizable: the Chinese "social credit system" [37]—a reputation system that can, for example, bar people from taking planes or flights if their reputation is bad—raised the alarm of privacy advocates over the world, and has drawn comparisons to pieces of dystopic science fiction [74]. Similar comparisons were drawn for Peeple—a proposed application to leave reviews for people based on professional or personal relationships—which was harshly criticized by public opinion, and the company backtracked to the point of allowing people to veto the reviews they receive, making the usefulness of the application (not yet launched as of January 2020) questionable [57].

We consider the problem of designing a reputation system that does not suffer from the privacy shortcomings described above. We require the system to be *decentralized*, and we want users to be *in control* of whether and how they should appear in the system. The "web of trust" name was first proposed by Zimmerman [82] as a decentralized way of certifying other people's identity—as opposed to the hierarchical structure of trusted third parties like certification authorities that is used, for example, for TLS/SSL certificates. We extend this concept, and here we call "web of trust" a decentralized construction that keeps all kinds of assessments between users, with the goal of creating an efficient and privacy-conscious system without the need of any trusted third party. Garcia Lopez et al. [30] discuss the problems of incentives to cooperation, free riding and decentralized trust as key weaknesses of permissionless blockchains; we think that our effort can be useful in alleviating them.

Recent privacy regulations, such as the European Union's General Data Protection Regulation (GDPR) [26] and the recent California Consumer Privacy Act (CCPA [1], in turn inspired by the GDPR [48]) require that users are given clear and informed opportunities to give consent about using their personal data, and that they have access to granular controls that allows them to decide which of their personal data is shared with whom. The system that we plan to build is based on these concepts: information is shared in a decentralized fashion with trusted peers, through policies which are under control of users themselves.

This is an ambitious problem, and luckily an important corpus of research can be exploited to solve these problems: the goal of this paper is to organize the related work—in sometimes disparate communities—that can be harnessed to reach our goal, and to highlight the most important open questions.

We tackle the problem of representing user reputation, as discussed in Sect. 2, along with ways to formalize it in such a way that there exist sound incentives to cooperation even in a completely decentralized setting. We then discuss in Sect. 3 the security and privacy issues connected to this, in particular as connected to the question of pseudonimity and the opportunity for *whitewashing*— i.e., discarding a user's past bad reputation—and Sybil attacks—i.e., creating large numbers of fake users to subvert the system. We then move on to architectural concerns dealing with decentralization and scalability, discussed in Sect. 4, including decentralized approaches to represent social networks in a privacy-aware way. In Sect. 5, we discuss how our design can be helped by distributed ledgers such as blockchains, and smart contracts on top of it, in order to provide consistency in a completely decentralized architecture. The conclusions of Sect. 6 summarize the state of the art, with potential problem, solutions, and open issues.

2 Formalizing Reputation

Here we provide an overview of the concepts and formalisms used to represent trust and reputation in a computational fashion. For more in-depth discussions, we refer the interested reader to more comprehensive works [20,39].

It is known that reciprocative behavior can make cooperation evolve between selfish actors. For example, the game-theoretic work of Axelrod and Hamilton [3] has shown that simple "tit-for-tat" strategies—where players rewards peer that cooperate and punish those that defect—are successful in various settings of the iterated prisoner's dilemma. Cohen [14] applied successfully this strategy when designing the BitTorrent P2P file-sharing protocol.

Simple reciprocation is effective when two users interact frequently with each other, such that opportunities for reciprocation happen often. Unfortunately, this is not always the case: for one-off interactions, tit-for-tat strategies are not enough. *Reputation*, in this case, can be a means to enable *indirect reciprocation*, based on the idea that my cooperation with others will boost my reputation, and when I have a high reputation others will be more cooperative with me.

In the absence of central authorities that attribute a reputation score to everybody, the concept of reputation is still viable. Consider the example by

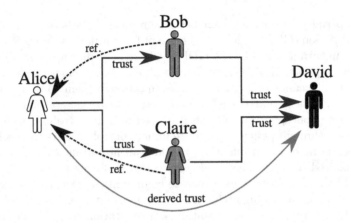

Fig. 1. Transitive trust propagation.

Jöang et al. [39] in Fig. 1: Alice trusts Bob, and Bob trusts David. Bob, therefore, recommends David to Alice, who obtains derived trust in David. Also Claire recommends David to Alice, giving her another reason to increase her trust in David. Since now Alice trusts David to some extent, she might also want to put trust in further people recommended by him. Note that, in this framework, reputation is *subjective*, depending on the subject that evaluates it—to put it another way, there are *no pre-trusted entities*, and everybody can *choose their trust anchors freely*; in the example, Alice's trust anchors are Bob and Claire.

In the following, we will consider a *web of trust* as a graph $G = (V, E)$ where the nodes V are our users and the edges E are *feedback* given by a user for others. A *reputation scoring function* $r : V \times V \to \mathbb{R}$, such that $R(a, b)$ is the reputation for user b as seen by a, will be the way that we use to compute a reputation score. If the transitive trust propagation pattern is used, r will be such that it will depend on paths in G from a to b. There are other possible trust propagation patterns: for example, when judgments are a matter of taste (say, we consider evaluating how somebody cooks), we may want to trust more people that have tastes, and hence judgments, similar to ours. The HITS [45] and SALSA [49] algorithms use a zig-zag propagation pattern that can be used to reflect this.

In our view, users should be free to adjust the parameters of the reputation score function—or choose different reputation score functions altogether—depending on their own preferences and on the domain at hand: for example, which types of endorsements to consider, how to aggregate them, etc. Choosing a suitable reputation scoring function is not trivial, in particular because they should be defined in such a way that they cannot be manipulated by attackers: results on security of reputation metrics are discussed in Sect. 3.

3   Privacy, Robustness and Accountability

Reputation systems should of course not be gameable by adversaries; here we give an overview of the issues we consider most closely related to our problems; for a more in-depth look we defer to Ho man et al. [36].

The Cost of Cheap Pseudonyms. A key trade-off between privacy and accountability is the possibility of creating cheap pseudonyms: from a user's privacy point of view it is of course desirable to have several different, unlinked and possibly disposable identities. This, however, means that identities with bad reputation can simply be forgotten (*whitewashing*) and will not be linked with another user's profiles, giving them the opportunity to misbehave without paying consequences. Friedman and Resnick [29] found that, in this case, *"a large degree of cooperation can still emerge, through a convention in which newcomers "pay their dues" by accepting poor treatment from players who have established positive reputations."* Cheap pseudonyms, hence, do not make reputation systems useless but they limit their positive impact by introducing a kind of "cold-start" problem, as also corroborated by Feldman et al. [28] in the context of P2P systems.

Reputation systems can still be useful when whitewashing is present, but this essentially rules out large transactions with important losses in case somebody misbehaves (think, e.g., of a large loan). In our scenario, we consider we should handle *both* persistent and disposable identities, handling them distinctly in the reputation system.

An interesting possibility with respect to privacy is the field of zero-knowledge proofs, with cryptographic constructs such as zk-SNARKs [7] and zk-STARKs [4]: we will investigate to which extent they can be used to prove a user's reputation score without disclosing too much information about their other past interactions. Another interesting approach to provide anonymity in reputation systems is the mix-net strategy adopted by AnonRep [79]; unfortunately, besides not allowing subjective reputation evaluation, AnonRep is susceptible to Sybil attacks. Lifting this restriction would be an interesting research direction.

Sybil Attack. A problem related to cheap pseudonyms is the Sybil attack [23], where a system, or parts of it, is subverted by creating a large—and possibly unlimited—number of fake identities. Cheng and Friedman [11] show that some reputation mechanisms—e.g., those based on the MaxFlow measure—are immune to Sybil attacks, in the sense that attackers cannot gain reputation score by creating fake identities; Dell'Amico and Capra [21] show that metrics such as Personalized PageRank (PPR) also give some guarantees against Sybil attacks, and propose new metrics that are Sybil-resistant while also employing the trust propagation pattern observed in HITS, SALSA and the large majority of recommender systems. A related line of research is the one by Yu et al. [77,78], who use social networks to limit the number of Sybil users that are accepted into a system. This approach is based on the assumption that the benign part of a social network will be *fast-mixing*, i.e., random walks will quickly become uncorrelated with the place they started from; measurement studies have shown that this property is not always verified, in particular when the creation of a link in a social network requires co-location, resulting in geographically clustered networks [22].

Since we consider a system that allows for disposable identities, we must take into account the Sybil attack. Rather than building on the possibly non-verified hypothesis of a fast-mixing network, we find preferable the more solid guarantees of Sybilproof or Sybil-resistant mechanisms [11,21].

Negative Feedback. Reports of bad experiences should be taken into account as well [2,31], but we need to make sure that the feature shouldn't be abused, for example through blackmail or retaliation [44]. This can be done by designing asymmetric systems (e.g., only one partner in an interaction can give negative reviews [12]), by associating feedback with only verified interactions, and/or by hiding user reviews until all those involved in a transaction are also committed.

4   Decentralization and Scalability

Computing reputation poses scalability issues: with the approach described in Sect. 2, reputation is a function of the paths on the Web of trust between two nodes; if the edges of this social network (assessments) are not public or they are simply too many, then finding them becomes tricky.

This problem—finding paths in social networks in a decentralized fashion—goes back to 1967, when it was popularized as the "small-world problem" [73]: in fact, social networks connect seemingly remote people through rather short chains of acquaintances and, perhaps surprisingly, people are able to efficiently find those chains (i.e., short paths in the social network) even without knowing the full network; Kleinberg [46] provided a mathematical model that possesses these properties, whereby nodes in a graph are placed as points in a circle, and each node has short-range links to their neighbors and long-range links to far-away nodes. If a node knows the circle position of the destination and each of its neighbor, a simple *greedy* routing strategy routing towards the neighbor that is closest to the destination is sufficient to quickly reach the destination. We can see the circle positions as a *network embedding* in a space that is in this case one-dimensional; while the circular embedding of Kleinberg is a good one for the particular kind of synthetic small-world networks created in that work, however, the same kind of embedding is not ideal for real-world social networks that can be better represented in more complex spaces.

Besides computing reputation, our problem of routing in opaque networks arises for routing in friend-to-friend networks [5,13,63], and to discover suitable paths for off-chain payment channels [60,62]. In most cases, the problem is solved through an embedding: a set of coordinates associated to each node such that close nodes in the embedding are likely to be also close in the original graph. The routing algorithm can be the simple greedy approach described before, or some generalization of it (for example, keeping a queue of discovered nodes to limit the likelihood of getting stuck in a local minimum, like the solution adopted by Malkov et al. [52]).

The problem of finding a good embedding for a graph is a recurrent and important one in computer science [32, 35], with a variety of applications such as visualization, link prediction, community detection in addition to finding shortest paths in a graph [6, 18, 34, 50, 80, 81]. Several recent approaches, such as Deep-Walk [58], LINE [72], PTE [71] and node2vec [33] have been unified as related to the factorization of network's Laplacian matrices [61].

A related field is the one of Internet coordinate systems [15, 55, 56, 59, 69], which assign coordinates to Internet nodes, with the goal of making the distance between any pair of nodes an estimation of the Internet network latency between them; a few fully decentralized approaches exist [9, 16, 17, 53]. Approaches taken in this space can be of inspiration for our problem, even though assumptions are different. In particular, (i) Internet coordinate systems are based on a real-world infrastructure with geographical constraints, hence the final layout will be influenced by those geographical characteristics; (ii) nodes can freely ping each other and so-called *beacons* that serve as references, in order to obtain better precision in network distance estimation; (iii) in Internet coordinate systems nodes can only lie in one direction: while they can artificially make their latencies appear higher, they cannot answer pings faster than what the network infrastructure allows. In short, while techniques used for Internet coordinate systems are certainly a good source of inspiration, we cannot directly use these approaches for our goal.

Fortunately, there exist decentralized approaches to network embeddings that do not leverage on the assumptions above. In the following, we outline the ones that we are aware of:

- Sandberg's approach based on Kleinberg's model for routing in the Freenet friend-to-friend network ("darknet"), embedding nodes in a circle [67]. This clean and simple approach, however, appears not very well suited to some more complex social networks [19];
- Approaches based on spectral analysis: as discussed before, Qiu et al. [61] showed that many network embedding approaches can be unified as ones based on spectral properties of the graph adjacency matrix or some related ones, like its Laplacian matrix. Dell'Amico [19] proposes a decentralized implementation of an embedding algorithm by Koren [47] (initially conceived for graph drawing) and evaluates the approach in the context of finding short paths in social networks; Kempe and McSherry [42] describe a generic approach for distributed network factorization. Ling et al. [51] propose an alternative approach which however appears less suited to our case, because the number of nodes in the network (and hance, users in the social network) is required to be fixed and known a priori.
- A couple of approaches based on spanning trees. Roos et al. [64] show how one can build multiple spanning trees for the same graph and use them for routing in friend-to-friend networks; a subsequent work [65] adapts the same

approach to payment networks. These approaches appear effective, but they have a possible limitation on the side of centralization, because the number of spanning trees that can be built is small (the papers experiment with around 10 spanning trees per network); the roots of those spanning trees introduce an element of centralization.

- A piece of work by Kermarrec et al. [43] based on a force-based layout: nodes repel each other while edges bind them together with a force proportional to their weight. Here, it is critical to find efficient ways of discovering other nodes that are close in the embedding to compute the repulsive forces; Kermarrec et al. propose a gossip-based approach inspired by Van Steen [75], which may be problematic for our privacy requirements as it would require to share information with strangers. Alternative solutions (e.g., one based on a solution where all communication is tunneled through paths in the social network) may be possible, but scalability trade-offs should be evaluated.

It is interesting to see that while these approaches attempt to solve the same of similar problems, work that compares and contrasts them is lacking–these pieces of work actually rarely even reference each other. We are working on bridging this gap by implementing and comparing these approach, in order to gain further insight on the weaknesses and merits of each.

Of course, in an adversarial setting like ours, security is a key requirement: malicious users shouldn't be able to subvert the routing algorithm such that paths that would discover trusted users are not found. Kaafar et al. [41] show that decentralized network coordinate systems can be compromised by malicious nodes, and propose a system based on pre-trusted supernodes to mitigate this problem [40], while Sherr et al. [70] propose a fully decentralized countermeasure based on voting. Chen et al. [10] discuss attacks to matrix factorization-based network coordinates approaches, and interestingly propose a reputation-based countermeasure to counter them: this style of defense may be effective in a network whose very purpose is to compute reputation and whose edges do represent trust relationships. Evans et al. [27] and Schiller et al. [68] discuss attacks to Sandberg [67]'s Freenet routing algorithm, and propose countermeasures to secure it. Finally, in a recent piece of work, Bojchevski and Günnemann [8] discuss attacks on centralized node embeddings through the lenses of adversarial machine learning.

In summary, we see that an impressive amount of relevant work exists in terms of network embeddings. In our view, what is needed is a comprehensive and systematic evaluation in light of our goal of computing reputation in a privacy-aware way. Four properties are fundamental to our goals, and should be evaluated: level of decentralization, scalability, security and privacy. Once this comparison is made, we will be able to evaluate the best architectural choice for this problem, and outline if there are any major problems that still need to be solved.

5   Consistency: Distributed Ledgers and Smart Contracts

The problem of finding a consistent state in a decentralized network was an unsolved problem, until 2008, when Nakamoto [54] introduced the disruptive concept of blockchain. Blockchains allow creating a *distributed ledger* (DL), that is, an append-only, unmodifiable data structure that is readable and writeable by everybody. While the concept of distributed ledger was famously created to enable cryptocurrencies, the data structure itself lends itself to several other important uses: a rather trivial one—which is indeed the cornerstone for many others—is providing a place where transactions are sorted and recorded forever univocally.

Probably the most generic way application of a distributed ledger is using it as input to a Turing-complete virtual machine: this is the approach taken by Ethereum [76], which is centered on the concept of *smart contracts*, which are programs for a "world computer", as the Ethereum creators informally call the Ethereum Virtual Machine (EVM) [25]. In this way, anything that can be written in software can be represented, in a consistent and completely decentralized way, in the state of the EVM. Among the software running on Ethereum, Decentralized Autonomous Organizations (DAOs) [24,38]—completely self-organizing, decentralized organizations—are particularly fascinating experiments; we think that efforts that try to build sustainable economies on DAOs [66] may benefit from a distributed reputation metric.

Distributed ledgers and smart contracts are certainly powerful and flexible constructs, but they also have shortcomings: all data and programs for them need to be written on a DL, and writing on the DL is expensive and has high latency (improving latency and throughput of distributed ledgers is a very active area of research). The consequence is that we think that our architecture can and should benefit from DLs in order to achieve features like non-repudiable ratings (for example, this avoids that a user associates different ratings to the same transaction when reporting it to different recipients); similarly, smart contracts can be used to obtain agreement on computations when otherwise it would be problematic. Another use case where DLs are beneficial is associating ratings between users in the web of trust to transactions that already happened on DLs: since creating those transactions is expensive, this gives us a higher confidence that those transactions actually happened, and they are not part of a Sybil attack aimed to subvert the reputation system. Ironically, in a case like this, a shortcoming of a DL (the cost of writing on it) makes them more apt to our use case.

In general, rather than centering the design on a DL-based solution, we envision a system that should avoid the costs of DLs as much as possible, and use them only when and where they are essential to create a completely decentralized architecture.

6 Conclusion

We have explored the challenges that arise when designing a global-scale web of trust for reputation, together with a discussion of related pieces of work and directions towards its implementation. While the objective is ambitious, it is encouraging to see that many difficult sub-problems have been tackled by an impressive array of research, in many cases from different communities.

Our immediate plan now is evaluating and comparing the approaches to decentralized routing discussed in Sect. 4, in order to find to what extent these approaches are usable for our tasks, and which ones would be preferable: we think that this could be the core of a system that can be used effectively.

This document has been written with the goal of inspiring discussion, critique, and collaboration; while much has to be done, we think that this document can provide useful information on key design issues and related work with the goal of developing an open, decentralized and privacy-conscious reputation system for the Internet.

References

1. California States Assembly: The California Consumer Privacy Act of 2018 (2018). https://leginfo.legislature.ca.gov/faces/billTextClient.xhtml?bill_id=201720180AB375
2. Avesani, P., Massa, P., Tiella, R.: Moleskiing. it: a trust-aware recommender system for SKI mountaineering. Int. J. Infonom. **20**(35), 1–10 (2005)
3. Axelrod, R., Hamilton, W.D.: The evolution of cooperation. Science **211**(4489), 1390–1396 (1981)
4. Ben-Sasson, E., Bentov, I., Horesh, Y., Riabzev, M.: Scalable, transparent, and post-quantum secure computational integrity. CryptolePrint Arch., Technical report 46, 2018 (2018)
5. Bennett, K., Grothoff, C., Horozov, T., Patrascu, I., Stef, T.: Gnunet-a truly anonymous networking infrastructure. In: Proceedings of the Privacy Enhancing Technologies Workshop (PET). Citeseer (2002)
6. Berchenko, Y., Teicher, M.: Graph embedding through random walk for shortest paths problems. In: Watanabe, O., Zeugmann, T. (eds.) SAGA 2009. LNCS, vol. 5792, pp. 127–140. Springer, Heidelberg (2009). https://doi.org/10.1007/978-3-642-04944-6_11
7. Bitansky, N., Canetti, R., Chiesa, A., Tromer, E.: From extractable collision resistance to succinct non-interactive arguments of knowledge, and back again. In: Proceedings of the 3rd Innovations in Theoretical Computer Science Conference, ITCS 2012, pp. 326–349. ACM, New York (2012). https://doi.org/10.1145/2090236.2090263, http://doi.acm.org/10.1145/2090236.2090263. ISBN 978-1-4503-1115-1
8. Bojchevski, A., Günnemann, S.: adversarial attacks on node embeddings via graph poisoning. In: International Conference on Machine Learning, pp. 695–704 (2019)
9. Chen, Y., Wang, X., Shi, C., Lua, E.K., Fu, X., Deng, B., Li, X.: Phoenix: a weight-based network coordinate system using matrix factorization. IEEE Trans. Netw. Serv. Manage. **8**(4), 334–347 (2011)

10. Chen, Y., Wu, S., Li, J., Fu, X.: NCShield: protecting decentralized, matrix factorization-based network coordinate systems. IEEE Trans. Serv. Comput. **10**(2), 244–257 (2017). https://doi.org/10.1109/TSC.2015.2437383. ISSN 1939–1374
11. Cheng, A., Friedman, E.: Sybilproof reputation mechanisms. In: Proceedings of the 2005 ACM SIGCOMM Workshop on Economics of Peer-to-Peer Systems, pp. 128–132. ACM (2005)
12. Chwelos, P., Dhar, T.: Caveat emptor: Differences in online reputation mechanisms. Technical report, Working Paper, Sauder School of Business, University of British Columbia (2006)
13. Clarke, I., Sandberg, O., Wiley, B., Hong, T.W.: Freenet: a distributed anonymous information storage and retrieval system. In: Federrath, H. (ed.) Designing Privacy Enhancing Technologies. LNCS, vol. 2009, pp. 46–66. Springer, Heidelberg (2001). https://doi.org/10.1007/3-540-44702-4_4
14. Cohen, B.: Incentives build robustness in bittorrent. Workshop Econ. Peer-to-Peer Syst. **6**, 68–72 (2003)
15. Costa, M., Castro, M., Rowstron, R., Key, P.: PIC: practical internet coordinates for distance estimation. In: Proceedings of the 24th International Conference on Distributed Computing Systems, pp. 178–187. IEEE (2004)
16. Cox, R., Dabek, F., Kaashoek, F., Li, J., Morris, R.: Practical, distributed network coordinates. ACM SIGCOMM Comput. Commun. Rev. **34**(1), 113–118 (2004)
17. Dabek, F., Cox, R., Kaashoek, F., Morris, R.: Vivaldi: a decentralized network coordinate system. ACM SIGCOMM Comput. Commun. Rev. **34**, 15–26 (2004)
18. Das Sarma, A., Gollapudi, S., Najork, M., Panigrahy, R.: A sketch-based distance oracle for web-scale graphs. In: Proceedings of the Third ACM International Conference on Web Search and Data Mining, pp. 401–410. ACM (2010)
19. Dell'Amico, M.: Mapping small worlds. In: Seventh IEEE International Conference on Peer-to-Peer Computing, P2P 2007, pp. 219–228. IEEE (2007)
20. Dell'Amico, M.: Exploiting Social Networks in Robust P2P Applications. Ph.D. thesis, Università degli Studi di Genova (2008). https://www.disi.unige.it/person/DellamicoM/research/phd-thesis.pdf
21. Dell'Amico, M., Capra, L.: Dependable filtering: philosophy and realizations. ACM Trans. Inf. Syst. (TOIS) **29**(1), 5 (2010)
22. Dell'Amico, M., Roudier, Y.: A measurement of mixing time in social networks. In: Proceedings of the 5th International Workshop on Security and Trust Management, Saint Malo, France, p. 72 (2009)
23. Douceur, J.R.: The sybil attack. In: Druschel, P., Kaashoek, F., Rowstron, A. (eds.) IPTPS 2002. LNCS, vol. 2429, pp. 251–260. Springer, Heidelberg (2002). https://doi.org/10.1007/3-540-45748-8_24
24. DuPont, Q.: Experiments in algorithmic governance: a history and ethnography of "the dao," a failed decentralized autonomous organization. In: Bitcoin and Beyond, pp. 157–177. Routledge (2017)
25. Ethereum: Ethereum: the world computer (2015). https://www.youtube.com/watch?v=j23HnORQXvs
26. European Union: Regulation (EU) 2016/679 of the European Parliament and of the Council of 27 April 2016 on the protection of natural persons with regard to the processing of personal data and on the free movement of such data, and repealing Directive 95/46/EC (General Data Protection Regulation). Official Journal of the European Union (2016)
27. Evans, N.S., GauthierDickey, C., Grothoff, C.: Routing in the dark: pitch black. In: Twenty-Third Annual Computer Security Applications Conference (ACSAC 2007), pp. 305–314. IEEE (2007)

28. Feldman, M., Papadimitriou, C., Chuang, J., Stoica, I.: Free-riding and white-washing in peer-to-peer systems. IEEE J. Sel. Areas Commun. **24**(5), 1010–1019 (2006)
29. Friedman, E.J., Resnick, P.: The social cost of cheap pseudonyms. J. Econ. Manage. Strategy **10**(2), 173–199 (2001)
30. Garcia Lopez, P., Montresor, A., Datta, A.: Please, do not Decentralize the Internet with (Permissionless) Blockchains! In: 2019 IEEE 39th International Conference on Distributed Computing Systems (ICDCS), pp. 1901–1911, July 2019. https://doi.org/10.1109/ICDCS.2019.00188. ISSN 1063–6927
31. Golbeck, J.A.: Computing and applying trust in web-based social networks. Ph.D. thesis, University of Maryland (2005)
32. Goyal, P., Ferrara, E.: Graph embedding techniques, applications, and performance: a survey. Knowl.-Based Syst. **151**, 78–94 (2018)
33. Grover, A., Leskovec, J.: node2vec: scalable feature learning for networks. In: Proceedings of the 22nd ACM SIGKDD International Conference on Knowledge Discovery and Data Mining, pp. 855–864. ACM (2016)
34. Gubichev, A., Bedathur, S., Seufert, S., Weikum, G.: Fast and accurate estimation of shortest paths in large graphs. In: Proceedings of the 19th ACM International Conference on Information and Knowledge Management, pp. 499–508. ACM (2010)
35. Hamilton, W.L., Ying, R., Leskovec, J.: Representation learning on graphs: methods and applications. arXiv preprint arXiv:1709.05584 (2017)
36. Hoffman, K., Zage, D., Nita-Rotaru, C.: A survey of attack and defense techniques for reputation systems. ACM Comput. Surv. (CSUR) **42**(1), 1 (2009)
37. Hvistendahl, M.: Inside China's vast new experiment in social ranking. Wired (2017). https://www.wired.com/story/age-of-social-credit/
38. Jentzsch, C.: Decentralized autonomous organization to automate governance. White paper, November 2016
39. Jösang, A., Ismail, R., Boyd, C.: A survey of trust and reputation systems for online service provision. Decis. Support Syst. **43**(2), 618–644 (2007)
40. Kaafar, M.A., Mathy, L., Barakat, C., Salamatian, K., Turletti, T., Dabbous, W.: Securing internet coordinate embedding systems. ACM SIGCOMM Comput. Commun. Rev. **37**, 61–72 (2007)
41. Kaafar, M.A., Mathy, L., Turletti, T., Dabbous, W.: Real attacks on virtual networks: Vivaldi out of tune. In: Proceedings of the 2006 SIGCOMM Workshop on Large-Scale Attack Defense, pp. 139–146. ACM (2006)
42. Kempe, D., McSherry, F.: A decentralized algorithm for spectral analysis. J. Comput. Syst. Sci. **74**(1), 70–83 (2008)
43. Kermarrec, A.M., Leroy, V., Trédan, G.: Distributed social graph embedding. In: Proceedings of the 20th ACM International Conference on Information and Knowledge Management, pp. 1209–1214. ACM (2011)
44. Klein, T.J., Lambertz, C., Spagnolo, G., Stahl, K.O.: Last minute feedback. Technical report, SFB/TR 15 Discussion Paper (2006)
45. Kleinberg, J.M.: Authoritative sources in a hyperlinked environment. J. ACM **46**(5), 604–632 (1999)
46. Kleinberg, J.M.: Navigation in a small world. Nature **406**(6798), 845 (2000)
47. Koren, Y.: On spectral graph drawing. In: Warnow, T., Zhu, B. (eds.) COCOON 2003. LNCS, vol. 2697, pp. 496–508. Springer, Heidelberg (2003). https://doi.org/10.1007/3-540-45071-8_50
48. Lapowsky, I.: California Unanimously Passes Historic Privacy Bill. Wired, June 2018. https://www.wired.com/story/california-unanimously-passes-historic-privacy-bill/

49. Lempel, R., Moran, S.: SALSA: the stochastic approach for link-structure analysis. ACM Trans. Inf. Syst. (TOIS) **19**(2), 131–160 (2001)
50. Liao, Y., Du, W., Geurts, P., Leduc, G.: DMFSGD: a decentralized matrix factorization algorithm for network distance prediction. IEEE/ACM Trans. Networking (TON) **21**(5), 1511–1524 (2013)
51. Ling, Q., Xu, Y., Yin, W., Wen, Z.: Decentralized low-rank matrix completion. In: 2012 IEEE International Conference on Acoustics, Speech and Signal Processing (ICASSP), pp. 2925–2928. IEEE (2012)
52. Malkov, Y., Ponomarenko, A., Logvinov, A., Krylov, V.: Approximate nearest neighbor algorithm based on navigable small world graphs. Inf. Syst. **45**, 61–68 (2014). https://doi.org/10.1016/j.is.2013.10.006, http://www.sciencedirect.com/science/article/pii/S0306437913001300. ISSN 0306-4379
53. Mao, Y., Saul, L.K., Smith, J.M.: Ides: an internet distance estimation service for large networks. IEEE J. Sel. Areas Commun. **24**(12), 2273–2284 (2006)
54. Nakamoto, S.: Bitcoin: a peer-to-peer electronic cash system (2008). https://bitcoin.org/bitcoin.pdf
55. Ng, T.E., Zhang, H.: Predicting internet network distance with coordinates-based approaches. In: Proceedings of the Twenty-First Annual Joint Conference of the IEEE Computer and Communications Societies, vol. 1, pp. 170–179. IEEE (2002)
56. Ng, T.E., Zhang, H.: A network positioning system for the internet. In: USENIX Annual Technical Conference, General Track, pp. 141–154 (2004)
57. Pearson, J.: Peeple has backtracked to the point of pointlessness. Motherboard (2015). https://motherboard.vice.com/en_us/article/vv74z3/peeple-has-backtracked-to-the-point-of-pointlessness
58. Perozzi, B., Al-Rfou, R., Skiena, S.: Deepwalk: Online learning of social representations. In: Proceedings of the 20th ACM SIGKDD International Conference on Knowledge Discovery and Data Mining, pp. 701–710. ACM (2014)
59. Pias, M., Crowcroft, J., Wilbur, S., Harris, T., Bhatti, S.: Lighthouses for scalable distributed location. In: Kaashoek, M.F., Stoica, I. (eds.) IPTPS 2003. LNCS, vol. 2735, pp. 278–291. Springer, Heidelberg (2003). https://doi.org/10.1007/978-3-540-45172-3_26
60. Poon, J., Dryja, T.: The Bitcoin Lightning network: Scalable off-chain instant payments (2016). https://lightning.network/lightning-network-paper.pdf
61. Qiu, J., Dong, Y., Ma, H., Li, J., Wang, K., Tang, J.: Network embedding as matrix factorization: unifying DeepWalk, LINE, PTE, and Node2vec. In: Proceedings of the Eleventh ACM International Conference on Web Search and Data Mining, WSDM 2018, pp. 459–467. ACM, New York (2018). https://doi.org/10.1145/3159652.3159706. ISBN 978-1-4503-5581-0; Event-place: Marina Del Rey, CA, USA
62. Raiden: What is the Raiden network? (2019). https://raiden.network/101.html
63. Rogers, M., Bhatti, S.: How to disappear completely: a survey of private peer-to-peer networks. RN **7**(13), 1 (2007)
64. Roos, S., Beck, M., Strufe, T.: Anonymous addresses for efficient and resilient routing in F2F overlays. In: IEEE INFOCOM 2016-The 35th Annual IEEE International Conference on Computer Communications, pp. 1–9. IEEE (2016)
65. Roos, S., Moreno-Sanchez, P., Kate, A., Goldberg, I.: Settling payments fast and private: efficient decentralized routing for path-based transactions. arXiv preprint arXiv:1709.05748 (2017)
66. Rozas, D., Tenorio-Fornés, A., Díaz-Molina, S., Hassan, S.: When Ostrom meets blockchain: exploring the potentials of blockchain for commons governance. Available at SSRN 3272329 (2018)

67. Sandberg, O.: Distributed routing in small-world networks. In: 2006 Proceedings of the Eighth Workshop on Algorithm Engineering and Experiments (ALENEX), pp. 144–155. SIAM (2006)

68. Schiller, B., Roos, S., Hofer, A., Strufe, T.: Attack resistant network embeddings for darknets. In: 2011 IEEE 30th Symposium on Reliable Distributed Systems Workshops, pp. 90–95. IEEE (2011)

69. Shavitt, Y., Tankel, T.: Big-bang simulation for embedding network distances in euclidean space. IEEE/ACM Trans. Networking (TON) 12(6), 993–1006 (2004)

70. Sherr, M., Blaze, M., Loo, B.T.: Veracity: practical secure network coordinates via vote-based agreements. In: Proceedings of the 2009 Conference on USENIX Annual Technical Conference, p. 13. USENIX Association (2009)

71. Tang, J., Qu, M., Mei, Q.: PTE: predictive text embedding through large-scale heterogeneous text networks. In: Proceedings of the 21th ACM SIGKDD International Conference on Knowledge Discovery and Data Mining, pp. 1165–1174. ACM (2015)

72. Tang, J., Qu, M., Wang, M., Zhang, M., Yan, J., Mei, Q.: Line: large-scale information network embedding. In: Proceedings of the 24th International Conference on World Wide Web, pp. 1067–1077. International World Wide Web Conferences Steering Committee (2015)

73. Travers, J., Milgram, S.: The small world problem. Phychol. Today 1(1), 61–67 (1967)

74. Vincent, A.: Black Mirror is coming true in China, where your 'rating' affects your home, transport and social circle. The Telegraph (2017). https://www.telegraph.co.uk/on-demand/2017/12/15/black-mirror-coming-true-china-rating-affects-home-transport/

75. Voulgaris, S., van Steen, M.: Epidemic-style management of semantic overlays for content-based searching. In: Cunha, J.C., Medeiros, P.D. (eds.) Euro-Par 2005. LNCS, vol. 3648, pp. 1143–1152. Springer, Heidelberg (2005). https://doi.org/10.1007/11549468_125

76. Wood, G.: Ethereum: a secure decentralised generalised transaction ledger. Ethereum Proj. Yellow Paper 151, 1–32 (2014)

77. Yu, H., Gibbons, P.B., Kaminsky, M., Xiao, F.: Sybillimit: a near-optimal social network defense against sybil attacks. In: 2008 IEEE Symposium on Security and Privacy (S&P 2008), pp. 3–17. IEEE (2008)

78. Yu, H., Kaminsky, M., Gibbons, P.B., Flaxman, A.: Sybilguard: defending against sybil attacks via social networks. ACM SIGCOMM Comput. Commun. Rev. 36, 267–278 (2006)

79. Zhai, E., Wolinsky, D.I., Chen, R., Syta, E., Teng, C., Ford, B.: AnonRep: towards tracking-resistant anonymous reputation. In: 13th USENIX Symposium on Networked Systems Design and Implementation (NSDI 2016), pp. 583–596. USENIX Association, Santa Clara, Mar 2016. https://www.usenix.org/conference/nsdi16/technical-sessions/presentation/zhai. ISBN 978-1-931971-29-4

80. Zhao, X., Sala, A., Wilson, C., Zheng, H., Zhao, B.Y.: Orion: shortest path estimation for large social graphs. Networks 1, 5 (2010)

81. Zhao, X., Sala, A., Zheng, H., Zhao, B.Y.: Efficient shortest paths on massive social graphs. In: 7th International Conference on Collaborative Computing: Networking, Applications and Worksharing (CollaborateCom), pp. 77–86. IEEE (2011)

82. Zimmerman, P.: PGP user's guide (1994)

Italian National Framework
for Cybersecurity and Data Protection

Marco Angelini[1,2], Claudio Ciccotelli[1,2], Luisa Franchina[2],
Alberto Marchetti-Spaccamela[1,2], and Leonardo Querzoni[1,2(✉)]

[1] Department of Computer Control and Management Engineering - CIS,
Sapienza University of Rome, Rome, Italy
{angelini,ciccotelli,alberto,querzoni}@diag.uniroma1.it
[2] CINI Cybersecurity National Lab, Rome, Italy
blustarcacina@gmail.com

Abstract. Data breaches have been one of the most common source of
concerns related to cybersecurity in the last few years for many organizations. The General Data Protection Regulation (GDPR) in Europe,
strongly impacted this scenario, as organizations operating with EU citizens now have to comply with strict data protection rules.

In this paper we present the Italian National Framework for Cybersecurity and Data Protection, a framework derived from the NIST Cybersecurity Framework, that includes elements and tools to appropriately take
into account data protection aspects in a way that is coherent and integrated with cybersecurity aspects. The goal of the proposed Framework
is to provide organizations of different sizes and nature with a flexible
and unified tool for the implementation of comprehensive cybersecurity
and data protection programs.

Keywords: Cybersecurity · Data protection · GDPR

1 Introduction

Organizations of all types are increasingly subject to data theft and loss, whether
the asset is customer information, intellectual property, or sensitive company
files. In fact, cybersecurity threats exploit the increased complexity and connectivity of critical infrastructure systems, placing security, economy, and public
safety and health at risk. Similar to financial and reputational risk, cybersecurity risk affects a company's bottom line: it can drive up costs and negatively
impact revenues; it can harm an organization ability to innovate and to attract
and maintain customers. As a consequence, average expenditures on cybercrime
are increasing dramatically and, quite often, current spending priorities fail to
deliver the expected levels of effectiveness (see for example [1]).

L. Antunes et al. (Eds.): APF 2020, LNCS 12121, pp. 127–142, 2020.
https://doi.org/10.1007/978-3-030-55196-4_8

In fact, there are many organizations and companies with little or no experience in cyber protection; they may have security practices in place, but they are most likely not sure if those practices establish a comprehensive security program. They need to know the necessary requirements and actions (or at least the most important ones) from an information security perspective. This stimulated the development of documents, guidelines and tools to support companies and organizations in a cost effective way that takes into account specific characteristics of the organization. To answer this need, several proposals have been recently presented (see Sect. 2). Among these proposals we focus on the Cybersecurity Framework originally proposed by the US National Institute of Standards and Technology (NIST) to support the development of a industry-led set of standards, guidelines, best practices, methodologies, and processes to cost-effectively reduce cyber risks of critical infrastructures. NIST released version 1.0 of the Cybersecurity Framework in 2014, describing it as a voluntary, risk-based approach to manage cybersecurity risk for organizations of all shapes and sizes. The Framework has been proposed for protecting critical infrastructures but its approach has a much broader applicability for industries and organizations and it has been widely adopted by non-critical infrastructure organizations [19]. Version 1.1 has been recently published [17]. In 2015, the Research Center for Cyber Intelligence and Information Security (CIS) at Sapienza University of Rome presented the Italian National Framework for Cybersecurity [4], the result of a collaboration between academy, public bodies, and private companies. The Italian National Framework for Cybersecurity is based on the NIST Cybersecurity Framework and provides an operational tool for organizing cybersecurity processes suitable for public and private organizations of any size; in particular, it has been customized and improved with a focus on the Italian economic system, mainly formed by small-to-micro manufacturing companies that have limited IT expertise.

The Italian National Framework for Cybersecurity provides organizations with a unified point of view from which other standards, guidelines, and best practices can be applied effectively. It does not provide a unique set of rules that should be applied by all organizations, but rather enables organizations, regardless of size, cybersecurity risk, or cybersecurity sophistication, to improve their security and resilience to cyber attacks.

As of May 2018, with the application of the General Data Protection Regulation [10] (GDPR), there is one single set of data protection rules to be enforced for all companies operating with EU citizens. The GDPR regulates the processing and circulation of personal data related to natural and legal persons, identifying roles and responsibilities. The GDPR explicitly requires organizations to demonstrate that they have embedded the principle of data protection by design and by default; for example, Article 8 requires that data controllers shall implement appropriate technical and organizational measures to ensure that processing of data is performed in accordance with the Regulation.

Security and data protection have complementary and mutually-reinforcing objectives with respect to managing the confidentiality, integrity, and availability of personally identifiable information (PII). When applied to securing PII, security controls provide privacy protection and are, therefore, a mandatory requirement for the protection of data of individuals. Indeed, from an implementation perspective of identifying and selecting controls, these controls are generally classified as security controls. However, there are also data protection concerns with no direct implications for cybersecurity (and cybersecurity concerns without implications for data protection). Therefore, the privacy of individuals cannot be achieved solely by securing PII. We finally observe that there are cases where security approaches may pose at risk personal information (e.g. extensively logging information about user activities on a web application for security monitoring purposes), potentially creating conflicting goals between security and data protection that need to be carefully considered. We refer the interested reader to [16] for a thorough discussion that demonstrate various types of privacy concerns apart from data security breaches. These concerns relate to the ways in which systems process PII and the effects such processing can have on individuals.

We observe that there is a significant number of standards, guidelines that address specific privacy aspects and/or security requirements that should be followed. However the situation is not satisfactory. A recent report by ENISA [8] explores how the standards-developing world has been responding to the fast-changing and demanding realm of privacy. The study provides insights into the state-of-the-art of privacy standards in the information security context by mapping existing standards available and standardisation initiatives alike. Main findings of the study include that *"there is an increasing need to analyse the mapping of international standards and European regulatory requirements, as references to standards in the EU legislation are becoming recurrent and there are considerable differences from jurisdictions outside of the EU"*; additionally, *"proving compliance with privacy standards in information security is not as straightforward as expected. While there are some approaches for conformity assessment available in specific sectors others are still lacking appropriate mechanisms"*.

Clearly, SMEs are facing additional difficulties since they often lack the expertise needed to cope with such complexity. As an example, for this issue we refer to the position of SMEUnited (the association of crafts and SMEs in Europe) that points out significant difficulties in complying to the GDPR. Namely, it is pointed out that the main challenge is that the regulation is extremely complex while *"the guidelines published may help to understand the rules, but do not offer guidance on how to apply the theory in the real life"*[1].

The above issues suggest that organizations should put in place an appropriate framework that ensures they are implementing technical and organizational measures such that data processing is performed in line with the GDPR.

---

[1] https://smeunited.eu/news/smes-say-gdpr-needs-reality-check.

1.1 Our Contribution

The above discussion motivates the need for a security framework that considers both the protection of the organization from cyber attacks and the requirements established by the GDPR. This paper presents the Italian National Framework for Cybersecurity and Data Protection (hereinafter referred to as *Framework*) to support organizations that need strategies and processes aimed at the protection of personal data and cybersecurity[2]. The goal is *to provide a flexible and unified tool to support organizations in the implementation of cybersecurity* **and** *data protection programs toward standards and regulations.*

The proposed Framework, that extends the one presented in [4], includes specific prescriptions necessary for an organization to implement a full cybersecurity and data protection program; its adoption can help organizations define a path toward cyber protection that is consistent with current regulations and that can be adapted taking into account the specific needs and maturity of the company. For organizations that already implement measures consistent with GDPR, the Framework can be used for guiding the necessary continuous monitoring activities. According to the GDPR, data security is an important part of wider compliance with data protection obligations (mainly considered in articles 5 and 32 of GDPR). However we observe that these aspects are quite often those that represent technical challenges especially for SMEs. The adoption of a cybersecurity framework may represent a best practice and a way to demonstrate that the organization adopted a well-grounded duty of care, an important step to properly face fines and the legal liability of lawsuits.

2 Related Work

Several frameworks dedicated to cybersecurity and data protection have been proposed in the past. Most of them provide technical indications, while others propose a more high level approach. In this section we briefly discuss those among them that have the largest similarities with the Framework proposed in this paper. We refer to [19] for a detailed comparison and discussion.

ISO/IEC 27000. The International Organization for Standardization (ISO) and the International Electrotechnical Commission (IEC) publish the 27000 family of documents and standards to help organizations keep their information assets secure. In particular, organizations can be certified to respect the standard ISO/IEC 27001 published in 2013. We observe that certification is a plus that however comes at a cost that might be non negligible for small companies. ISO/IEC 27001 and ISO/IEC 27002 provide a comprehensive lists of security controls discussing how to accomplish each control statement; namely, it includes more that one hundred control measures that address the most common information security risks. The controls are flexible and customizable and

---

[2] The Italian National Framework for Cybersecurity and Data Protection [5] is publicly available at http://www.cybersecurityframework.it/.

implemented as part of an organization-wide process to manage risk. ISO/IEC 27000 is a set of best practices with a focus on information security and provides practical advice on how to protect information and reduce cyber threats.

Recently, (August 2019) ISO/IEC published the document 27701 that complement the ISO/IEC 27000 family of standards by specifically addressing privacy issues and has the main goal of providing a unifying framework for implementing GDPR. The New ISO/IEC 27701 jointly with ISO/IEC 27001 proposes a consistent approach mixing information security and data protection (Privacy). ISO standards are well known and recognized in businesses worldwide and the market of auditors and certifiers is fully mature. This clearly sets an advantageous path for organizations that were already certified ISO/IEC 27001 compliant, to further embrace the new ISO standard and deploy startegies to protect personal identifiable information, in coherence with GDPR.

On the negative side, the ISO/IEC 27000 family of standard is known to be complex and expensive to implement and certify, limiting their general applicability to organizations with specific needs, or large size. This is particularly true for micro enterprises and SMEs, and in general for companies where IT is not the core business. For all these reasons accreditation with ISO/IEC 27001 is not widespread: in 2018 there were about 30,000 worldwide certifications, less than 9,000 in EU (including UK)[3]. Furthermore, an explicit adoption of ISO/IEC 27701 for GDPR certification by National supervisory authorities may pose problems in relation with Article 42/43 of the GDPR that state certification requirements must be made *"publicly accessible by the supervisory authorities in an easily accessible form"* and that authorities should take special care of *"specific needs of micro, small and medium-sized enterprises"*. Lauchad discusses these and further threats and opportunities on this topic in [7].

HITRUST CSF. The HITRUST Alliance is an independent organization based in the United States whose partners develop and maintain HITRUST CSF [11] a security framework that is based on ISO/IEC 27001 and 27002 that are integrated with other major information security standards, regulations, and requirements. Historically, they have focused on the healthcare industry but are also considering the financial services industry. Recent versions of the framework incorporate GDPR and privacy regulations in other countries. We note that HITRUST CSF targets heavily regulated markets and its implementation is rather complex. Organizations that are involved in healthcare delivery and payments would be well-suited to evaluate HITRUST for adoption since it covers many of the unique regulations of these industries; on the other side HITRUST CSF is not suited for organizations in other areas.

Other NIST Frameworks. The NIST Risk Management Framework (NIST RMF) [14] is a US federal government policy and standards to help secure information systems developed by National Institute of Standards and Technology. It provides a disciplined and structured process that integrates information security and risk management activities into the system development life cycle through

---

[3] See ISO survey for details; available at https://www.iso.org/the-iso-survey.html.

six steps. During its life cycle, an information system will encounter many types of risk that affect the overall security posture of the system and the security controls that must be implemented. The RMF process supports early detection and resolution of risks. We note that this framework is more complex to implement than the NIST Cybersecurity Framework and that it could take external expertise to assist with implementation for most organizations.

NIST recently published the Privacy Framework [18] that specifically addresses compliance with privacy regulation though has not been designed to directly address GDPR requirements. The framework also provides cross references between the Privacy Framework and the Cybersecurity Framework; such references are directly applicable to our framework as well.

Finally, concerning technical proposals, ENISA reports a list of third-party tools tied to Risk Management and Risk Assessment, eventually encompassing Data Protection aspects [9]; After a review of these tools, we concluded that they mainly cope with technological aspects considered during policy implementation. Our proposal is positioned at a higher modeling level and can benefit from those tools in implementing the security controls. The above discussion motivates the relevance of the Cybersecurity Framework originally proposed in [17] for its generality and flexibility that makes it applicable to all organizations independent of the size, the cybersecurity maturity, the specific area etc.

3   Background on the Framework

This section introduces key elements of the first version of the Italian National Cybersecurity Framework referring to [4] for a more detailed presentation. The Framework inherits the three fundamental elements of the NIST Cybersecurity Framework, namely *Framework Core*, *Profiles* and *Implementation Tiers*, and introduces three additional concepts: *Priority Levels*, *Maturity Levels* and *Contextualization* (Fig. 1).

Framework Core. The Framework Core represents the life cycle structure of the cybersecurity management process, both from a technical and organizational point of view; it is hierarchically structured into functions, categories and subcategories. The five functions (*IDENTIFY, PROTECT, DETECT, RESPOND, RECOVER*) are concurrent and continuous and represent main security topics to be addressed; the cybersecurity enabling activities (e.g. processes and technologies) that should be executed are defined. Namely, for each subcategory the Core presents informative references that link the subcategory to known cybersecurity practices provided by industry standards (e.g. ISO/IEC 27000 [13], NIST SP 800-53 rev. 4 [15], COBIT 5 [12], CIS CSC [3]) or general legal regulations. The 5 functions group together categories and subcategories linked to the following themes:

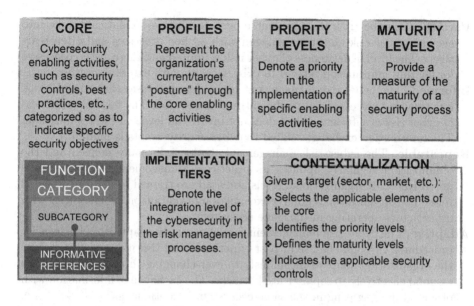

Fig. 1. Key elements of the Framework.

IDENTIFY - identification of business processes and associated risks with the goal of defining resources and investments coherent with risk management strategy and business objectives.

PROTECT - implementation of measures aimed at protecting business processes and corporate assets, regardless of their IT nature.

DETECT - definition and implementation of appropriate activities to promptly identify cybersecurity incidents.

RESPOND - definition and implementation of the appropriate activities to contain and mitigate impact when a computer security incident has been detected.

RECOVER - definition and implementation of activities for the recovery of processes and services impacted by an accident. The objective is to support the timely recovery of business operations.

Profiles. Profiles are the result of an organization's selection of specific subcategories based on several factors: the risk assessment, the business context, the applicability of the various subcategories. Profiles can be used to improve the security status by comparing the *current profile* with the desired (*target*) profile. The current profile can be used to define priorities and to measure progress towards the target. Profiles can be also used to communicate cyber risk posture within or outside the organization.

Implementation Tiers. Implementation Tiers provide context on the integration level of cyber risk management processes within the organization. There are four levels of evaluation, from the weakest to the strongest.

Partial. The cyber risk management model does not systematically take into account cyber risk and it is managed with ad hoc processes and often reactively. The level of awareness of cyber risk is limited and there are no processes for sharing information related to cybersecurity with external entities.

Informed. The cyber risk management model has processes that consider risk but they are not extended to the entire organization. The level of awareness of cyber risk is sufficient, but it does not involve all levels of the organization. The information exchange related to cybersecurity events is limited.

Repeatable. The cyber risk management model is formally defined and the organization regularly updates its practices. Management of cyber risk is pervasive at all organizational levels and staff are trained to manage assigned roles. The organization regularly exchanges information on cybersecurity with other actors operating in the same ecosystem.

Adaptive. The cyber risk management model regularly adapts its cybersecurity procedures through the use of past experience and risk indicators; moreover the organization adapts continuously to ever-changing threats and is able to respond effectively to sophisticated attacks. The exchange of information with other actors operating in the same ecosystem is continuous.

Priority Levels. Priority levels allow organizations and companies to support the definition of an implementation program to reach a target profile that prioritize those actions that most reduce the risk level. There are three key factors:

1. exposure to threats, determining the actions that decrease the likelihood of the threat;
2. probability (i.e. frequency) of threat occurrence;
3. impact of the damage resulting from a cybersecurity incident.

The above classification is used to set priorities on the basis of two specific criteria:

- ability to reduce cyber risk by acting on one or more key factors for its determination;
- implementation costs and impact for specific actions.

The Framework suggests three simple priority levels: *High, Medium, Low.* High priority actions significantly reduce one of the three key factors of cyber risk that must be implemented independently of the complexity of the implementation. Medium (Low) interventions make it possible to achieve a reduction of one of the three key factors of cyber risk and are simple (complex and costly) to implement.

Maturity Levels. Maturity levels provide a reference point by which each organization can evaluate its own subcategory implementation and set goals and priorities for its improvement. They measure the maturity of a security process, of a specific technology, of the amount of adequate resources used to implement a given subcategory. We observe that an organization may have different maturity levels for different subcategories; moreover the maturity level of a subcategory requires that all specified security practices are implemented. This allows organizations to define their level of maturity and to identify the security actions necessary to achieve their desired goals.

Contextualization. Basic elements of the Framework are general and independent to the context characteristic (e.g. production sector, size or location of the organization). Contextualizing the Framework for an organization or an application area (e.g., a productive sector or a homogeneous category of organizations) requires specifying its core by selecting the relevant functions, categories and subcategories, and defining the desired priority and maturity levels for all the selected subcategories. A contextualization is defined through the following steps:

1. select the list of functions, categories and subcategories that are relevant to the organization on the basis of all or some of the previous elements (production sector, size and location of the organization, etc.);
2. define the priority levels for the implementation of the selected subcategories;
3. define guidelines at least for high priority subcategories;
4. specify maturity levels at least for high priority subcategories.

4 The Italian National Framework for Cybersecurity and Data Protection

The Framework presented in this paper introduces two main novelties:

- improves the Framework Core by introducing new categories and subcategories dedicated to data protection topics (Sect. 4.1);
- introduces *Contextualization Prototypes*, a new tool that support and facilitates the definition of contextualizations (Sect. 4.2).

4.1 Framework Core

As the original Italian National Cybersecurity Framework [4], the version presented in this document is also based on the Cybersecurity Framework developed by NIST [17]. In particular, changes made by NIST to the Framework Core with their recent v1.1 have been integrated: a new category has been added to manage security issues linked to supply chains; a category has been modified to strengthen the security of authentication and identity management processes by adding two subcategories; finally three new subcategories have been added to control the integrity of hardware devices, to meet resilience requirements and to manage information about vulnerabilities.

In addition to the modifications made by NIST, we introduced further categories and subcategories to integrate data protection elements in the Framework Core. To this end, nine new subcategories and a new category have been introduced which capture the following aspects related to data protection:

– data management processes, with particular reference to those applicable to personal data;
– methods for personal data processing;
– roles and responsibilities in the management of personal data;
– impact assessment on the protection of personal data;
– documentation and communication procedures following incidents that are considered a violation of personal data.

We observe that the proposed modifications extend the previous Framework Core and align it to the different standards that already deal with the problem of personal data protection and make it applicable even in contexts where general or sector regulations impose specific requirements on data processing.

4.2   Contextualization Prototypes

Contextualization prototypes are a new tool for simplifying and structuring the creation of a contextualization of the Framework. A contextualization, in general, requires to integrate several requirements, stemming from regulations, technical standards, best practices, etc. Prototypes can be defined such to embed these requirements in a general format that can be applied to independent contextualizations. Therefore, contextualization prototypes facilitate the definition of a contextualization by allowing to build it incrementally, coping with the different technical regulations, or legal regulations or best practices one at a time and then integrating them in the final result. Prototypes can be used, for example, to represent:

– general regulations that impose the implementation of specific practices of cybersecurity or data protection;
– technical standards or guidelines that indicate specific checks related to cyber-security or data protection;
– industry best practices related to cybersecurity or data protection.

For each subcategory a prototype defines an implementation class among the following options:

– **MANDATORY:** the subcategory must be included in all contextualizations that implement the prototype;
– **RECOMMENDED:** the inclusion of the subcategory in all contextualizations that implement the prototype is suggested;
– **FREE:** the inclusion of the subcategory in the contextualization that implements the prototype is optional.

For each subcategory a contextualization prototype might define a priority level for its implementation. Furthermore, a prototype is accompanied by an implementation guide, a document that describes:

– the prototype's application context;

- additional constraints on the selection of subcategories and the definition of priority levels;
- an optional list of security checks, for the considered subcategories, which will be opportunely organized in the different maturity levels during the implementation of the prototype.

Therefore, contextualization prototypes do not replace contextualizations, but provide a support tool that facilitates the creation and update of a contextualization through their composition as illustrated in Sect. 5.1. The contextualization prototypes maintain their compatibility with the form of a contextualization, and this feature allow their integration into tools that we already provided in the past for implementing the framework contextualizations, such as [6] and CRUMBS, a cybersecurity framework browser [2].

5   Implementation Methodology

The use of the Framework is achieved through two fundamental activities described in the following sections: (i) contextualization of the Framework to a specific application context and (ii) implementation of the Framework by an organization.

5.1   Contextualizing the Framework

The process of defining a contextualization is usually delegated to the single organization that decides to adopt the Framework, but it can also be provided by an association, a regulator or, more generally, by any actor able to identify and apply to the contextualization a set of characteristics belonging to one or more organizations. The process, shown in Fig. 2, requires the selection of one or more prototypes, the integration of aspects that they model in the contextualization, (legal or technical regulations, industry best practices etc.) and the refinement of the resulting contextualization with respect to the organization's specific aspects.

For each prototype of interest the following steps are performed:

1. all subcategories indicated as mandatory in the prototype are selected in the contextualization;
2. the inclusion in the contextualization of the subcategories indicated as recommended in the prototype must be assessed, considering the specific characteristics of the application context;
3. any further restrictions on the selection of the subcategories documented in the prototype's implementation guide must be applied;
4. any further restriction on the definition of priority levels documented in the prototype's implementation guide must be taken into account when adapting prototype's priority levels to the application context;
5. any security checks documented in the prototype's implementation guide can be integrated into the contextualization application guidelines.

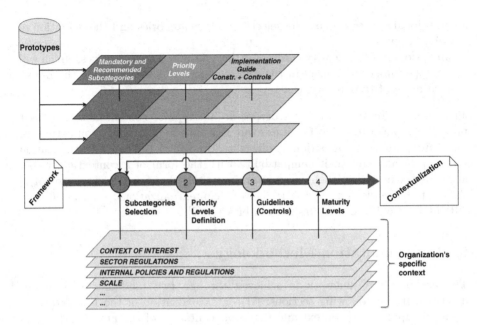

Fig. 2. Contextualization of the Framework through the implementation of prototypes.

At the end of this implementation process, repeated for all the contextualization prototypes of interest, the resulting contextualization can be further specialized where needed.

5.2   Implementing the Framework

Recall that the objective of the Framework is to provide a tool to support management of cyber risk management precesses. It is plausible that in many cases cybersecurity programs have already been implemented. In these cases the introduction of the Framework is to be intended not to replace what is already in place, but as further reference in order to:

- improve (or define, if not present) a cybersecurity and data protection program in a structured and integrated way, based on risk management, which can be implemented in the presence of pre-existing security governance models;
- determine the level of maturity of the cybersecurity and data protection activities, identifying appropriate improvements or rationalization of costs, in favor of a rational redistribution of resources;
- conduct benchmarking among companies and organizations operating in specific sectors or with similar characteristics that can favor the improvement of security levels, simultaneously enabling the cyber insurance market;

– facilitate communication with top management (e.g. directors and boards of directors, shareholders, etc.) and with external actors (e.g. rating agencies, suppliers and partners), so that the cyber risk levels to which the organizations are exposed are clearly represented and to identify the investments and resources to be put in place for an adequate risk reduction.

The implementation of the Framework follows a set of essential steps. The identification/creation of a contextualization (step A) has been thoroughly described in the previous sections and is the part more impacted by the contextualization prototypes. In the following the essential steps are reported:

A. **Identify a contextualization of the Framework.** If the organization belongs to a regulated sector, it should use one of the contextualizations provided by its own sector regulator, or define its own contextualization by implementing any prototypes that collect the applicable regulations. In the case in which the organization does not belong to a regulated sector, it can identify the contextualization to be used among the available ones, or define a specific one;

B. **Define priorities and scope.** Periodically identify the organization's strategic objectives and business priorities to select key areas and functions that require specific focus;

C. **Identify systems and assets.** Identify information and systems that the organization considers vital and critical to guarantee the organization's operations. This step is especially important for the subsequent phases, since it allows for the proper assessment of the impacts during the analysis of the risks and thus facilitating the understanding of the actual needed level of protection;

D. **Determining the current profile.** The implementation status and maturity level for each subcategory of the Framework is expected to be assessed. This allows to define one or more current profiles in relation to the areas/functions envisaged for the implementation of the program;

E. **Risk analysis.** Determine and evaluate risks by adopting an appropriate methodology in relation to the specific organizational and market characteristics in which the organization operates. Some ideas regarding the process of analysis and risk management are provided in [4] (Sect. 7.2);

F. **Determine the target profile.** Through the risk management process, the organization must be able to define a target profile that, unlike the current one, represents the level of implementation and maturity that it is intended to achieve for each subcategory of the Framework. It is desirable that the selection of these levels can be carried out having already integrated the cybersecurity risk management within the enterprise risk management program, so that the management of cyber risk can benefit from decisions taken at the higher organizational level (i.e., top management), using a comprehensive systemic view to support decision-making;

G. **Determine the gap with respect to the target profile.** Conduct a comparison between the target and the current profile to identify the gaps in the management of cybersecurity;

H. Define and implement a roadmap to reach the target profile. The application phase of the Framework implementation consists in defining the set of activities necessary to reach the target profile determined in phase F. This means developing a specific plan to implement the individual security checks of the Framework, following a time schedule that will vary according to the actual risks and the specific conditions in which the organization operates;

I. Measuring performance. In order to review actions taken and improve them to efficiently reach the target profile, it is necessary to define monitoring metrics that can also highlight operational costs. Evaluation of the efficacy of the current profile must be used to define the new target profile.

6   A GDPR Contextualization Prototype

We now present a GDPR contextualization prototype (hereinafter referred to as the GDPR prototype). Recall that prototypes represent a starting point for creating contextualizations by adapting the prototype to the specific context of the sector, organization or company under consideration. This requires to select the subcategories of interest, the priority levels, and define appropriate maturity levels, according to the specificity of the application context. As we already pointed out, a contextualization for an organization can be obtained by combining more prototypes.

The GDPR prototype supports the integration of the fundamental elements of the regulation and, therefore, can be applied in many contextualizations.

Due to space constraints the entire specification of the contextualization prototype cannot be included in this document; we refer to [5] for a detailed presentation.

Selection of Subcategories. The subcategory selection process is guided by the classification described in Sect. 4.2. The GDPR contextualization prototype organizes the subcategories according to the following criteria:

MANDATORY: these subcategories express requirements that are explicitly stated in the Regulation, and that must therefore be included in any contextualization that adheres to this prototype. As an example, subcategory DP-ID.AM-8 captures a fundamental aspect of Art. 30 from GDPR by stating that "records of personal data processing activities must be identified and maintained".

RECOMMENDED: this class gathers those subcategories which, while unable to completely encompass fundamental aspects of the Regulation when considered singularly, allow to consider those aspects on which the Regulation waives more freedom regarding the modalities of implementation when combined together (e.g., artt. 25 and 32). On the other hand, the term RECOMMENDED should not suggest that their implementation is, to some extent, "optional" or "marginal". Conversely, these aspects must be implemented according to the modalities that best suit the specific context under consideration (as long as compliant with the Regulation) by coherently selecting the

RECOMMENDED subcategories, and possibly integrating them with additional FREE subcategories if necessary or appropriate for the specific context.

FREE: all the other subcategories. For these subcategories there is no motivation which definitely support their selection in relationship with the Regulation. Nevertheless, this does not mean that the selection of these subcategories is "not recommended"; it means that their selection is subordinate to the specific context under consideration.

Priority Levels. The GDPR contextualization prototype specifies a "predefined" priority level for all MANDATORY and RECOMMENDED subcategories. During the creation of a contextualization these priority levels must be revised to appropriately fit the specificities of the context under consideration. Moreover, the priority levels for the selected FREE subcategories must be defined. The priority of each subcategory is defined on the three-level scale described in Sect. 3 (*High, Medium, Low*).

Moreover, the GDPR prototype's implementation guide defines the following constraint: "all MANDATORY subcategories must be set to *High* priority". Namely, their default priority level is *High* and cannot be changed. Their implementation should be a priority regardless of complexity and cost. Refer to [5] for the details of the priority levels assigned to the MANDATORY and RECOMMENDED subcategories.

Implementation Guide. The GDPR prototype provides a guide for supporting the implementation of contextualizations based on it (see Sect. 4.2). This defines for each MANDATORY subcategory a set of security and data protection *checks* that refer to one or more articles of the GDPR covering several fundamental areas of interests. The reader is encouraged to check the full details of the implementation guide on the supplementary material available at http://www.cybersecurityframework.it/supplemental_material.pdf.

7 Conclusions

In this paper we presented the Italian National Framework for Cybersecurity and Data Protection. Standing on top of the original Italian National Framework for Cybersecurity, this new proposal improves it by integrating elements linked to data protection and providing tools for its implementation in the current context where the General Data Protection Regulation (GDPR) provides a single source of data protection rules for all organizations that manage personal data from EU citizens. The framework has the goal of supporting organizations in the definition of a comprehensive cybersecurity and data protection program that is clearly structured, risk-based, goal-oriented and in line with current regulations and technical standards. The framework also supports the organization governance in monitoring the program implementation and assessing its evolution toward the intended targets.

Acknowledgements. The authors would like to thank Cosimo Comella, Marco Coppotelli and Dorotea Alessandra de Marco (representatives of the Italian Data Protection Authority) for their valuable feedback which helped improving the Framework and its relationship with data protection principles and requirements.

References

1. Accenture and Ponemon Institute: Cost of cybercrime study (2017). https://www.accenture.com/us-en/insight-cost-of-cybercrime-2017?src=SOMS
2. Angelini, M., Lenti, S., Santucci, G.: Crumbs: a cyber security framework browser. In: 2017 IEEE Symposium on Visualization for Cyber Security (VizSec), pp. 1–8, October 2017. https://doi.org/10.1109/VIZSEC.2017.8062194
3. Center for Internet Security: Critical Security Controls for Effective Cyber Defense (CIS Controls). https://www.cisecurity.org/
4. CIS Sapienza: 2015 Italian Cyber Security Report: Un Framework Nazionale per la Cybersecurity, February 2016. https://www.cybersecurityframework.it
5. CIS Sapienza: Framework Nazionale per la Cybersecurity e la Data Protection, February 2019. https://www.cybersecurityframework.it
6. CIS Sapienza: Tool for the implementation of Italian Cybersecurity Framework (2020). http://tool.cybersecurityframework.it
7. Lachaud, E.: ISO/IEC 27701: Threats and opportunities for GDPR certification (2020). https://research.tilburguniversity.edu/en/publications/isoiec-27701-threats-and-opportunities-for-gdpr-certification
8. ENISA: Guidance and gaps analysis for European standardisation (2019). https://www.enisa.europa.eu/publications/guidance-and-gaps-analysis-for-european-standardisation
9. ENISA: Inventory of risk management/risk assessment tools (2020). https://www.enisa.europa.eu/topics/threat-risk-management/risk-management/current-risk/risk-management-inventory/rm-ra-tools
10. European Union: Regulation (EU) 2016/679 of the European Parliament and of the Council of 27 April 2016 on the protection of natural persons with regard to the processing of personal data and on the free movement of such data, and repealing Directive 95/46/EC (General Data Protection Regulation), May 2016. http://eur-lex.europa.eu/legal-content/EN/TXT/?uri=OJ:L:2016:119:TOC
11. HITRUST Alliance: HITRUST CSF. https://hitrustalliance.net/hitrust-csf/
12. ISACA: Cobit 5. ISA (2012)
13. ISO/IEC 27000:2018: Information technology - Security techniques - Information security management systems - Overview and vocabulary, February 2018
14. NIST: Risk management framework overview. http://csrc.nist.gov/projects/risk-management/risk-management-framework-(RMF)-Overview
15. NIST: SP 800–53 Rev. 4 - Security and Privacy Controls for Federal Information Systems and Organizations, April 2013
16. NIST: An Introduction to Privacy Engineering and Risk Management in Federal Systems (NIST Interagency Report 8062), January 2017. https://csrc.nist.gov/publications/detail/nistir/8062/final
17. NIST: Framework for improving critical infrastructure cybersecurity (version 1.1), April 2018. https://www.nist.gov/cyberframework/framework
18. NIST: NIST Privacy Framework, January 2020. https://www.nist.gov/privacy-framework
19. Zaras, D.: Information Security Frameworks and Controls Catalogue (Impact Makers Report) (2018)

Operationalization of Privacy and Security Requirements for eHealth IoT Applications in the Context of GDPR and CSL

Oleksandr Tomashchuk[1,3]([⊠]), Yuan Li[2], Dimitri Van Landuyt[3], and Wouter Joosen[3]

[1] Philips Research, Eindhoven, The Netherlands
oleksandr.tomashchuk@philips.com
[2] University of Macerata, Macerata, Italy
y.li6@studenti.unimc.it
[3] imec-DistriNet, KU Leuven, Heverlee, Belgium
{dimitri.vanlanduyt,wouter.joosen}@kuleuven.be

Abstract. The Fourth Industrial Revolution imposes a number of unprecedented societal challenges and these are increasingly being addressed through regulation. This, in turn, lays the burden to adopt and implement the different concepts and principles (such as privacy-by-design) with practitioners. However, these concepts and principles are formulated by legal experts in a way that does not allow their direct usage by software engineers and developers, and the practical implications are thus not always obvious nor clear-cut. Furthermore, many complementary regulatory frameworks exist to which compliance should, in some cases, be reached simultaneously.

In this paper, we address this generic problem by transforming the legal requirements imposed by the EU's General Data Protection Regulation (GDPR) and the China's Cybersecurity Law (CSL) into technical requirements for an exemplar case study of a generic eHealth IoT system. The derived requirements result from an interdisciplinary collaboration between technical and legal experts and are representative of the types of trade-off decisions made in such a compliance process. By means of this exemplar case study, we propose a set of generic requirement-driven elements that can be applied to similar IoT-based architectures and thereby reduce the role of supervision from a legal point of view in the development of such architectures.

Keywords: IoT · eHealth · GDPR · CSL · Requirements

1 Introduction

The widespread proliferation of Internet-of-Things (IoT) raises a number of non-trivial societal challenges. IoT devices are embedded in the physical surroundings

---

O. Tomashchuk and Y. Li—The authors contributed equally.

© Springer Nature Switzerland AG 2020
L. Antunes et al. (Eds.): APF 2020, LNCS 12121, pp. 143–160, 2020.
https://doi.org/10.1007/978-3-030-55196-4_9

of human beings, and IoT-based applications in many cases are used to manage systems that directly affect human actors, e.g. in a smart home, smart city or smart traffic context. The common characteristics of such systems is that they systematically gather personal data in a continuous and fine-grained fashion, and thus they impose non-trivial risks to the fundamental privacy rights of involved data subjects.

The latter is especially true in the case of IoT-based health applications, which deal with health indicators, information related to physical state, the whereabouts and activities of individual patients. In the HEART project [1], we focus on a number of specific application cases driven by IoT. Some examples involve (i) sleep description analysis, (ii) gestational weight gain prediction, (iii) recommender system for pregnancy application. Each eHealth application case involves its own intrinsic design challenges, and given the nature of the involved data, these systems impose even more substantial risks to fundamental privacy rights.

Modern data processing activities efficiently leverage the massive amounts of computational power available in today's systems, and activities involving the large-scale collection (such as IoT) and Big Data analytics by design involve large amounts of personal data. To deal with the challenges and risks raised by these evolutions in technology, several Legislative and Regulatory efforts have emerged. In the context of the European Union (EU), the well-known General Data Protection Regulation (GDPR) has come into force in 2018. Similarly, in the context of China, the Cybersecurity Law (CSL) has established a number of fundamental rights related to the processing of personal information.

In contemporary development practices, the development of software-intensive systems and service is seldom restricted to a single geographical location. Furthermore, if different regulatory constraints are not explicitly taken into account, there is a significant risk that the created services will only be applicable within a single geographical area of application. The initial investment costs of compliance analysis vis-a-vis different regulations thus will drastically pay off if the created products and services will be viable across different markets.

The existing state-of-the-art offers some research towards operationalization of the GDPR and other legislations. For example, Hintze and LaFever [18] tried to elaborate on GDPR requirements. However, they focused on the concept of Controlled Linkable Data, which does not fully cover the broad variety of technical requirements that arise from the GDPR. Also, Brodin [9] introduced a framework for GDPR compliance for SMEs, but the influence of GDPR requirements on solutions architecture is not adequately highlighted by this work. Ayala-Rivera and Pasquale [6] tried to operationalize the GDPR requirements by proposing a 6-step approach for elicitation of requirements, although they did not propose the requirements themselves. A similar situation can be observed in [13]. Some requirements were extracted from the recitals and articles of the GDPR in [5,19,26,31], but the authors did not study the influence of obtained requirements on architectures. Furthermore, there were some trials for investigation on geographical implications [5,11,15,17,29], however, the authors did not extract the requirements and did not demonstrate their implications on architectures.

Problem Statement. The regulations establish core principles, to which compliance must be attained and demonstrated. However, there is a large distance between these principles and requirements that are understandable and can be addressed by software engineers in the development life-cycle of these systems. Commercial cooperations in the eHealth sector between the European Union and China that are rooted in completely different legal, cultural, and academic backgrounds can create new challenges: (i) operationalization of the principles and thus requirements is non-trivial and demands extensive expertise, and (ii) when dealing with solutions that are to be rolled out across multiple geographical locations, specific expertise is required on each applicable legislations.

Approach. In this paper, we address the identified problem through an *exemplar* eHealth case study. This is an abstracted system architecture that exhibits the most prominent characteristics of the eHealth system described above. We first discuss and compare the main implications of both the GDPR and the CSL in this specific context, and then we translate the implications into technical Privacy and Security requirements. Application of the latter is firstly investigated on simplified architecture (entities are limited to a human user, a database, and a stakeholder), and then spread to an extracted from the state-of-the-art reference eHealth IoT architecture.

The remainder of the paper is structured as follows: Sect. 2 provides an overview of the GDPR and the CSL and discusses commonalities and differences between them. Section 3 demonstrates the influence of GDPR and CSL requirements on architectures, and Sect. 4 concludes the paper and highlights future work.

2   A Comparison of the GDPR and the CSL: Two Sides of the Coin?

One impression about China is that it is like a privacy-vacuum territory where no data protection rules have been implemented. It is not the case until China released its Cybersecurity Law in 2015, six months after the GDPR was well known globally. This legislation slipped away under the radar due to its competence being limited inside the territory of the People's Republic of China, but its importance should not be undermined. This section outlines the core requirements of the GDPR and the CSL on personal information protection. It aims at providing legal implications for further technical interpretations.

The CSL is the highest-level standard framework on personal information protection in China. It is broader than the GDPR. The objectives are to govern everything within the country's digital infrastructure, from cyberspace information regulation to the data export. This legislation is an evolving project that is still being worked on by competent authorities such as the Cyberspace Administration of China (CAC), the Ministry of Industry and Information Technology (MIIT), together with active interactions among industrial entities.

As its name suggests, the CSL is mainly devoted to provisions involving the security of cyberspace networks. A special category of security procedures and requirements is mandated for the "critical information infrastructure operators" i.e. energy, transportation or public services sectors.[1] Except where these topics touch on personal information protection, they are not the subject of this article.

Due to certain commonalities laying between the GDPR and the CSL, it is easy to classify the two as similar frameworks at first glance. Scholars considered the CSL having been modelled based on the GDPR, or even claimed it as the "Chinese version of the GDPR" [32]. However, the provisions of the two laws are inconsistent, thus leading to different requirements for legal compliance. We reasoned this as follows.

2.1   GDPR and CSL: An Overview

The GDPR highlights the principle of the supremacy of data privacy by (i) greatly expanding the scope and protection mechanisms of data subjects' rights; (ii) significantly regulating the processing of personal data by data controllers and processors and; (iii) increasing the controllers' legal responsibilities for personal data management. The GDPR also clarifies some exceptions based on highlighting the private protection of personal data. When private rights conflict with public rights, public rights take precedence. For example, when the rights and principles of personal data protection conflict with national security, government surveillance, public security, public interest or judicial procedures, the needs of the latter should be met first.

The CSL's provisions relating to data privacy formed what China's most comprehensive and broadly applicable set of data privacy rules to date are. These provisions implanted many of the basic principles and requirements that can be found in other laws and regulations. However, its set of data protection provisions is extensive, including numerous normative texts scattered across various industries (such as the Administrative Measures for e-commerce, the Administrative Provisions on protection of children's online personal information, and the Provisions on mobile Apps personal information collection). This particular

---

[1] Five systems constitute the Cybersecurity Law: (1) Cybersecurity Multi-Level Protection Scheme – specific security measures need to be met according to the level of the activities that would affect the public, scaled from 1 the least risky to 5 the most risky; (2) Critical Information Infrastructure Security Protection System (Chapter 3); (3) Personal Information and Important Data Protection System (Chapter 4), which focuses on the scope of personal information protection and the according protection standard; (4) Network Products and Services Management – network products that are used in critical information infrastructure (see number 3) are required to go through a cybersecurity assessment; and (5) Cybersecurity Incident Management System – guidelines and measures are provided to be activated in response to cybersecurity incidents.

formation hints to observers of a field of law that it is in continuous development, but this trend can be traced back to the 1990s.

The development of the basic principles of personal information protection has gone through two generations [15], and it is now likely to enter the third one:

- The first generation of personal information protection principles is the OECD Guidelines in 1980 [4] and the Convention 108 issued by the Council of Europe in 1981 [12]. These two documents defined the basic regime for a "personal information protection law" in a modern sense.
- The representative legislation of the second generation of personal information protection principles is the EU Data Protection Directive 1995 [24]. It is expanded based on the first-generation principle, adding elements such as "data minimisation", "deletion", "sensitive data", and "independent personal data protection authority" among others.
- The third generation of personal information protection principles is still dominated by the European Union - the GDPR. Compared with the second generation, the GDPR has expanded, including "establishing a data protection officer within the enterprise", "data protection impact assessment", "reporting to data protection authorities after data security incidents and notifying individuals", "collective litigation system" and so on.

In addition to the EU-led progressing, the OECD released a new version of the privacy framework in 2013 without significant changes, mainly introducing the concept of data security breach notice to authority as well as to an individual being affected [4].

Against this background, we switched focus to the nine principles contained in the Asia-Pacific Economic Cooperation Privacy Framework [2]. The principles embodied by APEC are still aligned with the standard of the first generation. While we appreciate the EU's efforts in promoting the protection of personal information by "willing to do it alone", other countries seem to be satisfied that the first generation is sufficient. But empirical research shows that countries and regions outside the EU have achieved the personal data protection standard of the second generation by rectifying new/updated personal information protection laws [14]. It is not surprising to see that China's CSL followed the principles of the APEC privacy framework (see Appendix 1)[2] while the supplementary norms and state standards[3] are following the GDPR (see Appendix 2).

---

[2] All the appendices can be found online: http://bit.ly/39bGd8I.

[3] Within China, national standards play an important role in implementing higher-level laws and legislations. They are better understood as a quasi-regulation rather than a technical specification or voluntary frameworks typically presented in Western context. Although they are not legally binding, the competent authorities often refer to them when conducting assessments and approvals. The bundle of standards under the umbrella of the CSL in practice will function as a form of regulation where auditing and certification of the entities will be conducted based on the criteria. Up to date, over 240 national standards related to the field have been issued since 2010.

In order to include a reasonable scope of a comprehensive comparison for meaningful and practical discussion, we refer to China's personal data protection rules as to the requirements addressed in the CSL and its supplementary norms and standards.

2.2 Commonalities Between the GDPR and the CSL

Even though the GDPR and the CSL are established based on different origins, the convergence between Europe and China's approaches in personal information protection regime is ever-growing. One of the most glaring similarities between GDPR and China's data protection laws is the fundamental principles for the processing of personal information (see Appendix 1).

The CSL has also established a bundle of new or more explicit "personal information rights", including "data correction right", "right of deletion", "re-use and breach notification obligation". However, these principles are drafted in such a high-level that in practice it is unlikely to be directly applied. Instead, the "Information Security Technology - Personal Information Security Specifications" (referred to as "the Specification"), which came into effect in May 2018, turned to be an essential supporting document for the interpretation of Chapter 4 of the CSL. In drafting the Specification, it referenced and benchmarked the current international rules and legislative standards, as well as foreign legislations in the protection of personal information, including the GDPR, OECD Guidelines, APEC Privacy Framework [2], EU-US Privacy Shield agreement, American Consumer Privacy Bill of Rights Act [3].

2.3 Differences Between the GDPR and the CSL

Firstly, the CSL provides only ONE legal basis for the processing of personal information – the consent (Art. 41 CSL). The GDPR provides five other legal basis, including the "joker card" – a legitimate interest (Art. 5 GDPR). The requirements for obtaining the consent in the CSL, therefore, is relatively looser than the ones in the GDPR, since it applies to broader scenarios. The GDPR is more indulgent about certain kinds of consent requirements for collecting personal information. Particularly, consent is not strictly required for data sharing under the GDPR [30], Art. 49.

Secondly, "sensitive personal information" under China's data protection rules is more far-reaching. It is defined as "any personal information that would cause harm to individuals' reputation, and mental and physical health if illegally disclosed or misused" [28], Art 3(2). Interestingly, ID number, bank account number, credit information and geo-location are included in the category of sensitive personal information, of which the GDPR does not [30], Art. 9.

Thirdly, China's data protection rules contain more descriptive requirements with regard to security assessment and audit. This is consistent with a broader difference: the objectives of China's data protection regime overall are to safeguard national cybersecurity. These give it a much broader applicable scope, while GDPR does not.

Last but not least, the major difference between China's data protection rules and the GDPR is that they have different levels of legal effects. The former is a general description of principles (CSL) with a bundle of recommended standards, while the latter is the EU's supranational Regulation. Each part of the GDPR is legally binding, and this legal binding is not only manifested in its specific goal, but also in various ways and measures required to achieve that specific goal.

Additionally, several common elements that exist in other jurisdictions' data protection laws, such as the right to access, right of accuracy and special requirements for sensitive personal data, are still missing in the CSL. The CSL also does not establish a data protection authority at the national level.

3   Operationalization of GDPR and CSL Requirements in eHealth IoT Scenario

The legal requirements imposed by both the GDPR and the CSL (Appendix 3 and 4) can be divided into two main types: those that influence the processes that stakeholder (healthcare or research institution, hospital, care organization, insurance company, etc.) should execute in the context of a technical solution, and those that influence the design of architectures of IoT applications. The first we call organizational requirements and the second we call technical requirements.

Organizational requirements are the requirements that do not influence the architecture of applications. They are adhered through guidelines, questionnaires, documentation regarding description of processing, justification of the purpose of processing, establishing periodic data audits, informing data subjects on relevant matter, etc. The implementation of organizational requirements can be specific for every use case. Since they are not within the main area of focus, the extended list of these requirements as well as some explanations can be found in Appendix A.

Technical requirements are the requirements that directly influence the architecture of an application. They include establishing data flows for informing the subject, mechanisms for obtaining consent, mechanisms for setting restrictions for processing, authorization, etc. Considering that in contrast to organizational requirements, complying with the technical ones is far from being trivial, in the following subsections we (i) establish a reference eHealth IoT architecture, and (ii) investigate the influence of technical requirements on simplified and reference architectures.

3.1   Reference eHealth IoT Architecture

Practical adoption of IoT in the healthcare domain has started several years ago and draw reasonable attention. There were multiple trials for development of eHealth IoT solutions that obtained various levels of success and acceptance. Below we outline a number of related efforts. Habib and Leister [16] proposed an architecture for an eHealth patient monitoring scenario that is based on IoT. It includes the following key elements:

- Sensors (e.g. glucose, body temperature, blood pressure, ECG);
- Smartphone as a hub for sensors;
- Gateway (Wi-Fi or 3G/4G connectivity);
- Stakeholders (e.g. hospital, nursing home, transport, public venues);
- Backend EHR system;
- Health services;
- Corresponding data flows.

Another architecture was presented by Farahani et al. [7]. In that work, the authors introduced a holistic multi-layer IoT eHealth architecture with bidirectional data flows and offered a protocol stack. They split the architecture into three layers: device, fog, and cloud, which reasonably aligns with the ideas in [16].

eHealth IoT solutions rely a lot on wearable devices. This is also supported by Perez and Zeadally in [33]. In their paper that mainly focuses on privacy issues of consumer wearables, the system consists of a personal area network, wearable sensors, smartphones, base stations, cloud storage and analytics. Also, their system highlights a direct communication link between the wearable device and the base station, which is not observed in other publications. The data flows in their work are of both bidirectional and unidirectional types, while the latter observed only between the smartphone and wearables.

In [27], El-Sappagh et al. propose a comprehensive mobile health framework with an integrated clinical decision support system (CDSS) capability. They propose an ontology that is able to collect, formalize, integrate, analyse, and manipulate all types of patient data which provides patients with care plans. Also, the proposed CDSS provides real-time patient monitoring based on vital signs collected from patients' wireless body area networks. The architecture of the proposed framework includes the following elements:

- Wireless body area network (e.g. Bluetooth, Wi-Fi);
- Wireless base unit (e.g. smartphone);
- Wireless router (e.g. Wi-Fi access point);
- Cloud-based environment;
- Backend EHR system;
- Health services;
- Corresponding data flows.

In [22] Fernandez et al. propose a cloud-IoT architecture aiming at protecting the sensitive data of the user by allowing them to control which kind of data is transmitted by their devices and providing supportive tools for agreement visualisation and privacy-utility trade-off. The architecture consists of several layers, from IoT objects in the lower layer to web and mobile applications in the top layer, with regulated communication mechanisms to transfer data from the lower level to data processing services in the top level. The proposed architecture includes user, platform that manages data emanating from IoT devices, cloud repository, service provider, and corresponding data flows. Additionally, the proposed example considers multiple potential stakeholders.

Considering the state-of-the-art discussed above, we establish a reference eHealth IoT architecture (depicted on Fig. 1) that consists of:

- Human user - a person which operates the architecture and is a data subject in the solution's context;
- Firmware-driven device - a mobile or embedded device with limited functionality, connectivity scope, and computational resources which operates under commands of a firmware (smart watch/mattress/necklace/plate/glasses/scales/toothbrush/headband/scale, etc.)
- OS-driven device - a mobile device with broad functionality and connectivity scopes that offers advanced memory management (smartphone, smart hub, etc.);
- Gateway - a device or devices that are used for connection with the server's network;
- Controller's server - a device on which data controller stores or processes the data obtained from the user;
- Stakeholder's server - a device on which a stakeholder (governmental healthcare institutions, research institutions, hospitals, care organizations, insurance companies, etc.) user data obtained from the data controller.

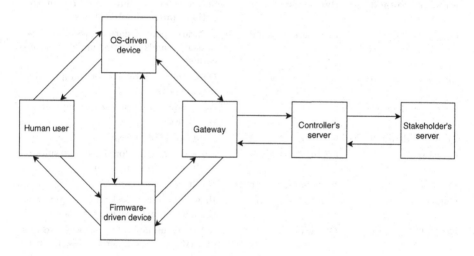

Fig. 1. Reference eHealth IoT architecture

In this architecture, both the firmware-driven and OS-driven devices are responsible for data collection and represent sensors that can be responsible for providing electroencephalogram (EEG), electrocardiogram (ECG), galvanic skin response (GSR), polysomnogram (PSG), temperature, pressure, humidity, and others.

In its turn, the controller's server, as well as OS-driven device, are expected to perform data-driven services like activity monitoring, sleep monitoring, medication intake monitoring, nutrition analysis, cough detection, fall detection, emotion monitoring, monitoring of physical parameters (heart rate, blood pressure, weight, etc.), monitoring of environment (air pressure/quality, water quality, humidity, CO_2 level, amount of light, noise level, etc.), and other potentially relevant services. In cases like fog computing, gateway may also be involved in performing some computations for the services. However, in this paper we consider it as a purely communicational element which puts the gateway out of the scope of elements that can be manipulated for satisfying the requirements.

The data flows that are also depicted on Fig. 1 also influence the architecture and may consist of various data types. To provide a better understanding of relations between the elements of the proposed reference eHealth IoT architecture, we introduce an overview of the data flows in Table 1.

Table 1. Overview of data flows

Origin	Destination	Type of information in the data flow
Human user	OS-driven device	User and sensor input
Human user	Firmware-driven device	User and sensor input
OS-driven device	Human user	Progress notifications, recommendations
Firmware-driven device	Human user	Short version or summary of recommendations, progress notifications
OS-driven device	Firmware-driven device	Software updates, data requests, application commands, progress updates, notifications
Firmware-driven device	OS-driven device	Data collected by sensors, application status updates
OS-driven device	Gateway	Raw or pre-processed sensor input from the devices
Firmware-driven device	Gateway	Data collected by sensors
Gateway	OS-driven device	Software updates for devices, results of analytics, recommendations
Gateway	Firmware-driven device	Notifications
Gateway	Controller's server	Raw or pre-processed sensor input from the devices, data collected by sensors
Controller's server	Gateway	Software updates for devices, results of analytics, recommendations, notifications
Controller's server	Stakeholder's server	Anonymized or pseudonymized data, raw or processed data that are sharable accordingly to the consent
Stakeholder's server	Controller's server	Data that are useful for improving quality of analytics

3.2 Influence of Technical Requirements on the Reference Architecture

The main principles behind privacy and data protection by design imply that the technical requirements extracted from the GDPR and the CSL should be taken into consideration from the initial stages of the development of eHealth IoT applications. Therefore, in this subsection we provide (i) an overview of the influence of the GDPR and the CSL requirements on data flows in a simplified architecture, and (ii) an extension of the reference eHealth IoT architecture with identified requirements-driven elements for simultaneous compliance.

Highlighting the influence of technical requirements on architectures is not a trivial task. Therefore, we focus our investigation on analysis of corresponding data flow diagrams (DFDs) that in its turn enable understanding of influence and consequences. This decision is driven by the fact that DFDs are the core elements of STRIDE [21] and LINDDUN [23] methodologies, which are also seen by us as potential drivers of continuous compliance. Additionally, LINDDUN is also used by Ekdahl and Nyman in [10] for an investigation on GDPR compliance, and by Bisztray and Gruschka in [8] for investigation related to Privacy Impact Assessment. Furthermore, Sion et al. in [20], as well as Dewitte et al. in [25], use this methodology for investigations related to Data Protection by Design.

In order to satisfy the technical requirements, we came up with the concepts of services and centres for data flow diagrams. We do not position them as an extension of existing DFD elements (entity, process, data store, data flow, trust boundary), but as aggregators of processes. Subsequently, the services are combinations of several processes that perform certain manipulations on data. In their turn, the centres are combinations of services that need to take place for performing necessary data manipulations.

Based on our findings, we introduce the following additional elements on the DFDs in this section:

- Consent centre – a collection of services responsible for obtaining consent from the user and interpreting it into suitable input for the processing;
- Access/disclosure centre – a collection of services responsible for logging and managing the access to the collected data for given entities under certain conditions (who can get the data);
- Centre of processing permissions/restrictions – a collection of services responsible for establishing lawful processing for involved entities in the context of a given solution (what can be done with the data);
- Data export centre – a collection of services responsible for providing disclosable data in a readable format to a 3rd party or the human user;
- Read/write service – a collection of processes responsible for inserting new data into the database and providing stored data to relevant entities;
- Data correction service – a collection of processes responsible for finding data that needs to be corrected in the database and sending corresponding requests to appropriate services;
- Data deletion service – a collection of processes responsible for finding and deleting certain data in the database;
- Keep data alive service – a collection of processes responsible for timely deletion of irrelevant data from the database;
- Database – an organized collection of data obtained from the data subject;

– Backup – a copy of database taken and stored elsewhere for restoring the
original data in case of a data loss event.

Influence of the Technical Requirements of GDPR. As discussed above,
the data flow diagrams are a suitable means for architecture analysis. Therefore,
in order to understand the implications of the technical requirements from the
GDPR, we extended a simplified reference architecture with relevant centres, services and related data flows (see Fig. 2). Furthermore, the usage of DFDs is even
strongly justified by the GDPR requirements on accountability documentation.

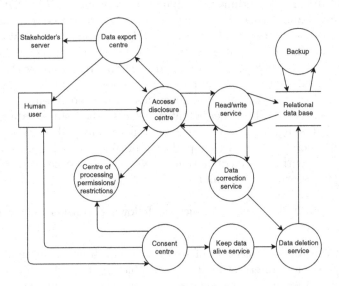

Fig. 2. Influence of technical requirements from the GDPR on DFDs

As mentioned above, Fig. 2 contains a simplified version of the reference
eHealth IoT architecture modified accordingly to the technical requirements. In
their turn, the relevant requirements can be grouped in the following categories:

1. Initialization (requirements 3, 11);
2. Data management (requirements 7, 8, 9, 13, 15, 16, 17);
3. Security (requirements 7, 9, 18, 19, 22).

The initialization category provides means for informing the user about what
data the application will collect, how the application will process the data, and
why such processing is required. Also, it provides information regarding the
data controller and data processors, as well as the legal basis and the purpose
of processing. The initialization, along with the consent collection, is covered by
the consent centre.

The data management category provides support for data storage, data correction and deletion, restriction of processing, logging, data export, and consent withdrawal. Additionally, due to the requirements 8 and 17 that demand logical separation of data entries that enables targeted deletion and usage of structured machine-readable formats, the database is expected to be relational. We recognize that this can be a strong technical constraint, but we leave further investigations on this issue for future work. All the additional elements on Fig. 2, except backup and data flows, are responsible for covering this category.

The security category provides support for authorization, data integrity, encryption, data loss prevention, and logging. This category is covered by access/disclosure centre, backup, and the data flows. The latter are expected to run on the protocols that provide data integrity and encrypted communication. Nevertheless, some of the GDPR requirements on security are formulated rather vaguely. For example, requirement 9 and 19 demands applying security best practices and state-of-the-art security measures considering risks and costs. We acknowledge that this was done to accommodate for the reality that best practices, as well as state-of-the-art, changes rapidly with the course of time, and regulations cannot adapt that fast, but this leads to additional efforts for finding reasonable security measures for every particular case and cannot be reflected on the given DFD.

Completeness of the proposed approach can be proven by the fact that the data subjects rights highlighted in the GDPR (the right to information access/accuracy/erasure, right to restrict processing, portability, and right to reject) can be provided by the introduced elements.

Influence of the Technical Requirements of CSL. In order to understand the implications of the technical requirements imposed by the CSL, we extended a simplified reference architecture with relevant centres, services and related data flows. Considering the smaller amount of requirements that arise from this law than from the GDPR, the influence of the CSL is smaller too, which is depicted on Fig. 3. Therefore, some of the elements that can be found on Fig. 2 can not be found on Fig. 3.

The technical requirements that arise from the Cybersecurity law include:

- Obtaining consent from the subject and informing him/her regarding the purpose, means, and scope of data collection (requirement 1) - covered by consent centre;
- Disclosing collected data only to authorized entities (requirement 2) - covered by access/disclosure centre;
- Preventing data leakages, and data losses (requirement 4) - covered by access/disclosure centre and backup;
- Deleting data in case of misuse (requirement 5) - covered by read/write service, data correction service, data deletion service;
- Correcting data in case of necessity (requirement 5) - covered by read/write service, data correction service, data deletion service.

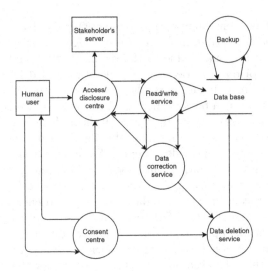

Fig. 3. Influence of technical requirements from CSL on DFDs

Completeness of the proposed approach can be proven by the fact that the data subjects rights highlighted in the CSL (the right to delete, and the right to rectification) can be provided by the introduced elements.

Simultaneous Compliance with the Technical Requirements of GDPR and CSL. Being compliant with both the GDPR and the CSL is of great interest for eHealth IoT solution providers that operate on European and Chinese markets. We investigated how the architecture of a solution should be adapted to be in line with both legislations. Such adaptation can be reached via extending the reference architecture depicted on Fig. 1 with our findings introduced on Figs. 2 and 3.

Extending the reference eHealth IoT architecture with the proposed centres and services requires positioning them under the boundaries of devices. Considering that the centres consist of complex processes, they may require partial execution on multiple devices. For example, the formulation of the consent shall take place on the controller's side, while obtaining the actual consent is expected to take place on the OS-driven device's side. Similar issues arise for other centres too. Therefore, access/disclosure, consent, and processing permissions/restrictions centres had to be represented in several instances across the devices that are involved in storing or processing of undisclosable data. Despite being very similar, their functionality may not be identical and is foreseen to be device- and solution-tailored.

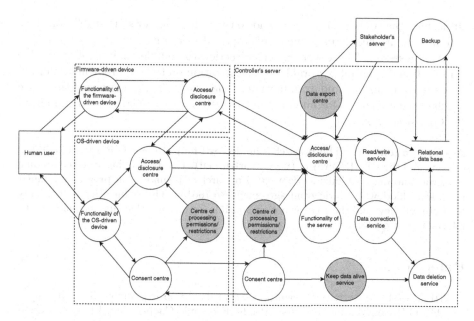

Fig. 4. DFD of a reference eHealth IoT architecture extended with the requirements-driven elements. Grey elements are optional for CSL-only compliance.

Furthermore, Fig. 4, on which the extended DFD of the reference architecture is depicted, contains an additional element - functionality of devices. This element represents processes, services, and software that eHealth IoT devices may normally have. They may include heart rate measurements, sleep analytics, notifications, progress reporting, etc.

Additionally, some of the elements on the diagram in question are toned in grey. Inclusion of those elements is obligatory for satisfying GDPR requirements but remain optional for satisfying the CSL.

4   Conclusion and Future Work

This paper presents a comparison of the GDPR and the CSL, and discusses requirements that can be obtained from them on the basis of a case study. Our findings show that simultaneous compliance with both legislations for the eHealth IoT solutions can be reached through (i) obtaining legal requirements from the regulations and laws, (ii) interpreting the legal requirements into technical and organizational ones, (iii) integrating the corresponding services and centres that satisfy technical requirements into solutions architecture.

Considering that our work contributes to the operationalization of the GDPR and the CSL, one of the key findings is that despite some clear differences between these legislations, simultaneous compliance with both of them can be reached in an effective manner. Furthermore, the integration of the proposed elements commits to reducing risks to the fundamental privacy rights of the data subjects in the context of eHealth, and to the reduction of risk that IoT solutions will only be applicable in a single geographical location.

We foresee our future work in this direction to include analysis of applicable standards and relevant sectoral laws, investigation on the requirements for cross-border data transfers, and examination of the practical implications of the usage of relational databases for human input as well as other unstructured content in the GDPR context.

Acknowledgements. This research is funded by Philips Research, Research Fund KU Leuven, and the HEART project (www.heart-itn.eu). This project has received funding from the European Union's Horizon 2020 research and innovation programme under the Marie Skłodowska-Curie grant agreement No 766139. This publication reflects only the authors' view and the REA is not responsible for any use that may be made of the information it contains.

References

1. HEalth related Activity Recognition system based on IoT. http://heart-itn.eu/
2. APEC Privacy Framework, Asia-Pacific Economic Cooperation, Electronic Commerce Steering Group (ECSG) (2005)
3. Consumer data privacy in a networked world: a framework for protecting privacy and promoting innovation in the global digital economy (2012)
4. OECD Guidelines on the Protection of Privacy and Transborder Flows of Personal Data (2013)
5. Handbook on European data protection law, European Union Agency for Fundamental Rights and Council of Europe (2018)
6. Ayala-Rivera, V., Pasquale, L.: The grace period has ended: An approach to operationalize GDPR requirements. In: Proceedings of 26th International Requirements Engineering Conference (RE). IEEE, Banff, August 2018
7. Farahani, B., Firouzi, F., Chang, V., Badaroglu, M., Constant, N., Mankodiya, K.: Towards fog-driven IoT eHealth: promises and challenges of IoT in medicine and healthcare. Future Gener. Comput. Syst. **78**, 659–676 (2018)
8. Bisztray, T., Gruschka, N.: Privacy impact assessment: comparing methodologies with a focus on practicality. In: Askarov, A., Hansen, R.R., Rafnsson, W. (eds.) NordSec 2019. LNCS, vol. 11875, pp. 3–19. Springer, Cham (2019). https://doi.org/10.1007/978-3-030-35055-0_1
9. Brodin, M.: A framework for GDPR compliance for small and medium-sized enterprises. Eur. J. Secur. Res. **4**(2), 243–264 (2019)
10. Ekdahl, A., Nyman, L.: A methodology to validate compliance to the GDPR. Master's thesis, Department of Computer Science and Engineering, Chalmer University of Technology, University of Gothenburg, Gothenburg, Sweden (2018)
11. Erickson, A.: Comparative analysis of the EU's GDPR and Brazil's LGPD: enforcement challenges with the LGPD. Brooklyn J. Int. Law **44**, 859–888 (2019)
12. Secretary General of the Council of Europe: Convention for the protection of individuals with regard to automatic processing of personal data (1981)
13. Fernandes, M., da Silva, A.R., Gonçalves, A.: Specification of personal data protection requirements: analysis of legal requirements based on the GDPR regulation (2018)

14. Graham Greenleaf, S.L.: China's New Cybersecurity Law - Also a Data Privacy Law? (2016)
15. Greenleaf, G.: Asian Data Privacy Laws. Oxford University Press, United Kingdom (2014)
16. Habib, K., Leister, W.: Threats identification for the smart internet of things in ehealth and adaptive security countermeasures. In: Proceedings of the 7th International Conference on New Technologies, Mobility and Security (NTMS), vol. 555. IEEE, Nashville, Tennessee (2015)
17. Han, S.W., Munir, A.B.: Information security technology - personal information security specification: China's version of the GDPR. Eur. Data Protect. Law Rev. (EDPL) **4**, 535–541 (2018)
18. Hintze, M., LaFever, G.: Meeting upcoming GDPR requirements while maximizing the full value of data analytics (2017)
19. Huth, D., Matthes, F.: Appropriate technical and organizational measures: identifying privacy engineering approaches to meet GDPR requirements. In: Proceedings of 25th Americas Conference on Information Systems (2019)
20. Sion, L., Dewitte, P., Van Landuyt D., Wuyts, K., Emanuilov, I., Valcke, P., Joosen, W.: An architectural view for data protection by design. In: Proceedings of the 2019 IEEE International Conference on Software Architecture (ICSA). IEEE, Hamburg, Germany (2019)
21. Loren Kohnfelder, P.G.: The threats to our products. Microsoft Interface, April 1999
22. Maribel Fernandez, J.J., Thuraisingham, B.: Privacy-preserving architecture for Cloud-IoT platforms. In: Proceedings of the International Conference on Web Services (ICWS), vol. 555. IEEE (2019)
23. Deng, M., Wuyts, K., Scandariato, R., Preneel, B., Joosen, W.: A privacy threat analysis framework: supporting the elicitation and fulfillment of privacy requirements. Requirements Eng. J. **16**, 3–32 (2011)
24. European Parliament Council: Directive 95/46/EC of the European Parliament and of the Council of 24 October 1995 on the protection of individuals with regard to the processing of personal data and on the free movement of such data (1995)
25. Dewitte, P., Wuyts, K., Sion, L., Van Landuyt, D., Emanuilov, I., Valcke, P., Joosen, W.: A comparison of system description models for data protection by design. In: SAC 2019: Proceedings of the 34th ACM/SIGAPP Symposium on Applied Computing, pp. 1512–1515 (2019)
26. Ringmann, S.D., Langweg, H., Waldvogel, M.: Requirements for legally compliant software based on the GDPR. In: Panetto, H., Debruyne, C., Proper, H.A., Ardagna, C.A., Roman, D., Meersman, R. (eds.) OTM 2018. LNCS, vol. 11230, pp. 258–276. Springer, Cham (2018). https://doi.org/10.1007/978-3-030-02671-4_15
27. El-Sappagh, S., Ali, F., Hendawi, A., Jang, J.-H., Kwak, K.S.: A mobile health monitoring-and-treatment system based on integration of the SSN sensor ontology and the HL7 FHIR standard. BMC Med. Inform. Decis. Mak. **19**, 97 (2019)
28. Standing Committee of the People's Congress: Cybersecurity Law (2016)
29. Tovino, S.A.: The HIPAA privacy rule and the EU GDPR: illustrative comparisons. Seton Hall Law Rev. **47**(4), 973–993 (2017)
30. European Union: Regulation 2016/679 of the European Parliament and of the Council of 27 April 2016 on the protection of natural persons with regard to the processing of personal data and on the free movement of such data, and repealing Directive 95/46/EC (General Data Protection Regulation). Official Journal of the EU (L 119), 1–88, May 2016

31. Voigt, P., von dem Bussche, A.: The EU General Data Protection Regulation (GDPR). Springer, Cham (2017). https://doi.org/10.1007/978-3-319-57959-7
32. Wang Han, S., Munir, A.: Practitioner's corner information security technology - personal information security specification: China's version of the GDPR? Eur. Data Protect. Law Re. **4**, 535–541 (2018)
33. Zeadally, S., Perez, A.J.: Privacy issues and solutions for consumer wearables. IT Prof. **20**, 46–56 (2018)

Transparency

Purposes in IAB Europe's TCF: Which Legal Basis and How Are They Used by Advertisers?

Célestin Matte[1]([✉]), Cristiana Santos[1,2], and Nataliia Bielova[1]

[1] Inria, Paris, France
{celestin.matte,nataliia.bielova}@inria.fr
[2] Université Côte d'Azur, Nice, France
cristianasantos@protonmail.com

Abstract. The General Data Protection Regulation (GDPR), Data Protection Authorities (DPAs) and the European Data Protection Board (EDPB) discuss purposes for data processing and the legal bases upon which data controllers can rely on: either "consent" or "legitimate interests". We study the purposes defined in IAB Europe's Transparency and Consent Framework (TCF) and their usage by advertisers. We analyze the purposes with regard to the legal requirements for defining them lawfully, and suggest that several of them might not be specific or explicit enough to be compliant. Arguably, a large portion thereof requires consent, even though the TCF allows advertisers to declare them under the legitimate interests basis. Finally, we measure the declaration of purposes by all advertisers registered in the TCF versions 1.1. and 2.0 and show that hundreds of them do not operate under a legal basis that could be considered compliant under the GDPR .

1 Introduction

As a response to the General Data Protection Regulation (GDPR) [25] that came into force in May 2018, the *Internet Advertisement Bureau* (IAB) Europe introduced an open-source framework called the *Transparency and Consent Framework* (TCF) in April 2018 [28]. This framework introduces *Consent Management Providers* (CMPs), new actors collecting consent through the use of so-called "cookie banners", and transmitting this consent to advertisers by implementing an API defined in the framework. The TCF became popular and is actively used on 1,426 out of top 22,000 EU websites [38], and in 680 UK websites [39].

Any advertiser willing to be involved in the TCF and wishing to appear in CMP-based cookie banners must register therein. Thereupon, an advertiser must select one or more of the predefined purposes for data processing. These purposes are presented to website users in cookie banners when collecting their consent. For each purpose, advertisers must choose a legal basis for processing:

C. Matte and C. Santos—Co-first authors listed in alphabetical order.

© Springer Nature Switzerland AG 2020
L. Antunes et al. (Eds.): APF 2020, LNCS 12121, pp. 163–185, 2020.
https://doi.org/10.1007/978-3-030-55196-4_10

consent or legitimate interest. The choice of the purposes and their legal basis hold strong legal compliance implications – both on the advertisers, but also on the publishers side, as the latter include third-party resources in their websites.

According to Article 8 of the Charter of Fundamental Rights of the European Union [23], personal data must be processed fairly for *specified purposes* and on the basis of a *lawful ground*. Article 5(1)(b) of the GDPR predicates the *"Purpose Limitation"* principle which mandates personal data to be collected for specified, explicit and legitimate purposes. Identifying the appropriate legal basis that corresponds to the purpose of the processing is of essential importance. Thereby, in this work, we make the following contributions:

- We identify the legal requirements for defining purposes based on the GDPR, the 29 Working Party (now EDPB endorsed) and Data Protection Authorities guidance that help us to answer the following questions: *"Does a purpose satisfy the requirements of the purpose specification principle?"* and *"Which is the legal basis for a specific purpose?"* (Sect. 2);
- We analyse the purposes defined in IAB Europe's TCF versions 1.1 and 2.0, discuss whether such purposes comply with the legal requirements and which purposes should rely on consent (Sect. 3);
- We collect data about all advertisers registered in both versions of the TCF in order to measure which purposes are selected by advertisers and which legal bases are declared. We show that hundreds of advertisers rely on legitimate interest for purposes that instead should rely on consent (Sect. 4).

Our work demonstrates the persistence of the advertising industry in non-compliant (with GDPR and ePrivacy Directive) methods for tracking and profiling, bundled in often complex and vague presentation of purposes. The importance of this is further underlined by the extended prior work, guidance, as well as enforcement actions and court decisions in the field.

2   Legal Requirements for Defining Purposes

In this section, we discuss the legal requirements to describe purposes lawfully. Article 5 (1)(b) of GDPR and the 29WP [4] elaborate on the *"Purpose Limitation"* principle. This principle mandates personal data to be collected (1) for specified, explicit and legitimate purposes only and (2) not further processed in a way incompatible with those purposes. In this work, we focus on the first component of this principle named *purpose specification*. This principle focuses on the initial purpose of collection [45] and mandates that eachpurpose needs to comply with the three criteria of explicitness, specificity, and legitimacy [4]. We analyze each requirement and corresponding violations to better discern its application in the TCF.

Explicitness. The following conditions must be met for a purpose to be explicit:

- Unambiguous. A purpose must be sufficiently unambiguous as to their meaning or intent;

- Exposed. Purposes need to be clearly expressed, revealed or explained, (e.g. not hidden from the data subjects).
- Shared common understanding. The definition of the purposes must be understood in the same way by everybody involved. This ensures that everyone has the same unambiguous understanding of the purposes.

Violation: Hidden or defined with confusion, ambiguity as to their meaning or intent (i.e. purposes that leave doubt, difficulty in understanding).

Specificity. To fulfill the specificity requirement, purposes should be identified precisely, i.e. clearly defined. Their formulation must be detailed enough to determine what kind of processing is and is not included within them [4].

Violation: Vague, too general or overly legalistic purposes. The 29WP [4,10] give examples: "improving users' experience"; "marketing purposes", "IT-security purposes"; "we may use your personal data for research purposes"; etc.

Legitimacy. The purposes defined by the controller should conform to a legal basis for processing. Regarding the use of cookies and similar technologies, the eligible legal basis is informed consent (Article 5(3) of the ePD [19]).

Articles 4(11) and 7 of the GDPR establish the requirements for a valid consent: freely given, specific, informed, unambiguous, readable, accessible and revocable [44]. Whenever consent is exempted for concrete purposes, another legal basis might be applicable. Pursuant to the legitimate interest basis, the 29WP [6] recognizes the *usefulness* as a ground for lawful processing which in the right circumstances and subject to adequate safeguards, may help to prevent misuse of, and over-reliance on other legal grounds. The 29WP postulates this basis should not be used sparingly as a "catch-all" provision to fill in gaps for rare and unexpected situations as "a last resort" where other grounds for legitimate processing are not applicable. Nor should it be seen as a preferred option, or its use unduly extended on the basis of a perception that it is less constraining than the other grounds to legitimize all data processing activities.

In effect, it requires a three-tiered test [35] that allows a processing operation consisting of:

1. Legitimate interest test. Interests must be "lawful", "sufficiently clearly articulated" (transparent) and "represent a real and present interest" [6, p. 25,52];
2. Necessity test. Any data not directly linked to accomplishing the specific purpose are therefore considered "unlawful"; and
3. Balancing test of these interests and the interests of the data subject [20].

The general provision on legitimate interest is open-ended (with a broad and unspecific scope), meaning that it can be relied upon a wide range of purposes – as long as its requirements are satisfied. In this paper, we focus on point (1), since (2) and (3) require a casuistic analysis under a concrete context.

Violation: Purpose(s) without (or incorrect) legal basis for processing.

Discussion. In line with the above clarifications, the purpose specification principle does not allow for open or vaguely defined purposes to govern data-processing practices. These requirements contribute to transparency, legal certainty and foreseeability and aims to protect data subjects by setting limits on how controllers are able to use collected data. This functional delimitation should prevent the use of personal data in a way (or for further purposes) that they might find unexpected, inappropriate or otherwise objectionable, assuring this way the data minimisation principle (Article 5, (1)(c)). However, the purpose specification principle only provides for abstract procedural norms for purposes definition. Since purpose specification is a *procedural* and not a substantive norm, it allows website owners considerable freedom to define their purposes in flexibly interpretable terms [37]. In this paper, we complement this prescriptive framework by analyzing the purposes deployed in the concrete context of the TCF.

3   IAB Europe's Transparency and Consent Framework

IAB Europe introduced two versions of the TCF: version 1.1 in April 2018, and version 2.0 in August 2019 [29]. Although version 1.1 is actively used by website publishers [38], IAB Europe announced version 1.1 will no longer be supported starting from June 30, 2020 [30]. Version 2.0 will plausibly become even more popular because Google will integrate it as well[1]. In this paper, we consider both versions 1.1 and 2.0.

Upon registration, advertisers must select one or more purposes for data processing from the TCF's pre-defined list of purposes. These purposes are presented to website users in cookie banners when collecting their consent. The list of purposes differ in each version and we will discuss them in detail in Sects. 3.1 and 3.2. For each purpose, an advertiser must choose a legal basis for processing: consent or legitimate interest. Advertisers can also declare "features", which correspond to supplementary types of user's data – this usage relies on different purposes of the framework. We discuss potential risks of such features in Sect. 3.3.

Legal Analysis and its Limitations. Even though we ground our legal analysis in both authoritative and also expert generated legal sources (GDPR, ePD, 29WP and DPAs guidelines) to discern whether the declared IAB purposes are compliant with the purpose specification principle, as mentioned in Sect. 2, this analysis is yet limited if not sustained judicially, where a more specific fact finding of each practice could render a final appraisal. We therefore deliberately leave space to legal uncertainty on the assessment made on each purpose and its legal basis. Finally, there are some purposes analysed in v1.1 that are reused in a more granular way in v2.0 and therefore the reasoning given to some of the purposes is still applicable where appropriate, as identified in the text.

---

[1] https://support.google.com/admob/answer/9461778, accessed on 2020.02.05.

3.1   Analysis of Purposes of the IAB Europe's TCF v1.1

In this section, we analyze the purposes dened in v1.1 that we show in Table 1.

Table 1. Purposes defined in IAB Europe's Transparency and Consent Framework, TCF v1.1 [26, p. 13].

Purpose number	Purpose name	Purpose description
1	Information storage and access	The storage of information, or access to information that is already stored, on your device such as advertising identifiers, device identifiers, cookies, and similar technologies
2	Personali-sation	The collection and processing of information about your use of this service to subsequently personalise advertising and/or content for you in other contexts, such as on other websites or apps, over time. Typically, the content of the site or app is used to make inferences about your interests, which inform future selection of advertising and/or content
3	Ad selection, delivery, reporting	The collection of information, and combination with previously collected information, to select and deliver advertisements for you, and to measure the delivery and effectiveness of such advertisements. This includes using previously collected information about your interests to select ads, processing data about what advertisements were shown, how often they were shown, when and where they were shown, and whether you took any action related to the advertisement, including for example clicking an ad or making a purchase. This does not include personalisation, which is the collection and processing of information about your use of this service to subsequently personalise advertising and/or content for you in other contexts, such as websites or apps, over time
4	Content selection, delivery, reporting	The collection of information, and combination with previously collected information, to select and deliver content for you, and to measure the delivery and effectiveness of such content. This includes using previously collected information about your interests to select content, processing data about what content was shown, how often or how long it was shown, when and where it was shown, and whether the (sic) you took any action related to the content, including for example clicking on content. This does not include personalisation, which is the collection and processing of information about your use of this service to subsequently personalise content and/or advertising for you in other contexts, such as websites or apps, over time
5	Measurement	The collection of information about your use of the content, and combination with previously collected information, used to measure, understand, and report on your usage of the service. This does not include personalisation, the collection of information about your use of this service to subsequently personalise content and/or advertising for you in other contexts, i.e. on other service, such as websites or apps, over time

Purpose 1 *"Information storage and access"* is not specific, but could require consent. This purpose does not provide enough information. In fact, it only mentions the technical tools that collect data (such as advertising identifiers or cookies) without explaining at all for which purpose the data will be used. According to the *"specificity"* requirement denoted in Sect. 2, the GDPR requires a purpose to be sufficiently and clearly defined, i.e. it must be detailed enough to determine what kind of processing is and is not included. In effect, this purpose conveys the impression to be unspecified: it is too general and possibly violates the specificity requirement.

Nevertheless, we can argue that this purpose requires consent as a legal basis due to Article 5(3) of the ePD. However, due to its lack of specificity, it's still unclear whether the final usage of the stored or accessed data falls under any of the exceptions of the ePD. Moreover, this reasoning may differ within EU member States due to the implementation of this ePD in national law.

Purpose 2 *"Personalisation"* is not explicit, nor specific, and so we cannot derive its legal basis. Although its name is clear, its description is ambiguous and vaguely-worded: this purpose bundles a host of separate processing purposes under a single name – it implies both advertising *and/or* content personalization. We hereby decompose such purpose. Regarding personalization (also called customization or preferences), the 29WP [5] cautioned that cookies storing user's preferences of a service are explicitly enabled by the user (e.g. clicking a button or ticking a box to keep a language, display format, fonts, etc.). Only session (or short-term) cookies storing such information can be exempted. Regarding advertising, we cautiously conjecture that *"personalization for advertising"* conflates two different purposes. Taking the positioning (advocated by both 29WP and DPAs) that advertising requires consent, we further account the requirement for consent to be *specific* (Article 4(11) of the GDPR). It mandates granularity of the consent request in order to avoid a catch-all purpose acceptance, so that the user is able to give consent for an independent and specific purpose [7]. Moreover, Recital 43 clarifies the need for a separate consent for different processing operations. Recital 32 states consent should be given per purpose (or set of purposes). The 29WP [22] instructs further that *"a controller that seeks consent for various different purposes should provide a separate opt-in for each purpose, to allow users to give specific consent for specific purposes"*. Finally, Planet49 Judgment of the Court of Justice of the EU [18] determined that consent should be granular for each purpose. In the light of the above, we argue that this multi-purpose might be non-specific.

This multipurpose seems ambiguous, leaving room for doubt and confusion as to its meaning and intent and may possibly violate the *explicitness* requirement. As such, it is complex to determine which is the applicable legal basis.

Purpose 3 *"Ad selection, delivery, reporting"* is not explicit, not specific, but should require consent. We argue that this purpose requires consent because it describes collection of data with the purpose of selection and delivery of advertisement. Pursuant to this purpose, the 29WP stated that third-party advertising cookies are not exempted from consent [5][2]. The ICO (UK DPA) also contended that data collection for advertising is not "strictly necessary" from the point of view of a website user, and hence this purpose cannot rely on legitimate interest, requiring consent [36]. The same reasoning holds for the German [12] and Dutch DPAs [1].

Furthermore, the description afforded in this purpose induces to consider that we might be across multipurpose advertising with adjacent profiling that is not disclosed explicitly. While the documentation excludes "personalization", its description seems instead to accommodate profiling. It is perceivable that considering the user's interests and his reactions towards ads and the combination of the user's includes profiling. To ascertain this argument, we call forth the definition of profiling in Article 4 (4) (and Recital 30 of the GDPR): *"any form of automated processing of personal data consisting of using those data to evaluate certain personal aspects (...), in particular to analyse or predict aspects concerning that natural person's (...) personal preferences, interests, reliability, behaviour, location or movement."* We deduct the personal data to be collected and combined with a previous user profile is meant to analyze or predict (i.e. some form of assessment) aspects concerning the user's interests and likely behavior towards ads. In the light of the above, this purpose seems not explicit and non-specific. Morevoer, users would need to be informed of the purpose of profiling (and the legal basis of consent), pursuant to Article 13 (1)(c), and (2)(f).

Purpose 4 *"Content selection, delivery, reporting"* might be exempted from consent (if session-only). This purpose's name suggests it might be exempted of consent because it only mentions personalization of content (and not of ads as in purpose 3) based on the previously collected information about user interests, clicks, etc. According to the 29WP [5], customization cookies storing user's preferences regarding a service that is explicitly enabled by the user are exempted of consent. However, we note that only session (or short-term) cookies storing such information are exempted. These purposes can instead rely on other legal bases (e.g. legitimate interests) if these pass both the necessity and the balancing tests.

Purpose 5 *"Measurement"* requires consent. It covers the collection of information and combination with previously collected information. We are aware that the entities who will collect information are advertisers– hence third-party content providers for a website publisher. The 29WP regarded that cookies used for "analytics" are not "strictly-necessary" to provide a functionality explicitly requested by the user, because the user can access all the functionalities provided by the website when such cookies are disabled, especially when they are used by third-party services [5]. Moreover, according to the CNIL [15], analytics cookies require consent when collected data is combined or merged with other types of data. Both the ICO [36], and the German DPA [12] sustain the same position that third-party analytics cookies are not strictly necessary and require consent.

---

[2] In our work, the denomination of "cookies" covers all tracking technologies.

3.2   Analysis of Purposes the IAB Europe's TCF V2.0

Version 2.0 introduces 12 purposes (as opposed to 5 purposes in v1.1) and a new category of *"special purposes"* that do not allow users to opt out therefrom. In v2.0, advertisers declare which purposes they use under which legal basis. For each purpose, advertisers can choose to be "flexible", i.e. to leave the choice of the legal basis to publishers who embed TCF banners in their websites. Table 2 lists all purposes and special purposes from v2.0. TCF v2.0 also proposes "special features" that require user opt-in (we analyse features separately later in Sect. 3.3).

Purpose 1 *"Store and/or access information on a device"* **is not specific, but could require consent.** We reproduce the same observations as for purpose 1 in TCF v1.1. Its description seems to be contradictory: it states this purpose requires consent but it confirms that *"Purpose 1 is not a data processing purpose, is technically treated the same way for signalling purposes"*. Also, it mentions that *"any personal data stored and/or accessed via Purpose 1 still requires another Purpose to actually be processed"*; this statement renders it as a condition to other listed purposes. This suggests to be an unspecified purpose: we adduce it seems too general and it might violate the specificity requirement.

Interestingly, v2.0 introduces a special mechanism to prevent disclosing this purpose 1 depending on the publisher's country: when the publisher estimates that its country's jurisdiction does not require consent for this purpose, it will not be shown in cookie banners. As a result, purpose 1 is likely to require consent due to the national implementation of the ePD.

Purpose 2 *"Select basic ads"* **is specific, explicit and requires consent.** It relates to advertisement which requires consent (like purpose 3 of v1.1.)

Purpose 3 *"Create a personalized ads profile"* **and 4** *"Select a personalized ads"* **may require explicit consent.** They may trigger significant effects to end users under the set of assumptions interpreted below, which also apply to Purposes 2 and 3 of version 1.1. The 29WP [3] identified occasions where targeted behavioural advertising (as it is the case conducted by the TCF), could be considered as having *"significant effects"* on users. Where significant and solely automated decisions are made about an individual, *explicit consent* is required (as per Article 22 (1) and (2) c)). This holds specially where vulnerable individuals are targeted with ads of services that may cause them detriment (such as gambling or certain financial products). The 29WP [3] further illustrates that in many typical cases, targeted ads based on profiling might have significant effects on users depending upon the particular characteristics of the case, suchlike:

- the intrusiveness of the profiling process, including the tracking of individuals across different websites, devices and services;
- the expectations and wishes of the individuals concerned;
- the way the advert is delivered; or
- using knowledge of the vulnerabilities of the data subjects targeted" [3].

Table 2. Purposes defined in IAB Europe's TCF v2.0 [27, p .25]

(a) Purposes

Purpose number	Purpose name	User-friendly text
1	Store and/or access information on a device	Cookies, device identifiers, or other information can be stored or accessed on your device for the purposes presented to you
2	Select basic ads	Ads can be shown to you based on the content you're viewing, the app you're using, your approximate location, or your device type
3	Create a personalised ads profile	A profile can be built about you and your interests to show you personalised ads that are relevant to you
4	Select personalised ads	Personalised ads can be shown to you based on a profile about you
5	Create a personalised content profile	A profile can be built about you and your interests to show you personalised content that is relevant to you
6	Select personalised content	Personalised content can be shown to you based on a profile about you
7	Measure ad performance	The performance and effectiveness of ads that you see or interact with can be measured
8	Measure content performance	The performance and effectiveness of content that you see or interact with can be measured
9	Apply market research to generate audience insights	Market research can be used to learn more about the audiences who visit sites/apps and view ads
10	Develop and improve products	Your data can be used to improve existing systems and software, and to develop new products

(b) Special purposes

1	Ensure security, prevent fraud, and debug	Your data can be used to monitor for and prevent fraudulent activity, and ensure systems and processes work properly and securely
2	Technically deliver ads or content	Your device can receive and send information that allows you to see and interact with ads and content

This cognition of the 29WP holds significant interest for profiling. It advises the following relevant elements to account when profiling: the level of detail of the prole (broad, or segmented, granular); its comprehensiveness (does it describe merely one aspect of the data subject, or a more comprehensive picture); the impact of the profiling (effects on the data subject); the safeguards aimed at ensuring fairness, non-discrimination and accuracy in the profiling process.

We argue that the amount and variety of personal information collected under the aegis of these two purposes (as described in the specification policies) across websites, devices and services, might have a significant effect on individuals (even larger when conjugating with features and special features).

The TCF specification allows the use of legitimate interest for personalized advertising. Against this reasoning, the 29WP [22] suggested that "*it would be difficult for controllers to justify using legitimate interests as a lawful basis for intrusive processing and tracking practices for marketing or advertising purposes, for example those that involve tracking individuals across multiple websites, locations, devices, services or data-brokering*".

Purposes 5 "*Create a personalized content profile*" and 6 "*Select personalized content*" might be exempted from consent. With reference to them (the "content" in purpose 6 is shown to the user based on a profile), the 29WP [3, p .14] acknowledged profiling (that is not solely done by automated means resulting in legal or significant effects) can be legitimized under a legitimate interest.

From both versions of the TCF, we presume that only Purposes 5 and 6 from v2.0 and Purpose 4 from v1.1 are exempted of consent and thus, are hypothetically capable of being legitimized under a necessity of a legitimate interest of the controller or a third-party.

However, according to Recital 47 of the GPDR, when using legitimate interest as a legal basis for processing, the controller (in the balance test) has to consider the reasonable expectations of data subjects based on their relationship with the controller. Such legitimate expectations could exist, for example, where there is a relevant and appropriate relationship between the data subject and the controller, e.g. when the data subject is their client or in their service. This means that the data subject needs to have a "reasonable expectation" that their own personal data is being used by a company for a specific purpose. This expectation must exist at the time and in the context of the collection of her personal data. Meanwhile, the collection of data from unknown sources, by third-parties that users have never heard of and do not have a direct relationship with – to profile them and share these "insights" with other advertisers – is not plausibly within the individuals' reasonable expectations. Hence, we suppose that processing personal data of users that have no relationship with third-party advertisers, which is the case in the TCF, will, in practice, make that balance weight towards the interest and rights of users. As posited by the Norwegian Consumer Council [24], "*although consumers may know that many "free" digital services are funded by advertising, this does not mean that most people will have a "reasonable expectation" of the amount of sharing and processing going on behind the scenes (...) Companies are virtually unknown to most consumers, so one can hardly consider this a relationship at all."* Thus, the potentially unique purpose (from the specification of the TCF) that would rely on legitimate interest could, in practice, fail the requirements of such a legal basis. Lastly, Purpose 6 named *"Select personalized content"* would require consent in case of non session-only cookies.

Purposes 7 *"Measure ad performance"*,8 *"Measure content performance"* and 9 *"Apply market research to generate audience insights"* require consent. We argue that they fall into the broader category of measurement purposes. Hence, we reproduce the same reasoning of Purpose 5 in v1.1. Based on the argument of the 29WP [6, p .47], consent is always required for third-party analytics and tracking-based digital market research: *"opt-in consent would almost always be required [...] for tracking and profiling for purposes of direct marketing, behavioural advertisement, location-based advertising or tracking-based digital market research"*. We also claim that this latter purpose *"Apply market research to generate audience insights"* is not specific and is defined in a broad way and with ambiguity as to its intent.

Purpose 10 *"Develop and improve products"* is not specific, and so we cannot derive its legal basis. It seems vague and might be qualified unspecified, since it is not detailed enough to determine its kind of processing (to allow compliance with the law to be assessed). In fact, this purpose is a typical example of a violation of the specificity requirements, as indicated in [4,9]. Accordingly, deriving its legal basis is intricate. It follows therefrom that this purpose would facilitate non-specific, hypothetical processing of personal data under a broad designation of undefined purpose of product improvement or new product development. As an example, a recent EDPB guidance [21] only proposes legitimate interest or consent (depending on a concrete case and the legal requirements demanded) for the purpose of *"Service improvement"* under a motivation that online services often collect detailed information on how users engage with their service through a collection of organizational metrics that need to be justified contextually for a concrete service, also grounding the way to improve it.

Special Purpose 1 *"Ensure security, prevent fraud, and debug"* is not specific, but could be exempted from consent. It seems to cover a broad range of purposes which could be made autonomous in the TCF. These purposes could supposedly rely on legitimate interest since these have been the most consensual and prevalent interests sustained across industries [13], by the EDPB [21], other DPAs guidance [1,6,12] and proposed in GDPR Recitals. Recitals 47 and 49 mention fraud prevention, network and information security could "constitute" legitimate interest. These purposes would still need to pass the necessity and balancing tests for processing to be lawful under legitimate interest.

As a remark, the specification policies do not permit to exert the right to object to processing under legitimate interest via the TCF. Such right exists in the GDPR, unless the controller can demonstrate "compelling legitimate grounds" (Article 21(1)) that override the interests or rights and freedoms of the data subject, or for the establishment, exercise or defence of legal claims [3].

Special Purpose 2 *"Technically deliver ads or content"* **is not specific and could require consent.** It bundles separate data processing purposes under a single name: it implies both advertising *or* content delivery. We reproduce the same reasoning of Purpose 2 in version 1.1.

We summarize our analysis of all purposes of IAB Europe TCF v1.1 and v2.0 in Table 3.

3.3   Features and Special Features Defined in Versions 1.1 and 2.0

In this section, we briefly comment on the use of features and special features defined in the framework on both versions. We exclude a crossed analysis of the features with each purpose as it requires extensive work and is out of scope of this paper. Table 4 presents features for TCF v1.1 and v2.0.

Feature 1 of v1.1 "Matching Data to Offline Sources"

i) Definition of "matching" is problematic. This feature allows to combine data from offline sources that were collected in other contexts, without explaining what data and which context are at stake. Additionally, matching implies offline but *also* online data (*"data from offline data sources can be combined with your online activity in support of one or more purposes"*). Finally, the purpose description in the specification does not suffice to render probable *consequences* of such a feature.

ii) Profiling. Disparate and seemingly innocuous data from online and offline sources can ultimately be combined to create a meaningful comprehensive profile of a person. On this feature, Johnny Ryan [43] formulated that *"these notices fail to disclose that hundreds, and perhaps thousands, of companies will be sent your personal data. Nor does it say that some of these companies will combine these with a profile they already have built about you. Nor are you told that this profile includes things like your income bracket, age and gender, habits, social media influence, ethnicity, sexual orientation, religion, political leaning, etc. Nor do you know whether or not some of these companies will sell their data about you to other companies, perhaps for online marketing, credit scoring, insurance companies, background checking services, and law enforcement"*.

Feature 1 of v2.0 "Match and combine offline data sources" and Feature 2 of v1.1 and of v2.0 "Linking devices"

i) Personal data. Both features configure technical means to process personal data (considering its broad definition predicated in Article 4(1) and Recital 26 of the GDPR [2]), as matching data to offline sources and linking devices are means that could reasonably enable identification of individuals.

ii) Profiling. An advertiser able to track and link people's interests and/or behavior across different devices (e.g. laptops, computers, phone, smart TV, etc.) is able to get a fine-grained view of an individual's activities throughout a day. To this scope, whenever companies process data using these technical means, is plausible they are processing personal data and they need to be GDPR compliant, e.g. to the lawfulness and purpose limitation principles.

Table 3. Purposes defined in IAB Europe's TCF v1.1 and v2.0. The "Allowable Lawful Bases" column indicates the official documentation guidelines of IAB regarding the use of legal basis in v2.0 [27, p .25]. The "Requires Consent" column sums up our analysis. We indicate the default legal basis, and add parentheses if exceptions occur.

(a) Purposes (TCF v1.1)			
Purpose number	Purpose name	Allowable Lawful Bases	Requires Consent
1	Information storage and access	-	(✓)
2	Personalisation	-	?
3	Ad selection, delivery, reporting	-	✓
4	Content selection, delivery, reporting	-	(✓)
5	Measurement	-	✓
(b) Purposes (TCF v2.0)			
1	Store and/or access information on a device	Consent	(✓)
2	Select basic ads	Consent, LI	✓
3	Create a personalised ads profile	Consent, LI	✓
4	Select personalised ads	Consent, LI	✓
5	Create a personalised content profile	Consent, LI	(✓)
6	Select personalised content	Consent, LI	(✓)
7	Measure ad performance	Consent, LI	✓
8	Measure content performance	Consent, LI	✓
9	Apply market research to generate audience insights	Consent, LI	✓
10	Develop and improve products	Consent, LI	?
(c) Special purposes (TCF v2.0)			
1	Ensure security, prevent fraud, and debug	LI	(✗)
2	Technically deliver ads or content	LI	?

Table 4. Features defined in IAB Europe's TCF v1.1 and v2.0.

(a) Features in TCF v1.1 [26, p. 13]

Feature number	Feature name	User-friendly text
1	Matching Data to Offline Sources	Combining data from offline sources that were initially collected in other contexts with data collected online in support of one or more purposes
2	Linking Devices	Processing of a user's data to connect such user across multiple devices
3	Precise Geographic Location Data	Processing of a user's precise geographic location data in support of a purpose for which that certain third party has consent

(b) Features in TCF v2.0 [27, p .25]

1	Match and combine offline data sources	Data from offline data sources can be combined with your online activity in support of one or more purposes
2	Link different devices	Different devices can be determined as belonging to you or your household in support of one or more of purposes
3	Receive and use automatically-sent device characteristics for identification	Your device might be distinguished from other devices based on information it automatically sends, such as IP address or browser type

(c) Special features in TCF v2.0 [27, p .25]

| 1 | Use precise geolocation data | Your precise geolocation data can be used in support of one or more purposes. This means your location can be accurate to within several meters |
| 2 | Actively scan device characteristics for identification | Your device can be identified based on a scan of your device's unique combination of characteristics |

Feature 3 of v1.1 and Special Feature 1 of v2.0 "Precise Geographic Location Data"

i) Requires consent. Gaining access to information stored in the device of a user requires consent (under Article 5(3) of the ePD).

ii) Personal data. The GDPR also applies whenever the provider collects location data from the device and if it can be used to identify a person, which distinctively occurs with "precise geolocation data". The broad definition of "personal data" specifically includes location data as one of the elements that can identify a person. The 29WP [8] sets out that providers of geolocation based services gain *"an intimate overview of habits and patterns of the owner of such a device and build extensive profiles."*

iii) Profiling. Using location data may involve "profiling" within the meaning of Article 4(4) and Recital 72 which specifically includes analyzing location data.

iv) Special categories of personal data. In particular contexts, location data could be linked to special categories of personal data, requiring explicit consent (Article 9 of the GDPR), e.g. location data may reveal visits to hospitals or places of worship or presence at political demonstrations.

Feature 3 of v2.0 "Receive and use automatically-sent device characteristics for identification" and Special Feature 2 of v2.0 "Actively scan device characteristics for identification"
Consent is required. Due to browsers behavior, cookies are automatically sent to websites. These cookies can store user identifiers based on the device characteristics. Such features in principle require consent (under Article 5(3) of the ePD). This applies irrespective of whether or not the location data is personal data.

4 Evaluation of the Usage of Purposes of IAB Europe's Transparency and Consent Framework by Advertisers

In this section, we analyze the purposes declared by all the advertisers registered in IAB Europe's Transparency and Consent Framework. Our goal is to bring transparency to the use of purposes and features by advertisers, to raise concerns derived from the legal analysis in Sect. 3 and the practical usage measured herein. To do so, we take advantage of the fact that all data regarding different advertisers of the TCF is made public, and notably the Global Vendor List (GVL, the list of all registered advertisers). This list includes data about advertisers, what purposes they use and under which legal basis they operate. In Appendix A we show the evolution of the number of advertisers registered in TCF.

In TCF v1.1, only advertisers can choose which legal basis to use for each purpose. In TCF v2.0 however, advertisers can decide to declare some purposes as "flexible" – in that case publishers can impose "restrictions" and require a specific legal basis for such purposes [33][3].

4.1 Purposes and Legal Basis of Processing Declared by Advertisers

In this section, we measure the legal basis for purposes declared by advertisers in the Global Vendor List: in v1.1 (version 183) [31] and v2.0 (version 20) [32].

---

[3] We do not study the legal bases of purposes declared by publishers in this paper.

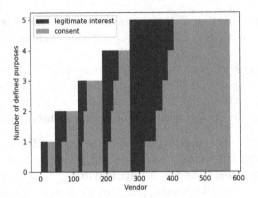

Fig. 1. Number of defined purposes and their legal basis per advertiser in the Global Vendor List for v1.1 (version 183) [31], January 2020.

Figure 1 shows the legal basis of processing for all advertisers: 46% (267) of them operate on legitimate interest for at least one purpose, and 19% (111) of advertisers rely on legitimate interest for all the purposes they declare (i.e., they do not operate on the basis of consent for any purpose). Overall, 54% (308 advertisers) operate on consent only and 27% (156) base their processing on both consent and legitimate interest. We present the list of all 267 third-party advertisers that rely on legitimate interests for at least one purpose in attachment [11].

Next, we measure the purposes self-declared by advertisers in the TCF's GVL in Fig. 2. Figure 2a details the results presented above for each individual purpose in v1.1 [31]. We observe a difference in the use of the different legal bases among purposes: while 72% of advertisers rely on consent for purpose 1 ("Information storage and access"), 38% do so for purpose 4 ("Content selection, delivery, reporting"). Interestingly, 22% of advertisers rely on legitimate interest for purpose 1 and 35% do so for purpose 5 ("Measurement"). We identified in Sect. 3 that purposes 3 and 5 of TCF v1.1 ("Ad selection, delivery, reporting" and "Measurement") require consent. However, we detect a particularly worrisome number of advertisers: 175 and 199 advertisers respectively rely on legitimate interests for purposes 3 and 5.

Figure 2b renders an analysis of purposes for the Global Vendor List of v2.0 [32]. The number of advertisers registered in this version is smaller, but we still see that a significant portion of advertisers use legitimate interest for purposes that require consent. For example, 17% advertisers rely on legitimate interest for purpose 2 ("Select basic ads"), and 25% advertisers do it for purpose 7 ("Measure ad performance"), while our legal analysis in Sect. 3 demonstrated that purposes 2 and 7 require consent. It is also notable that 32% of advertisers use "flexible purposes" for at least one purpose thus allowing publishers to change the legal basis for such purposes [33].

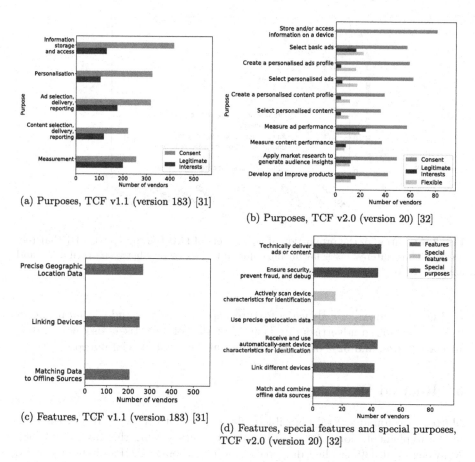

(a) Purposes, TCF v1.1 (version 183) [31]

(b) Purposes, TCF v2.0 (version 20) [32]

(c) Features, TCF v1.1 (version 183) [31]

(d) Features, special features and special purposes, TCF v2.0 (version 20) [32]

Fig. 2. Purposes, features and legal basis of processing declared by the registered advertisers in IAB Europe's Transparency and Consent Framework v1.1 and v2.0, January 2020.

As DPAs criticized the use of legitimate interest as a lawful basis for online advertising [34], it is interesting to see the evolution of this use over time. In Fig. 3, we show that the proportion of advertisers registered in the TCF that rely on legitimate interest for each purpose slowly decreases over time.

4.2 Additional "features" of Processing

Figure 2c shows the prevalence of features used by registered advertisers in TCF v1.1. Our analysis shows that 66% (377) of advertisers declare at least one of these features in v1.1 [31]. We present a list of 118 advertisers that use all three features of v1.1 in a public repository [11]. Such advertisers might require a deeper inspection by the DPAs, since consent is not requested for using these features in the TCF. We also present the list of all 377 advertisers that use at least one feature in v1.1 [11].

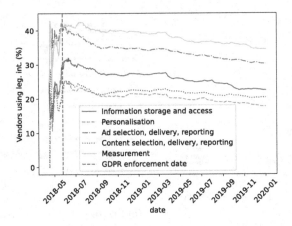

Fig. 3. Evolution of the proportion of advertisers of IAB Europe's TCF v1.1 that rely on legitimate interest as a lawful basis for data processing, between April 2018 and January 2020.

Figure 2d shows prevalence of features, special features and special purposes used by registered advertisers in TCF v2.0: 45% of advertisers use at least one special feature, and 52% of advertisers use at least one special purpose.

5   Related Work

Matte et al. found several plausible violations of both the GDPR and the ePD in the implementations of cookie banners by actors using this framework [38]. Nouwens et al. [39] studied dark patterns in 5 popular CMPs of the TCF and estimated that only 11.8% of banners met minimum legal requirements. Other works on cookie banners briefly mentioned the framework [17,44].

On the legal side in 2018 several complaints were lodged in Europe by NGOs against the Real-Time Bidding (RTB) scheme supported by IAB. These complaints alleged that IAB is in breach of the GDPR, as broadcasting of personal data takes place every time an RTB-driven ad is shown [42]. The French and UK DPAs both criticized the framework. In 2018, the CNIL pronounced a relevant decision determining that Vectaury, acting as a TCF CMP, failed to demonstrate that valid consent had been obtained for the processing of data used for targeted advertising, and had not complied with the principle of transparency with respect to the purposes of processing [14,41]. The ICO studied the TCF, most notably criticizing the use of legitimate interest as a lawful basis for data processing for online advertising [34]. The Panoptykon Foundation filed complaints against Google and IAB Europe [40] to the Polish DPA related to the online behavioural advertising (OBA) ecosystem. These complaints focus on the role of IAB as an organization that sets standards for other actors involved in the OBA market, insisting they should be treated as data controllers responsible for GDPR infringements. The network of data protection expertise lodged a complaint to the German DPA about data processing in the context of personalized online advertising, adducing that providers who are members of IAB Europe incur into possible violations of the GDPR [16].

6   Conclusions

In this paper, we assessed the scope of the principle of purpose specification in the predefined purposes of IAB Europe's TCF v1.1 and v2.0. Our analysis shows that some purposes, e.g. "Personalisation" are not specific and explicit enough to be used as legally-compliant ones and might not be exempted of consent. Nonetheless, we measured that 175 advertisers out of 575 registered in the TCF v1.1 declare the legitimate interest basis for this purpose.

All the actors using such frameworks need to be aware of the legal implications of the usage of predefined purposes and choices they make regarding the legal basis of processing personal data.

We hope these findings may be useful for policy-makers to design better guidelines regarding (i) the specification of purposes in the TCF and similar frameworks, and (ii) the legal basis to be used per purpose.

Acknowledgements. We thank Johnny Ryan for his comments on the analysis of the purposes. We thank anonymous reviewers of APF 2020 for their useful feedback. This work has been partially supported by ANR JCJC project PrivaWeb (ANR-18-CE39-0008), ANSWER project PIA FSN2 No. P159564-2661789/DOS0060094 between Inria and Qwant, and by the Inria DATA4US Exploratory Action project.

A   Evolution of the Number of Advertisers

We leverage the fact that all versions of the Global Vendor List of the TCF are public and dated – we can therefore display the evolution of the number of registered advertisers (vendors) in Fig. 4. We observe a fast increase in the first three months following the release of IAB Europe's TCF in April 2018 (one month before GDPR came in force in the EU), followed by a slow increase until March 2020. Version 2.0 was announced in August 2019 and is supposed to operate alongside version 1.1 until the end of March 2020. The increase in registered advertisers is far from being as fast as for the release of version 1.1, and as of January 16th 2020, only 92 advertisers are registered, compared to 574 for version 1.1. This is surprising if we consider that advertisers do not have to pay the registration fee a second time to register for version 2.0.

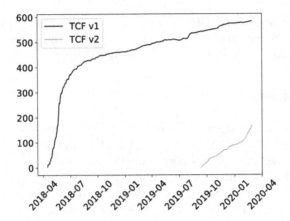

Fig. 4. Evolution of the number of registered advertisers in the IAB Europe's Global Vendor List between May 2018 and March 2020.

B   Attachments

We report several lists of advertisers collected in this work in a publicly available repository [11]:

- the list of 377 advertisers declaring that they use features,
- the list of 118 advertisers declaring that they use all features,
- the list of 267 advertisers declaring that they use legitimate interests,
- the list of 111 advertisers using only legitimate interests,
- the list of 308 advertisers using consent only.

This analysis has been done for the Global Vendor List for TCF v1.1 (version 183) [31].

C   Purposes, Features, Special Purposes and Special Features of TCF v2

We present definitions of the following notions as quotations from the TCF v2's policy [27]:

- "Purpose means one of the defined purposes for processing of data, including users' personal data, by participants in the Framework that are defined in the Policies or the Specifications for which Vendors declare a Legal Basis in the GVL and for which the user is given choice, i.e. to consent or to object depending on the Legal Basis for the processing, by a CMP"
- "Special Purpose means one of the defined purposes for processing of data, including users' personal data, by participants in the Framework that are defined in the Policies or the Specifications for which Vendors declare a Legal Basis in the GVL and for which the user is not given choice by a CMP."

- "Feature means one of the features of processing personal data used by participants in the Framework that are defined in the Policies or the Specifications used in pursuit of one or several Purposes for which the user is not given choice separately to the choice afforded regarding the Purposes for which they are used"
- "Special Feature means one of the features of processing personal data used by participants in the Framework that are defined in the Policies or the Specifications used in pursuit of one or several Purposes for which the user is given the choice to opt-in separately from the choice afforded regarding the Purposes which they support."

References

1. AP (Dutch DPA), Standard explanation of the basis of the legitimate interest
2. Article 29 Working Party, EDPB opinion 4/2007 on the concept of personal data (WP136). Accessed 20 July 2007
3. Article 29 Working Party, Guidelines on automated individual decision-making and profiling for the purposes of regulation 2016/679 (WP251 rev.01)
4. Article 29 Working Party, Opinion 03/2013 on purpose limitation (WP203)
5. Article 29 Working Party, Opinion 04/2012 on cookie consent exemption (WP 194). Accessed 7 June 2012
6. Article 29 Working Party, Opinion 06/2014 on the notion of legitimate interests of the data controller under article 7 of directive 95/46/EC (WP217)
7. Article 29 Working Party, Working document 02/2013 providing guidance on obtaining consent for cookies
8. Article 29 Working Party, Opinion 13/2011 on Geolocation services on smart mobile devices (WP 185) (2011). Accessed 16 May 2011
9. Article 29 Working Party, Guidelines on Consent under Regulation 2016/679 (wp259rev.01) (2016)
10. Article 29 Working Party, Guidelines on transparency under Regulation 2016/679 (WP260 rev.01) (2018). Accessed 11 April 2018
11. Attachments to the paper (dropbox repository). https://www.dropbox.com/sh/0g1qlsaatc8yplz/AACAaFLJNrwRH3eWRmGm_zqsa?dl=0
12. BfDI (German DPA), Guidance from German authorities for telemedia providers
13. Centre for Information Policy Leadership, CIPL examples of legitimate interest grounds for processing of personal data
14. CNIL, Décision n MED 2018–042 du 30 octobre 2018 mettant en demeure la société VECTAURY (2018)
15. Décision n MED 2018–042, Délibération n 2019–093 du 4 juillet 2019 portant adoption de lignes directrices relatives à l'application de l'article 82 de la loi du 6 janvier 1978 modifiée aux opérations de lecture ou écriture dans le terminal d'un utilisateur (notamment aux cookies et autres traceurs) (rectificatif) (2019)
16. Decision of the conference of independent data protection supervisors of the federal and state governments - 07.11.20191, Datenshutzkonferenz
17. Degeling, M., Utz, C., Lentzsch, C., Hosseini, H., Schaub, F., Holz, T.: We value your privacy... now take some cookies: measuring the GDPR's impact on web privacy. In: Network and Distributed System Security Symposium (NDSS) (2019)
18. Judgement of the court of justice of the EU, Case c-673/17

19. Directive 2009/136/ec of the european parliament and of the council of 25 november 2009 amending directive 2002/22/ec on universal service and users' rights relating to electronic communications networks and services
20. Judgment of the court (second chamber) of 4 May 2017, Case C-13/16
21. European Data Protection Board (EDPB), Guidelines 2/2019 on the processing of personal data under article 6(1)(b) gdpr in the context of the provision of online services to data subjects
22. European Data Protection Board (EDPB), Guidelines on consent under regulation 2016/679 (wp259 rev.01). Accessed 10 April 2018
23. European Parliament, the Council and the Commission, Charter of Fundamental Rights of the European Union, Official Journal of the European Communities, 18 December 2000 (2000/C 364/01)
24. Forbrukerrådet, Out of control - how consumers are exploited by the online advertising industry (2020)
25. Regulation (EU) 2016/679 of the European Parliament and of the Council of 27 April 2016 on the protection of natural persons with regard to the processing of personal data and on the free movement of such data (2016)
26. IAB Europe, IAB europe transparency & consent framework policies. https://iabeurope.eu/wp-content/uploads/2019/08/IABEurope_TransparencyConsentFramework_v1-1_policy_FINAL.pdf. Accessed 20 Nov 2019
27. IAB Europe transparency & consent framework policies, IAB Europe transparency & consent framework policies. https://iabeurope.eu/wp-content/uploads/2019/08/TransparencyConsentFramework_PoliciesVersion_TCFv2-0_2019-08-21.3_FINAL-1-1.pdf. Accessed 21 Jan 2020
28. IAB Europe transparency & consent framework policies, Transparency and consent framework (2018). https://github.com/InteractiveAdvertisingBureau/GDPR-Transparency-and-Consent-Framework
29. IAB Europe transparency & consent framework policies, Transparency and consent framework (v2), August 2019. https://github.com/InteractiveAdvertisingBureau/GDPR-Transparency-and-Consent-Framework/tree/master/TCFv2
30. IAB Europe transparency & consent framework policies, Dates you need to know for the TCF V2.0 switchover (2020). https://iabeurope.eu/tcf-2/dates-you-need-to-know-for-the-tcf-v2-0-switchover/
31. IAB Europe and IAB Tech Lab, Global vendor list (GVL, v1.1, version 183), January 2020. https://vendorlist.consensu.org/v-183/vendorlist.json
32. IAB Europe and IAB Tech Lab, Global vendor list (GVL, v2.0, version 20), January 2020 .https://vendorlist.consensu.org/v2/archives/vendor-list-v20.json
33. IAB Tech Lab and IAB Europe, Transparency and consent string with global vendor & CMP list formats, December 2019. https://github.com/InteractiveAdvertisingBureau/GDPR-Transparency-and-Consent-Framework/blob/master/TCFv2/IAB%20Tech%20Lab%20-%20Consent%20string%20and%20vendor%20list%20formats%20v2.md#the-core-string
34. ICO, ICO report into adtech and real time bidding. Accessed 20 June 2019
35. ICO report into adtech and real time bidding, Lawful basis for processing legitimate interests (2018)
36. ICO report into adtech and real time bidding, Guidance on the use of cookies and similar technologies, July 2019
37. Koops, B.-J.: The (in) flexibility of techno-regulation and the case of purpose-binding. Legisprudence 5(2), 171–194 (2011)

38. Matte, C., Bielova, N., Santos, C.: Do cookie banners respect my choice? measuring legal compliance of banners from IAB Europe's transparency and consent framework. In: IEEE Symposium on Security and Privacy (IEEE S&P 2020) (2020)
39. Nouwens, M., Liccardi, I., Veale, M., Karger, D., Kagal, L.: Dark patterns after the GDPR: scraping consent pop-ups and demonstrating their influence. In: Conference on Human Factors in Computing Systems (CHI 2020) (2020)
40. Panoptykon Foundation, Panoptykon files complaints against Google and IAB Europe (2019). https://en.panoptykon.org/complaints-Google-IAB
41. Ryan, J.: French regulator shows deep flaws in IAB's consent framework and RTB (2018). https://brave.com/cnil-consent-rtb/. Accessed 28 Mar 2019
42. French regulator shows deep flaws in IAB's consent framework and RTB, Regulatory complaint concerning massive, web-wide data breach by google and other "ad tech" companies under europe's gdpr (2018). https://brave.com/adtech-data-breach-complaint/. Accessed 02 May 2020
43. French regulator shows deep flaws in IAB's consent framework and RTB, Brave answers us senators questions on privacy and antitrust (2019). https://brave.com/senate-qrfs-june2019/. Accessed 02 May 2020
44. Santos, C., Bielova, N., Matte, C.: Are cookie banners indeed compliant with the law? deciphering eu legal requirements on consent and technical means to verify compliance of cookie banners, ArXiv, vol. abs/1912.07144 (2019)
45. von Grafenstein, M.: The Principle of Purpose Limitation in Data Protection Laws: The Risk-Based Approach, Principles, and Private Standards as Elements for Regulating Innovation, 1st edn. Nomos Verlagsgesellschaft mbH (2018)

Towards Transparency in the Internet of Things

Stephan Escher$^{(\boxtimes)}$, Benjamin Weller, Stefan Köpsell, and Thorsten Strufe

TU Dresden, Dresden, Germany
{stephan.escher,benjamin.weller,stefan.kopsell,
thorsten.strufe}@tu-dresden.de

Abstract. The establishment of IoT devices in all areas of public and private life raises, besides many new possibilities, also a number of new privacy issues. In particular, the establishment of almost invisible audio-visual sensors, like in smart speakers or smart cars, affects not only the user who purchases these IoT devices, but all those who are within the recording radius of them. At present, it is almost impossible for such uninvolved users to recognize all the surrounding recording IoT devices and their data processing, let alone object to this recording. This means, there currently is exclusively foreign control of the personal data of bystanders. Therefore we present our work in progress, to get towards transparency about the capturing and processing of audiovisual data by surrounding IoT devices one step closer. In this we assume that in the future such devices will have to identify themselves and their respective privacy policies. We have implemented a first prototype of our concept and show the need of such transparency solution by pre-evaluating it.

Keywords: Internet of Things · Transparency Enhancing Tools · Privacy · Biometric data

1 Introduction

Visions of ubiquitous computing and the Internet of Things (IoT) have existed since the end of the 20th century [15]. Today, these visions are turning into reality. Small, unobtrusive and networked sensors that measure and monitor their environment or users are continuously integrated into all types of physical objects, thereafter called smart devices. This development enables many new possibilities and increased efficiency, for example in mobility (self-driving cars), in energy supply (smart meters), in production (smart manufacturing), in medicine (mHealth) or in home automation (smart home).

The integration of IoT devices in all areas of public and private life, however, also raises a number of new privacy issues, especially in terms of unnoticed, ubiquitous data capturing that people cannot escape. The reason for this is that with the sensors becoming invisible, the data acquisition, transfer, processing and storage remain invisible to the user at the same time. In particular, the

© Springer Nature Switzerland AG 2020
L. Antunes et al. (Eds.): APF 2020, LNCS 12121, pp. 186–200, 2020.
https://doi.org/10.1007/978-3-030-55196-4_11

constant capturing and processing of *acoustic and visual signals*, e.g. through cameras and microphones in smart home devices, augmented reality glasses or smart cars[1], affects not only the user who purchases these IoT devices, but all those who are within the recording radius of them. May the owner of such devices still be informed about terms of use and data protection declarations when purchasing or setting up these devices, the independent user who is now constantly surrounded by these devices, currently has no possibility to intervene against the recording of his personal data. It is probably even impossible to just recognize all devices and their functionalities, let alone the involved companies and related privacy policies. There currently is exclusively foreign control of the personal data of bystanders, interference is hard, giving consent difficult, and being informed about its ramifications impossible, in consequence.

Therefore in this paper we want to present our work in progress to get towards transparency about audiovisual data capturing and processing in the world of the Internet of Things. The aim is to develop a concept that informs the user transparently and comprehensibly about the current situation regarding nearby devices with audio and/or video recording functionality, i.e. the possible recording of biometric data such as voice or face, as well as their processing and storage, and to evaluate this solution with the user according to its comprehensibility and usefulness.

2   Related Work

To design a suitable transparency solution for such audiovisual devices, first of all several challenges have to be considered:

1. How can such recording devices be recognized?
2. How could the information about data processing be transmitted to the user?
3. Which information should be transmitted?
4. How could transmitted information be presented in an understandable way?

Therefore, in the following, we take a closer look at state-of-the-art solutions for these questions.

2.1   Detecting Recording Devices

To be able to give the user a transparent overview of his environment, first of all, surrounding audiovisual capturing IoT devices have to be detected. On the one hand this could be done using technical approaches. Possibilities are for example object detection via augmented reality glasses or by wireless traffic pattern analysis [3]. However such technical approaches only work for certain recording devices, cannot give a complete overview and are therefore not suitable for daily usage.

---

[1] github.com/tevora-threat/scout.

Another approach is the assumption of regulation of IoT devices. Several proposals have been made out of mostly ethical reasons, to give people the possibility of being informed, and thus can allow or deny access to their personal information [6,8,14]. In 2018, the EU settled on the General Data Protection Regulation (GDPR) [1]. One of its main goals is the protection of natural persons in regard to their personal data. Article 13[2] states, that if personal data is collected from a data subject, they shall be provided with information about the data controller as well as insights into data processing and storage. Recent studies base their work on the assumption of regulation due to the GDPR [2,5,11] which mostly means, that IoT devices need to make themselves noticeable, e.g. through some kind of broadcast signal. In contrast, other work questions whether the GDPR alone may not be concise enough to deal with the complexity of IoT yet, due to the imbalance between data controller (the person owning the recording device) and data processor (the company, which handles the processing of the data) [10].

2.2 Information Transmission

If we assume that the identification of such IoT devices is regulated, we need a channel to transmit the information about data collection and processing to the user. On the one hand, this can be implemented analogously, like current warning signs for video surveillance in public areas (e.g. regulated in Germany through BDSG[3]). For example, the data controller (owner of the device) could offer a sign for possible data acquisition, as in their smart home, or the data processor/manufacturer could integrate a light signal in the IoT device that visualizes active data acquisition. However, we argue that such analogues information transmission is not suitable for the dynamic IoT world. Such concepts would lack on information, are not suitable for mobile IoT devices, flexible and adaptable.

On the other hand, the information transmission could be done via a digital communication channel. Such a channel could be either direct or indirect [11]. Using *direct communication*, a channel between the IoT device and a user device (e.g. smart phone) is constructed whenever they are in range. Therefore the IoT devices reveal themselves via broadcasting all needed information (e.g. recorded data type, range, privacy policies etc.). Alternatively, an identification number is transmitted, and additional information is queried via an external database. The user devices listen on this channel and display the information to the user.

Langheinrich proposed one of the first transparency systems for IoT [8]. For audiovisual data recordings, which he calls *active policy announcement*, he proposes a *privacy beacon*, which communicates with the user device over a short-ranged wireless link. Thereby a service id is transmitted to the user device, which will in turn communicate with a service proxy on the network to request the privacy policy. Several technologies for the communication between IoT and user

---

[2] gdpr.eu/article-13-personal-data-collected/.

[3] www.gesetze-im-internet.de/englisch_bdsg/englisch_bdsg.html#p0044.

device are proposed, such as Infrared, Bluetooth, Wireless LAN, and ZigBee. His decision to use infrared was also due to the fact, that the technology was readily available in then-common PDAs.

Morel et al. describe another design of a transparency and consent system for IoT [11]. Similarly to Langheinrich, they use a direct communication between IoT and user device. As the communication channel, Bluetooth Low Energy (BLE) is proposed over alternative short-ranged wireless technologies, due to high availability in today-commonplace smartphones, and privacy benefits due to no involvement of other systems. IoT devices are enhanced with a *Privacy Beacon*, which is responsible for the declaration of this device. Beacons use *advertisement packets* (a specification of BLE), which are able to carry data, and sent out as a broadcast in set intervals. All information required by the GDPR is transmitted using the advertisement packets.

In contrast, Das et al. offer a solution for transparency and consent tracking in IoT, using an *indirect communication* setup [5]. For this, they introduce IoT Resource Registries (IRR), where IoT devices are registered and their privacy policies are held. They decided to use an indirect approach for openness and scalability. IoT device owners are expected to register their device in the local IRR. A *Personalized Privacy Assistant* (PPA) is proposed as a smartphone app, which queries the local IRR and notifies the user about functionality, position, privacy policy etc. of surrounding IoT devices. The PPA is designed with mobile app privacy preferences in mind. In their implementation, the user devices detect specific WiFi access points and Bluetooth beacons to determine the location of the user.

If we consider the time of transparency relative to the time of data collection and processing, transparency solutions could be distinguish between Ex Ante (transparency before data collection) and Ex Post/Real-time (after/during data collection) [16]. Thereby direct communication only allows real-time transparency since the user is informed when he is already in range of data capturing, indirect communication on the other hand is conceivable to achieve ex-ante transparency, but the implementation for mobile IoT devices is more difficult.

2.3 Information Content

Next we have to think about the information which has to be transmitted to the user. The GDPR requires, that the data subject must be informed about the processing of their personal data by the data controller. Such information includes, but is not limited to, identity and contact details of the data controller, purposes of the processing, recipients, data retention time, as well as information regarding rectification and erasure of personal data. Morel et al. [11] represent the point of view, that position and range of the IoT device should be included as well, to make the given information more contextual.

Further, we argue, that for IoT transparency even the information about the data processor are almost more important than about the data controller, cause in most cases the data controller (the one who deploys the IoT device) does not have complete control over the data process owed to the current design of IoT devices. This means there are multiple responsible actors which should be considered.

For transparency it could also be interesting, next to explicit information about data processing, to think about predicted data, especially in the field of biometric data, where sensitive data could potentially be inferred, such as the health status of the user [4].

Depending on the information which is transmitted, additional privacy issues concerning the device owners have to be addressed. As already said, the data controller has to provide information regarding the circumstances and processing of personal data. Whenever a data controller broadcasts data, information about them is inevitably leaked, e.g. about available devices in his smart home, device types or traces of his movement via mobile IoT devices. The more specific the transmitted information becomes, the higher the risk for the device owner.

2.4 Information Visualization

If the content is determined the information has to be presented to the user understandable and intuitive. Since IoT devices are ubiquitous, the transparency solution must also be omnipresent. Therefore the solution needs to be unobtrusive enough and must provide a usable interface in an everyday scenario without overwhelming the user. This has to be kept in mind when designing user interfaces (UIs) and experience (UX). Research on application use in everyday situations reflects this [6,8,9,14]. These can be combined with general usability paradigms (e.g. by Krug [7]) to achieve a well-integrated UI and UX. Further, not every bit of information needs to be immediately presented, as user interfaces rely on comprehensibility and ease of use [7].

In addition to a UI that can be used daily, the information transmitted must also be easily accessible and quickly understood. It is conceivable that most users do not want to constantly read privacy policies about nearby IoT devices in their daily routine. Therefore most Transparency Enhancing Tools abstract and simplify the information [12]. Thus, various projects aim to make privacy policies more accessible and easier to understand. *ToS;DR*[4], for example, is an initiative, which grades websites and companies according to their privacy policies. They define various aspects of user privacy from which a final *privacy grade* is derived. The websites or companies are then classified by marks from A (best) to E (worst privacy practices). *DuckDuckGo Privacy Essentials*[5] is an extension for web browsers, which utilizes the ToS;DR framework and further extends the rating with the presence of connection encryption and integrated tracking networks of the website. In this way, the user receives a quick, comprehensible and unobtrusive indication of the current privacy situation when visiting the website. Others attempt to simplify the individual provisions of a privacy policy, such as the mozilla privacy icons project[6], which has created icons for privacy policy

---

[4] tosdr.org.

[5] duckduckgo.com/app.

[6] wiki.mozilla.org/Privacy_Icons.

settings such as the retention period to provide a quick and understandable view of ongoing data processing without reading the full privacy policy. Related work in this area is thereby mainly focused on web browsing or mobile app usage [12]. For IoT transparency their has to be done additional work, cause additional information could be important, like the usage of a wake-up word (like "Alexa") before data processing or local processing of biometric data (e.g. transcription of voice directly on the IoT device). Of course, simplification also leads to a loss of information, which must be taken into account when developing a transparency solution, i.e. weighing up between functionality and usability.

3   An Audit TET for IoT

In the following we want to present our work in progress of the development of an audit TET (Transparency Enhancing Tool) for IoT devices. Audit TET means thereby the transparent visualization of insights into data capturing, processing and storage at realtime without the possibility of interaction [16].

3.1   Information Transmission

Similar to related work, we assume a regulation of audiovisual IoT devices, which means that they have to identify themselves through some kind of broadcast signal. Due to the low energy consumption, the generally suitable range and the high availability in current mobile user devices, we have, like Morel et al. [11], decided to use a direct and digital BLE communication channel to transfer information from the IoT device to the user device. The main idea is that an IoT device continuously broadcasts a specific ID via BLE advertising mode whereas the user device is in scanning mode. The scan interval should be configurable, so that the user can weigh up the actuality of the transparency against the battery life of his device, or update the transparency status manually. If the device of the user receives such an ID, a database is queried anonymously, where the information about data capturing, processing, etc. has been deposited. The separate database is useful to be able to react flexibly to changes in data protection guidelines of IoT devices or legal requirements. After retrieving the information, the user device can directly inform the user about the current situation regarding nearby recording devices and their characteristics.

For the daily use of this transparency solution, our approach for notification and visualization is to support user devices that are directly accessible, i.e. wearables like smart watches or smart glasses. Thus, the user can be informed quickly and efficiently without being torn from his activities. For the concrete implementation, the user's smart phone would take over the scanning mode, query correlating information when devices are detected and then display a notification and/or forward important information to a wearable of the user. The whole communication setup is shown in Fig. 1.

Challenges for this communication setup are on the one hand to adjust the range of the BLE communication to the real recording range of the device and on the other hand the increased energy consumption especially for mobile IoT and user devices. Furthermore, users without a mobile user device still have no transparent overview of their current data recording. Fast moving IoT devices, such as integrated cameras of a smart car, might not be noticeable by the recorded user as they may not be able to react fast enough.

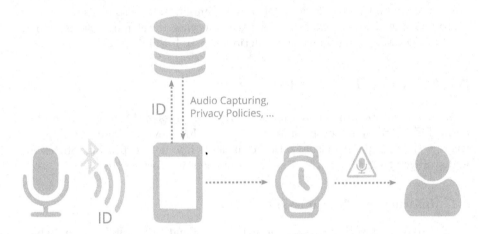

Fig. 1. Communication setup for transparency solution

3.2 Information Content

Transmitted content should at the best entail information and privacy policies about the data controller (the IoT device holder) as well as the data processor (the company which processes the data). For our first concept we focus on information about the nearby IoT device itself (device type, recording channel, ...) as well as the privacy policies of the specific data processor and exclude the data controller for now. Our scenario provides for the data processor to embed a BLE beacon with a corresponding transmission ID into the IoT device during production, and then to enter information about this ID (device type, range, recording channel, privacy policies, erasure etc.) into a corresponding database. The handling of the data controller is much more difficult, but has to be considered in future, because they of course have also (in part) access to the data, even though most of them probably have no idea how to handle them.

3.3 Information Visualization

In order to provide the user with an overview of nearby recording devices in a quick and understandable way, we have decided to use a hierarchical visualization structure.

The first level represents the corresponding device type respective *recording channel*, i.e. audio or video recording, and the number of devices of each type in the vicinity. This level corresponds to the well-known traditional warning signs (e.g. for video surveillance) and should always be accessible, e.g. as a notification of the smart phone or as a icon on the smart watch, in order to get a quick and transparent overview of which type of biometric data could be captured.

For more information the 2nd layer shows the IoT device type (e.g. smart speaker or smart tv) per recording category and the 3rd layer shows the device model and/or manufacturer of the specific IoT device (e.g. Amazon echo) and its specific privacy policies. Dependent on the device type (e.g. AR glasses) it is possible that also third party applications could have access to the capturing interface. Therefore additional application-based information has to be shared (4th layer) about the data processing of this third party apps involving their additional privacy policies. However, this layer cannot be realized with the separate database but the information has to be sent directly by the IoT device.

As already mentioned in Sect. 2.3, the lower the layer, the more details can be presented to the user, but they also carry a higher privacy risk for the IoT device owners.

Further, instead of simply linking the privacy policies of the data processor we want to simplify them and make them easier to understand, based on the work mentioned in Sect. 2.4 (see also Sect. 3.6).

3.4 A First Prototype

We decided to use a Fitbit smart watch for the first prototypical implementation, since our focus lies on wearable as the user device. These watches mainly function as fitness trackers, but offer high customizability of the user interface in a simple way. To be more specific, the whole UI is represented by HTML, CSS and JavaScript. For this work, we used a "Fitbit Ionic".

Regarding the detection of smart devices, we chose the approach of a mockup of the communication between smart device and watch app. Fitbit watches allow for remote shell access, and thus a change on the device can be triggered remotely in real-time.

For our prototype, we implemented layer 1 (represents recording channel, e.g. audio/video) and layer 3 (represents specific device information) of our information hierarchy. The UI is shown in Fig. 2. The left and middle image represents the default watch face, showing time and 2 *complications*. Complications are small badges, holding a specific part of information, which is usually represented with text and an icon.

The leftmost image shows the privacy state of the user. This is conveyed through a dashed eye icon, and enriched with a corresponding text denoting "private". The complication is also tinted in green, using a well-known color to indicate a good situation. The middle image shows an ear, as well as the text "Audio", showing that there might be devices **listening** to the user. For this, the typical warning color yellow is used. Using these colors, the privacy state is preliminary classified.

To convey the clickability of the complications, the privacy complication and the step counter can be tapped. The popup by tapping the privacy complication

Fig. 2. First smart watch prototype

is shown on the rightmost image. To make the concept of complications more intuitive, we decided to include a footstep counter as the right complication.

The popup consists of a short text describing the found smart device, i.e. its name. Additionally, a button allows for the user to request more information about the device. If it is tapped, the connected smartphone shows additional information about the device, e.g. data retention time, recording channel or whether it is activated with a wake word.

3.5   Pre-evaluation

To gain a first impression of the usefulness, we presented our solution to a group of 18 users (see Table 1) at the Dresden Science Night[7] and had them evaluate it.

Table 1. Overview of the participants

Age	10–20	20–30	30–40	40–50	50–60
Count	5	5	2	4	2

For this purpose, a booth was set up with an IoT sample device (Amazon Echo) and the implemented smart watch TET solution. The project was explained to the visitors and they could try out both the Amazon Echo and the smart watch. When the Amazon Echo was activated, the communication channel was also triggered and the transparency display of the smart watch visualized an audio recording device nearby. In addition, the user was prompted to visit different rooms, making the change in state of the transparency solution practically visible when leaving and entering the exhibition space. After the practical evaluation, the users were asked to fill out a small survey.

---

[7] www.wissenschaftsnacht-dresden.de.

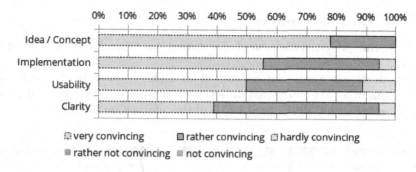

Fig. 3. Pre-evaluation of our TET solution by 18 test persons.

The overall feedback regarding the transparency solution developed was very positive (see Fig. 3). Especially the overall concept of the solution was felt to be very useful. In addition, 95 % of the test persons stated that they wanted to use this solution in daily life. More than half (59 %) of them said that they had already found themselves in a situation where the app would have been useful. The deficiencies in implementation, usability and comprehensibility were mainly due to the fact that many of the test persons wore a smart watch for the first time. In this regard, the implementation of the transparency solution for smart phones was started, which would also be preferred by most of the test persons (see Fig. 4).

Suggestions for improvements and remarks were in particular a desired control of the own data (e.g. by integrated switch-off function), as well as a listing of the range of the device located nearby. Furthermore different design suggestions were introduced.

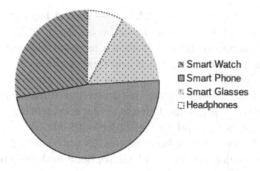

Fig. 4. Which device would you prefer for the transparent presentation?

3.6 Extending the Prototype

Based on the pre-evaluation we have started to expand our transparency solution.

First, as already mentioned, we started an implementation for smart phones based on Android. We integrated all levels of information (except third party applications). Figure 5 shows level 1 to 3 of the information hierarchy.

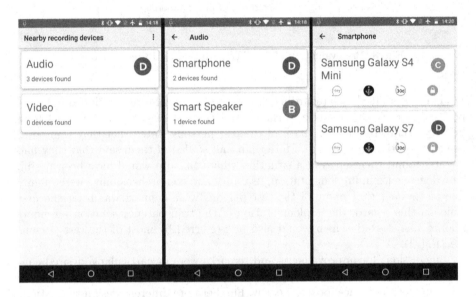

Fig. 5. Smart phone implementation (ltr: level 1, level 2, level 3)

The first layer is the main view, where the second layer can be accessed by clicking "Audio" or "Video". Layer 3 can be accessed by layer 2 respectively. Additionally, information of layer 1 is shown as a notification with a text and corresponding icon to allow for a quick overview of the users' privacy situation (see left image of Fig. 7).

The icons set were changed since it turned out during our pre-evaluation that they were partly ambiguous. Current icons representing the privacy state were chosen to be concise, and easily understandable: A mask represents no nearby recording devices, microphone represents only audio processing devices, eye respectively for video devices, and microphone and eye combined if audio and video processing devices are present.

Second we expand the smart watch solution for Wear OS devices. The implementation of the smart watch is shown in Fig. 6. Similarly to the pre-evaluation, a complication provides a quick overview of the current privacy state. The leftmost image shows a private state, without any recording devices nearby, whereas the middle image shows 3 recording devices nearby, with all being audio processing devices and no video processing devices. On click, the view on the right

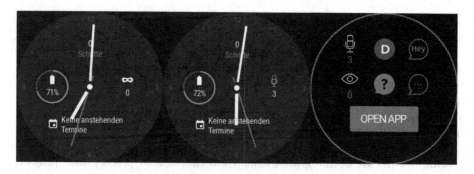

Fig. 6. Wear OS implementation

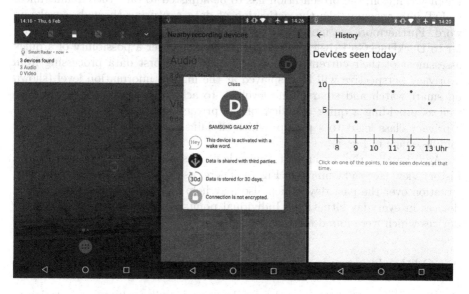

Fig. 7. Smart phone implementation (ltr: notification, popup view, history view)

image is shown, where the first information level is visualized, as well as the worst processing device from a privacy perspective and whether the device is always recording or is waiting for a wake word. Changes in the smartphone app are instantly reflected in the watch app.

The communication structure is implemented as shown in Fig. 1. The IoT-device broadcasts information using BLE GAP (Generic Access Profile), which defines the **central** and **peripheral** role. GAP offers 5 link layer states: Advertising, Scanning, Standby, Initiating and Connection. The advertising mode features 2 possible methods for inter-device communication: Advertising packets and Scan Response packets. The former can be sent in an interval from 20 ms to 10.24 s, and can contain up to 31 bytes of payload. IoT-devices use the peripheral role and broadcast information using this advertising packets, using an interval of 1 s. Advertising data contain an ID, which reflects device parameters and associated privacy policies.

User devices use the scanning mode to receive such broadcasts. Due to the short advertising interval, devices are detected in real-time. If data is received, the payload of the advertisement packet is extracted. Then, the included ID is queried in a database, which returns the privacy parameters of this IoT-device. We implemented this communication channel using separate bluetooth dongles from Nordic Semiconductor.

Further to simplify and visualize the important privacy parameters of the specific IoT-device we integrated icons from the Mozilla privacy icon project, as well as choosing icons which are more concise. To achieve an effective transparency solution, the presentation has to be adjusted to take the circumstances of IoT into account, like the activation of data capturing through a wake-up word. Furthermore we mock-up a scoring system (grades from A to F), similar to DuckDuckGo Privacy Essentials, to give the user a possibility of a quick assessment of their current privacy situation. The worst data processing from a privacy perspective will be displayed at the highest information level (shown on smart watch and smartphone level 1), to achieve a sense of awareness, as well as providing a quick overview of the privacy state. A tap action on such a privacy class leads to a popup, which explains the reason for the rating (see middle image in Fig. 7).

Additionally, the amount of found devices is recorded and presented in a history view (see right image in Fig. 7). There, users can reflect on their privacy situation over the past day, which also may help to raise awareness about IoT-devices in everyday situations. Individual points can be tapped, to reveal the devices which were found at this specific time.

4   Outlook

Continuing after completion of the development we will evaluate the solution to get answers to acceptability (is transparency important to the user), to usability and comprehensibility (is the visualization understood), to information requirements with regard to privacy issues for the device holder (what information is important to users), as well as to the impact of transparency in IoT to the user (do users feel better or worse if they can perceive their surrounding capturing devices, do they change their behavior).

Further UI design decisions should be carefully evaluated, as an evaluation in a clinical setting may not reflect the usage and usability of the tool in an everyday scenario, similar to the privacy paradox [13].

In addition, we are working on the rating system and the visualization/simplification of privacy policy parameters, which are better adapted to the IoT world and further, have to be evaluated.

Finally, we are working on concepts for integrating user-related interaction (opt-in/opt-out) to extend the audit TET to an interaction TET and thus give the user the opportunity for informed consent. Some concepts on interaction with IoT-devices in an everyday scenario have already been proposed [6,14]. This raises new challenges, as a connection has to be established between user device and IoT-device, where data regarding the consent of the user needs to be transmitted. This may include biometric data, e.g. a voice profile, enabling the IoT-device to filter specific information and to determine, how recorded information is to be processed.

5   Conclusion

Advancements in the Internet of Things introduces many positive aspects, such as alleviated life and efficiency, e.g. in mobility, energy supply or production. The integration of IoT-devices in all areas of public and private life, however, also raises a number of new privacy issues, especially in terms of unnoticed, ubiquitous data capturing that people cannot escape. May the owner of such devices still be informed about terms of use and data protection declarations, the independent user who is now constantly surrounded by these unobtrusively IoT-devices, does not even have the possibility to recognize them. Therefore in this paper we presented our work in progress for a first concept towards transparency in IoT, with focus on IoT-devices which capture acoustic and visual signals and thereby biometric data. Under the assumption of regulation, we define several challenges which a Transparency Enhancing Tool shall fulfill in order to be usable in an everyday scenario. A first prototype for a smart watch was then derived, which we tested at the Dresden Science Night. Visitors were able to try out the tool and voice their opinions and usability suggestions. The concept was well received, and thus we developed an extended implementation based on their feedback. Since many test persons stated interest in a smartphone app, the implementation is developed for watches and phones. Additionally, to support understandability and ease of use, given information is enriched with a classification of the users' current privacy state, depending on the privacy policies of surrounding IoT-devices.

References

1. General data protection regulation (2018). https://gdpr.eu/. Accessed on 02 Apr 2020
2. Castelluccia, C., Cunche, M., Le Metayer, D., Morel, V.: Enhancing transparency and consent in the IoT. In: 2018 IEEE European Symposium on Security and Privacy Workshops (EuroS&PW), pp. 116–119. IEEE (2018)
3. Cheng, Y., Ji, X., Lu, T., Xu, W.: DeWiCam: detecting hidden wireless cameras via smartphones. In: Proceedings of ASIACCS 2018 (2018)
4. Cohn, J.F., et al.: Detecting depression from facial actions and vocal prosody. In: 2009 3rd International Conference on Affective Computing and Intelligent Interaction and Workshops (2009)
5. Das, A., Degeling, M., Smullen, D., Sadeh, N.: Personalized Privacy Assistants for the Internet of Things: Providing Users with Notice and Choice. IEEE Pervasive Comput. **17**, 12 (2018)

6. Gomer, R., Schraefel, M.C., Gerding, E.: Consenting agents: semi-autonomous interactions for ubiquitous consent. In: Proceedings of the 2014 ACM International Joint Conference on Pervasive and Ubiquitous Computing Adjunct Publication - UbiComp 2014 Adjunct, pp. 653–658 (2014)
7. Krug, S.: Don't Make Me Think. A Common Sense Approach to Web Usability. Revisited. New Riders, Thousand Oaks (2014)
8. Langheinrich, M.: Personal privacy in ubiquitous computing: tools and system support. Ph.D. thesis, ETH Zurich (2005)
9. Lederer, S., Hong, J.I., Dey, A.K., Landay, J.A.: Personal privacy through understanding and action: five pitfalls for designers. Pers. Ubiquit. Comput. **8**, 440–454 (2004)
10. Lindqvist, J.: New challenges to personal data processing agreements: is the GDPR fit to deal with contract, accountability and liability in a world of the Internet of Things? Int. J. Law Inf. Technol. **26**, 45–63 (2018)
11. Morel, V., Cunche, M., Le Metayer, D.: A generic information and consent framework for the IoT. In: 2019 18th IEEE International Conference On Trust, Security And Privacy In Computing And Communications/13th IEEE International Conference On Big Data Science And Engineering (TrustCom/BigDataSE), pp. 366–373. IEEE (2019)
12. Murmann, P., Fischer-Hübner, S.: Tools for achieving usable ex post transparency: a survey. IEEE Access **5**, 22965–22991 (2017)
13. Norberg, P.A., Horne, D.R., Horne, D.A.: The privacy paradox: personal information disclosure intentions versus behaviors. J. Cons. Aff. **41**, 100–126 (2007)
14. Wegdam, M., Plas, D.J.: Empowering users to control their privacy in context-aware systems through interactive consent. CTIT Technical report Series, p. 10 (2008)
15. Weiser, M.: The Computer for the 21st Century, p. 13. Scientific American, New York (1991)
16. Zimmermann, C.: A categorization of transparency-enhancing technologies. arXiv (2015)

Tracking Without Traces—Fingerprinting in an Era of Individualism and Complexity

Florian Adamsky[1]([⊠]), Stefan Schiffner[2], and Thomas Engel[2]

[1] University of Applied Sciences Hof, Hof, Germany
florian.adamsky@hof-university.de
[2] University of Luxembourg, SNT, Luxembourg City, Luxembourg
{stefan.schiffner,thomas.engel}@uni.lu

Abstract. Fingerprinting is a ready-to-use technology that exploits the diversity and complexity of today's personal computing devices. Since fingerprinting leaves little to no trace, Do Not Track (DNT) policies are hard to enforce. The upcoming ePrivacy Regulation must consider this technological reality. In this opinion paper, we analyse technical use cases for device fingerprinting as an easy-to-deploy and hard-to-detect tracking technology. The EU has a longstanding tradition in strong data protection norms. To keep this high standards, we call on to the legislator to act, and illustrate vital points that must be considered in the legislative process.

1 Introduction

The General Data Protection Regulation (GDPR) [14] was a milestone for data protection and privacy regulations in the European Union (EU). Before its time, web operators were allowed to save tracking information on a web client without the user's consent. This allowed the web operator to track web clients around the web and invade the user's privacy. With the introduction of GDPR, every web operator needs at least consent before saving any tracking information. Legislators, however, are always one step behind the advances of technology.

With newer tracking techniques, such as fingerprinting, one can uniquely identify web clients without saving any data on the client. To make a fingerprint, the service provider collects multiple features of hardware or software to create a unique identifier. Currently, many service providers work under the assumption that the GDPR does not require consent for fingerprinting technologies. To the best of our knowledge, this assumption has not been challenged in front of a court.

We consider three converging main drivers that make fingerprinting easier and improve detection rates significantly: first, individualisation of devices and software to work more effectively; second, increasing complexity of software and hardware, e.g. current web browser have almost the complexity of a full operating system. and third, advances in machine learning (ML) techniques, leading to

L. Antunes et al. (Eds.): APF 2020, LNCS 12121, pp. 201–212, 2020.
https://doi.org/10.1007/978-3-030-55196-4_12

Machine Learning as a Service (MLaaS), which makes it easier to extract unique features from a big data set; These three developments make fingerprinting more dangerous than ever. Furthermore, technical countermeasures may even be counterproductive: every technical countermeasure that we use, generates more features and improves *fingerprintability*.

The EU is amending its related legislation. GDPR is key legislation if device fingerprinting is used to collect and process personal data. However, a grey area is left to whether certain metadata needs to be considered as personal data, especially for communication service providers. These are regulated by the ePrivacy directive [9], which is currently under review before it is into updated to a regulation. The increased harmonisation is positive, but it brings a requirement for more detail in the legal norms.

To this end, this paper aims to inform the discussion as to what is technically possible and the impact these possibilities already have today. Based on our research and literature review, we believe that technical countermeasures against fingerprinting are extremely difficult or even impossible to implement. The current legal framework is almost 20 years old and was drafted well before the reality of information society services and accurate fingerprinting techniques. Hence, there is a need for new legal countermeasures to include a clear statement about fingerprinting of hard- and software for all kinds of communication, including Machine to Machine (M2M).

2 Background

In this section, we provide a definition of fingerprinting and describe its different variations and techniques. Additionally, we sketch some use cases where fingerprinting is applied in the real world.

2.1 Definitions

Our definition is derived from Laperdrix et al. [24]. We define a fingerprint as set of information related to software, hardware or both. An attribute or a feature is a characteristic that contributes to the uniqueness of the fingerprint. We use attribute and feature interchangeably in this paper. Fingerprinting is the process of collecting information that results in a fingerprint. In general, there are two ways to collect a fingerprint.

Passive Fingerprinting requires no interaction to generate the fingerprint. The software or hardware spontaneously generates information that can be captured, e.g. network protocols that interact with their environment. This includes DNS Service Discovery (DNS-SD) [6], which provides enough information to capture a passive fingerprint. This is why, the latest draft concerning DNS-SD privacy and security requirements suggests *"avoid[ing] providing new fingerprinting information"* [20]. Another form of passive fingerprinting would be an Machinein- the-Middle (MitM) position, which allows an attacker to capture information and generate fingerprints. A more invasive way of collecting features is active fingerprinting.

Active Fingerprinting requires interaction with the device. It can be used if the device is not producing enough information, which could be used to generate a fingerprint on its own. An example for this technique is web browser fingerprinting. A web server sends specific JAVASCRIPT code to the web client; the client evaluates it and sends the result back to the web server. In this way the web server can actively collect features from a web client and generate a unique fingerprint. The distinction from passive techniques is not as clear-cut as it might seem from this definition: the extent, to which fingerprinting scripts can be obfuscated by interleaving them with the code for the actual service, remains an open research question. From a technical perspective, there are different techniques to generate a fingerprint and re-identity them.

2.2   Fingerprinting and Identification Techniques

To measure how much an attribute contributes to the uniqueness of a fingerprint, its entropy can be used. Attributes are represented as random variables X with their possible values x_i. The entropy H of discrete random variable X is defined as

$$H(X) = -\sum_i P(x_i) \log_b P(x_i), \tag{1}$$

where x_i are possible values of X and $P(x_i)$ the probability of this value. Analysing this formula, we can see that the entropy increases if the probability of the individual values decreases, or, in other words, the more surprising an element is for the observer, the more information it contains. This means the higher the entropy, the more unique is a feature in a fingerprint. The entropy helps to identify which attributes are more important than others and are effective in assessing the success of a given attack. Developing general privacy metrics, however, is an open research question that goes beyond this paper; a recent and exhaustive overview on this subject can be found in [33]. Attempts to estimate individual fingerprintability have been made by analysing systems of volunteers on the Internet [10] or browsers from different vendors [3].

In fingerprinting there are two phases: The first is the *learning phase* or *offline phase*, which generates fingerprints and saves them to a database. The second is the *identification phase* or *online phase*, which generates a fingerprint and compares it to the saved fingerprints in the database. Fingerprinting techniques depend on the characteristics of the attributes, which can be distinguished as follows:

Static Values are values of a attribute that do not change at all, or only insignificantly over time. The learning phase needs to capture the fingerprint once and save it to a database. The identification is simply a comparison with the saved values. It becomes more difficult, if the values are more dynamic.

Dynamic Values are values that have a specific range or change over time. For such values, one can manually select the features, collect them and save them to a database. The more data one has for a specific feature, the better, because according to the empirical law of large numbers one gets closer and closer to the *real* value. The identification can then be made with, for example, the Kullback-Leibler Divergence (KLD) [23]. There are a number of research Several studies [17,22,30] have used this technique.

Manual extraction of features, however, is cumbersome and time consuming. With the progress in ML algorithms, it is possible to detect features and generate fingerprints automatically. Popular algorithms, often used for this purpose are Support Vector Machine (SVM), Random Forrest (RF) and Long Short Term Memory (LSTM). Even without specialist knowledge of ML and access to high computing power, resources such as MLaaS make fingerprinting available to anyone. Such platforms cover pre-processing, model training, and model evaluation. However, all these fingerprinting techniques that we have covered, can be used in different use cases.

2.3   Use Cases

Fingerprinting has manifold use cases and is often deployed to the benefit of the user. However, it also carries privacy and security risks.

Security is a use case where a fingerprint can be used for authentication, either on its own or as an additional factor. For example, some websites require a username and password as a first factor and generate a web browser fingerprint for use as a second factor. If the browser fingerprint differs from a previously collected one, an additional step is needed for authentication. Other services try to generate fingerprints of malicious behaviour so as to filter and drop adversarial traffic as early as possible.

Positioning refers to fingerprinting used to localise persons or devices indoors. This is possible, since radio waves behave differently, depending on the environment. There are few research papers [18,26] that use fingerprinting to generate a fingerprint *of the environment*. Various radio technologies have been used for this purpose, e.g. IEEE 802.11 (WLAN), Bluetooth, Zigbee, and Ultra Wideband (UWB) [26].

Despite the similarity in names, these techniques deal with the opposite issue to the one we focus on in this paper: their aim is to recognise a change in the environment of a device. This indeed also has privacy and security implications, but is not in the scope of this paper.

Privacy Attack is a way to identify clients or persons by using the collected information. Fingerprinting is designed for this purpose. However, in this paper we look only at the privacy attack, which tries to use the collected fingerprint to uniquely identify a person. Here, the following applications can be observed: recognising a returning client at a certain virtual or physical location; and following a client over different locations, e.g. for targeted advertisement or price discrimination. In the next Section, we provide case studies which exploit fingerprinting to invade users' privacy.

3   Fingerprintability

In this section, we describe novel fingerprinting techniques that have been developed in recent years. We distinguish between software attributes and hardware attributes that can be used to generate a fingerprint.

3.1   Software Attributes

We start with web browser fingerprinting, since it has been investigated most thoroughly.

Browser Fingerprinting is the research domain of creating fingerprints of web browsers. To better combat the information overload we experience everyday on the Internet, we customise our browsers with different add-ons and plugins. The downside of this is that the diversity of internet browsing devices makes it difficult for developer to create web sites that perform well, provide similar look and feel, and functionality on all devices. This is the reason that current web browsers have rich JAVASCRIPT Application Programming Interfaces (APIs) to provide the best experience for every device. Both the individuality of the user including their customizations to the web browser and the richness of JAVASCRIPT APIs, make it possible to use fingerprinting to track browsers.

Since 2009, browser fingerprinting has been an active research area, having its origins in Mayer's bachelor thesis [27]. In his work, he conducted a small-scale experiment and collected different information, such as JAVASCRIPT objects (e.g. `navigator`, `screen`, `Plugin`, `MimeType`, among others) from 1,328 web browser to generate a fingerprint. The result of this experiment was that 96.23 % of the clients could be uniquely identified. A year later the Panopticlick [10] experiment conducted a large-scale experiment with 470,162 browser fingerprints with additional features with FLASH and JAVA. The result of this study was that 94.2 % could be uniquely identified. These studies were the beginning of a discipline the scientific community has improved fingerprinting continuously.

Over the years, the World Wide Web Consortium (W3C) has introduced new APIs to provide rich multimedia content on web pages. For example, the Canvas API *"provides objects, methods, and properties to draw and manipulate graphics on a canvas drawing surface"* [4]. Studies [1,28] discovered, that the Canvas API can be exploited to provide high-entropy attributes for a fingerprint. A website can send JAVASCRIPT code to the web browser leveraging the Canvas API and draw an image which is then sent back to the server. This image may contain different shapes, textual content, and smileys. Depending on the installed fonts, smiley themes and font rendering engine, the image will look different. This is because the font rendering engines from various operating system use different algorithms for sub-pixel hinting, anti-aliasing, and subpixel rendering.

With the introduction of the WebGL API, a graphics API to render 3D objects, the same thing has happened. A study [5] designed fingerprinting techniques based on this API. Additionally, this API can query the name of the graphics card and the driver used, which improves the fingerprint significantly. All newly introduced JAVASCRIPT APIs allow some kind of fingerprintability. We refer interested readers to [24] for a detailed survey of browser fingerprinting. Not only can a piece of software itself be fingerprinted, but also complex network protocols used in that software.

TLS Fingerprinting is a technique to create a unique identifier of the Transport Layer Security (TLS) implementation used. Researchers [13,21] have discovered that even complex network protocols such as TLS are fingerprintable. Before an encrypted transport can start, both client and server, must agree on the cryptographic parameters. Therefore, the purpose of the TLS handshake is to exchange the following information: list of supported TLS versions, list of supported cipher suits, compression methods, random nonce, and optional extensions. According to [31], TLS officially supports over 30 extensions. This handshake is not encrypted and therefore observable by a MitM attacker and passive observers. In [13], the authors collected over 11 billion TLS handshakes resulting in 230,000 unique fingerprints. Each fingerprint is not related to a user, but to a TLS implementation. Such unique TLS features have been used to block privacy-preserving tools such as Tor and Signal in repressive regimes [35]. In [21], the authors used TLS fingerprinting to identify the web browser being used. Consequently this could also be used as a feature in browser fingerprinting. The same techniques that are used to collect software attributes, can also be used for hardware.

3.2 Hardware Attributes

In this section, we describe different hardware fingerprints that are based on hardware imperfections resulting from the manufacturing process.

Wireless Device Fingerprinting is a research area which focuses on generating unique fingerprints from wireless devices. For a wireless transmission, a crystal oscillator is necessary to generate the required frequency. Due to the manufacturing process of these crystals, there are small imperfections causing carrier frequency offset (CFO) [25]. This CFO can be measured and a fingerprint can be generated which uniquely identifies a wireless device. In the past, high-precision measurement devices were needed to measure these small deviations. However, recent developments in wireless networks with Multiple Input, Multiple Output (MIMO) and the progress in ML makes fingerprinting easier than before.

With the introduction of IEEE 802.11n and the later standards, wireless Network Interface Controllers (NICs) support MIMO, which allows wireless frames to be sent and received over multiple antennas. To adapt the transmission to the current channel conditions and to optimise the transmission in general, modern NICs captures Channel State Information (CSI). With modified firmware versions [15,16] it is possible for a passive observer to capture this CSI. Which include a hardware timestamp, frame counter, number of receiving antennas, number of sending antennas, Received Signal Strength Indication (RSSI) of each antenna, noise, Automatic Gain Control (AGC), permutation matrix, rate, and the amplitude and phase for the first 30 subcarriers in form of a complex matrix. Recent studies [2,19] show that the CFO can be detected by ML and, together with CSI, identify a wireless device.

Sensor Calibration Fingerprinting focuses on the sensors in mobile devices. In a recent study [36], the authors investigated how far the sensors of a smartphone can be used as attributes for fingerprints. Smartphones are equipped with several sensors, i.e. accelerometer, gyroscope, motion sensor, and others. The precision of these sensors is important, which is why there is a need to calibrate these sensors to compensate the systematic errors introduced in the manufacturing process. An app or a webpage has access through different APIs to the sensors' raw data and does not need any special permissions. By analysing the sensor data carefully, the authors showed that it is possible to infer the per-device calibration and generate a unique fingerprint from that device. For iOS devices, they were able to extract attributes with 67 bits of entropy. This fingerprint is persistent, meaning that even a factory reset does not change these attributes. Their approach also works for Android devices such as the Google Pixel 2 and 3. In addition, the W3C introduced a candidate recommendation to standardize the generic sensor API and allow access to the raw motion data [34]. The authors of [36] foresees a significant privacy problem coming with these developments and propose mandatory mitigations.

4 Technical Countermeasures

From a technical perspective, countermeasures in these areas are difficult. Particularly, considering that any technical countermeasure results in an improvement in fingerprintabilty. This is what Peter Eckersley [10] called the *Paradox of Fingerprintable Privacy Enhancing Technologies*. Let us take browser fingerprinting as an example. The authors in [32] investigated whether it is possible to detect anti-fingerprinting plugins in browsers. They develop a novel testing framework and test the following six different anti-fingerprinting plugins: Random Agent Spoofer (RAS), User agent (UA) spoofers, CANVAS DEFENDER, FPRANDOM, BRAVE, and FIREFOX. The latest two are browsers with additional anti-fingerprinting settings that can be activated. The result of the study is that their testing framework detected all countermeasures, because of inconsistencies which the plugins introduce. For example, some plugins change the user agent string in the HTTP header, but not the value of the JAVASCRIPT object `navigator.userAgent`. Summarized, technical countermeasures are difficult, and this why we believe we need legal rather than technical countermeasures.

5   Recommendations on ePrivacy Regulation

Repealing the ePrivacy Directive. With the GDPR [14] coming into force in 2016, a legislative dissonance has been created: the currently effective Directive 2002/58/EC (ePrivacy) [9] complements the repealed Directive 95/46/EC (personal data protection) [8]. While references were mechanically mapped to the newer legislation, the updated scope of the GDPR does not match the scope of the old ePrivacy directive. This, in conjunction with technological advancements, created a legislative grey area. In order to rectify this issue, in early 2017 the European Commission (Com) proposed a new ePrivacy Regulation [29]. The Committee on Civil Liberties, Justice and Home Affairs (LIBE) of the European Parliament (EP) draw up a report [12], which was adopted by the EP on its first reading, resulting in that the position was being forwarded to Com, the Council of the European Union (Council) and member state parliaments in October 2017. However, since then the Council has been unable to reach a common position, which in turn puts the legislative process on hold. The situation only becomes more complicated, taking into account the latest attempt to find compromise by Finland [11], which has little overlap with Com's position and could be interpreted as diametrically opposite to the LIBE report.

The European Data Protection Supervisor (EDPS) wrote in its blog in October 2018: On one hand, *"A vast ecosystem has developed over the recent years, financed by advertising, for exploiting these special types of personal data without meaningful consent"* (which identify them self as information society services), while on the other hand, *"Traditional electronic communications services [..] cannot snoop on conversations over their networks."* The prolongation of this legislative void will only worsen the situation.

We can observe many conflict lines. Often, the definition of communication services is considered most relevant. In particular, the artificial distinction of communication from information services is often used to defend thew watering down of data protection standards for electronic communication services for the sake of 'fairness'. However, we argue here, that whatever finely nuanced definition, distinguishing services into these two broad categories, will soon be rendered obsolete by technological advances. Hence, we fall back to a general position that the legislator should ensure that services that are perceived as similar by users should be treated under the same legal framework. Following the expression of the duck test: if it looks like a duck, it swims like a duck, and quacks like a duck, it probably is a duck.

This out the way, for the matter at hand, we focus on the more relevant parts of the current EU legislative proposals dealing with the protection of users' terminal equipment information, namely Art 8 and recital 20 in [11,29], and the corresponding amendments in [12]. A sensible regulation to this end needs to cover tracking technologies that work without traces and storage on the device. This also needs to include passive fingerprinting, which we explained in Sect. 2.1, which is solely based on collateral data. Moreover, the very nature of these tracking technologies implies that browsers and other clients can only provide limited technical controls. Hence, transparency and purpose limitation is of utmost importance. The legislator might want to consider prohibiting certain applications of the techniques, in particular were the privacy impact for clients is not clear, or can be considered as out of proportion to their benefits.

6 Discussion and Conclusion

Fingerprinting techniques are mature and easy-to-use tracking technologies. They can and will be used to the benefit of ICT users, including to the benefit of criminal users and predatory marketing, and hence to the disadvantage of the end user. We have referenced multiple case studies in which fingerprinting has become a serious privacy threat. Advances in ML, especially the growing market provision of MLaaS, will further enable a wide range of actors to use these techniques to their benefit.

As we sketched in Sect. 4, technical countermeasures in these areas are hard to implement or sometimes even counterproductive: active countermeasures themselves induce suspicious behaviour that can actually enhance fingerprintabilty. This is what Peter Eckersley [10] called the *Paradox of Fingerprintable Privacy Enhancing Technologies*. Moreover, it seems to be a general pattern that cybersecurity protection measures have negative side effects, as shown in [7].

We would like to emphasise that fingerprinting is a dual-use technique; a general ban of the technique itself might be as harmful as its unregulated use. Legitimate use cases of fingerprinting range from indoor positioning systems to the detection of malicious activity. Thus dual use reality renders Do Not Track (DNT) options in browsers and devices ineffective. The harm for the end user does not necessarily result from the mere application of the technique, but rather from the later data processing.

A further complication for the privacy-aware user is that fingerprinting is hard to detect. By its very nature, using fingerprinting does not require the store of data on the user's device. Active fingerprinting, however, might result in suspicious function calls from web services. To the best of our knowledge, there has been little research on whether these fingerprinting calls can be hidden in the normal rendering of the service. Our educated guess would at least expect fruitful avenues of research in this direction.

The present paper aims to inform the stakeholders in the drafting process for the upcoming ePrivacy regulation. In order to allow the free market to police abuse of these techniques, the legal framework needs to set a high standard on transparency for users. Moreover, the user needs to be educated on the dangers of tracking. Lastly, not all users have the capacity to understand these dangers, so the legislator needs to protect the weaker members of society. In particular a clear decision needs to be taken as to the circumstances under which such a powerful and stealthy technique might be off limits for certain applications and under which frameworks it might be allowed only if a very clear cost-benefit analysis for the end user has been provided.

Acknowledgements. Parts of this work are supported by the Luxembourg National Research Fund (FNR) grant number C18/IS/12639666/EnCaViBS/Cole. We thank Dominic Dunlop for his review and comments that greatly improved the manuscript.

References

1. Acar, G., Eubank, C., Englehardt, S., Juarez, M., Narayanan, A., Diaz, C.: The web never forgets: persistent tracking mechanisms in the wild. In: Proceedings of the 2014 ACM SIGSAC Conference on Computer and Communications Security, pp. 674–689 (2014). https://doi.org/10.1145/2660267.2660347
2. Adamsky, F., Retunskaia, T., Schiffner, S., Köbel, C., Engel, T.: Poster: WLAN device fingerprinting using channel state information (CSI). In: Proceedings of the 11th ACM Conference on Security & Privacy in Wireless and Mobile Networks, WiSec 2018, New York, NY, USA, pp. 277–278. ACM (2018). https://doi.org/10.1145/3212480.3226099. ISBN 978-1-4503-5731-9
3. Al-Fannah, N.M., Li, W.: Not all browsers are created equal: comparing web browser fingerprintability. In: Obana, S., Chida, K. (eds.) IWSEC 2017. LNCS, vol. 10418, pp. 105–120. Springer, Cham (2017). https://doi.org/10.1007/978-3-319-64200-0_7
4. Cabanier, R., Mann, J., Hickson, I., Wiltzius, T., Munro, J.: HTML canvas 2D context, level 2. Technical report, W3C, September 2015. http://www.w3.org/TR/2015/NOTE-2dcontext2-20150929/
5. Cao, Y., Li, S., Wijmans, E.: (Cross-)browser fingerprinting via OS and hardware level features. In: Proceedings of the Network and Distributed System Security Symposium (NDSS) 2017, January 2017. https://doi.org/10.14722/ndss.2017.23152
6. Cheshire, S., Krochmal, M.: DNS-based service discovery. RFC 6763, RFC Editor, February 2013. http://www.rfc-editor.org/rfc/rfc6763.txt
7. Chua, Y.T., Parkin, S., Edwards, M., Oliveira, D., Schiffner, S., Tyson, G., Hutchings, A.: Identifying unintended harms of cybersecurity countermeasures. In: 2019 APWG Symposium on Electronic Crime Research (eCrime). IEEE (2020)
8. Data Protection Directive. Directive 95/46/EC of the European Parliament and of the Council of 24 October 1995 on the protection of individuals with regard to the processing of personal data and on the free movement of such data. Official Journal of the European Communities, L 281/31:37 (1995). https://eur-lex.europa.eu/legal-content/en/TXT/?uri=CELEX:31995L0046
9. Directive on Privacy and Electronic Communications. Directive 2002/58/EC of the European Parliament and of the Council of 12 July 2002 concerning the processing of personal data and the protection of privacy in the electronic communications sector (Directive on privacy and electronic communications). Official Journal of the European Communities, L 201/37:37 (2002). https://eur-lex.europa.eu/legal-content/EN/ALL/?uri=CELEX:32002L0058
10. Eckersley, P.: How unique is your web browser? In: Atallah, M.J., Hopper, N.J. (eds.) PETS 2010. LNCS, vol. 6205, pp. 1–18. Springer, Heidelberg (2010). https://doi.org/10.1007/978-3-642-14527-8_1

11. European Council Council of the European Union. Proposal for a Regulation of the European Parliament and of the Council concerning the respect for private life and the protection of personal data in electronic communications and repealing Directive 2002/58/EC (Regulation on Privacy and Electronic Communications) (2019). https://www.consilium.europa.eu/register/en/content/out?&typ=ENTRY&i=ADV&DOC_ID=ST-12633-2019-INIT

12. European Parliament. Report on the proposal for a regulation of the European Parliament and of the Council concerning the respect for private life and the protection of personal data in electronic communications and repealing Directive 2002/58/EC (Regulation on Privacy and Electronic Communications) (COM(2017) 0010 - C8–0009/2017 - 2017/0003(COD)) (2019). http://www.europarl.europa.eu/doceo/document/A-8-2017-0324_EN.pdf

13. Frolov, S., Wustrow, E.: The use of TLS in censorship circumvention. In: Proceedings 2019 Network and Distributed System Security Symposium (NDSS). Internet Society (2019). https://doi.org/10.14722/ndss.2019.23511

14. General Data Protection Regulation. Regulation (EU) 2016/679 of the European Parliament and of the Council of 27 April 2016 on the protection of natural persons with regard to the processing of personal data and on the free movement of such data, and repealing Directive 95/46/EC (General Data Protection Regulation). Official Journal of the European Communities, L 119/1:1–88 (2016). http://eur-lex.europa.eu/legal-content/EN/TXT/PDF/?uri=CELEX:32016R0679&from=DE

15. Gringoli, F., Schulz, M., Link, J., Hollick, M.: Free your CSI: a channel state information extraction platform for modern Wi-Fi chipsets. In: Proceedings of the 13th International Workshop on Wireless Network Testbeds, Experimental Evaluation & Characterization, WiNTECH 2019, New York, NY, USA, pp. 21–28 (2019). Association for Computing Machinery. ISBN 9781450369312. https://doi.org/10.1145/3349623.3355477

16. Halperin, D., Hu, W., Sheth, A., Wetherall, D.: Tool release: gathering 802.11n traces with channel state information. ACM SIGCOMM Comput. Commun. Rev. 41(1), 53 (2011)

17. Hjelmvik, E., John, W.: Statistical protocol IDentification with SPID: preliminary results. In: Swedish National Computer Networking Workshop (2009). http://www.cse.chalmers.se/~johnwolf/publications/sncnw09-hjelmvik_john-CR.pdf. Last Checked 12 May 2010

18. Hsieh, C., Chen, J., Nien, B.: Deep learning-based indoor localization using received signal strength and channel state information. IEEE Access 7, 33256–33267 (2019). https://doi.org/10.1109/ACCESS.2019.2903487. ISSN 2169–3536

19. Hua, J., Sun, H., Shen, Z., Qian, Z., Zhong, S.: Accurate and efficient wireless device fingerprinting using channel state information. In: Proceedings of the IEEE International Conference on Computer Communications (INFOCOM), p. 9 (2018)

20. Huitema, C., Kaiser, D.: DNS-SD privacy and security requirements (Draft Version 04). RFC, RFC Editor, January 2020. https://tools.ietf.org/html/draft-ietf-dnssd-prireq-04

21. Husák, M., Čermák, M., Jirsík, T., Čeleda, P.: HTTPS traffic analysis and client identification using passive SSL/TLS fingerprinting. EURASIP J. Inf. Secur. 2016(1), 6 (2016). https://doi.org/10.1186/s13635-016-0030-7. ISSN 1687–417X

22. Köhnen, C., Überall, C., Adamsky, F., Rakocevic, V., Rajarajan, M., Jäger, R.: Enhancements to statistical protocol identification (SPID) for self-organised QoS in LANs. In: Proceedings of the 19th International Conference on Computer Communications and Networks (ICCCN 2010) (2010)

23. Kullback, S., Leibler, R.A.: On information and sufficiency. Ann. Math. Stat. **22**, 49–86 (1951)
24. Laperdrix, P., Bielova, N., Baudry, B., Avoine, G.: Browser fingerprinting: a survey (2019). arXiv:1905.01051
25. Leen, S.: MIMO OFDM Radar-Communication System with Mutual Interference Cancellation. KIT Scientific Publishing, Karlsruhe (2017). ISBN 978-3-7315-0599-0
26. Lymberopoulos, D., Liu, J.: The microsoft indoor localization competition: experiences and lessons learned. IEEE Signal Process. Mag. **34**(5), 125–140 (2017). https://doi.org/10.1109/MSP.2017.2713817. http://ieeexplore.ieee.org/document/8026207/. ISSN 1053–5888
27. Mayer, J.R.: Any person... a pamphleteer: internet anonymity in the age of web 2.0, Bachelor thesis (2009)
28. Mowery, K., Shacham, H.: Pixel perfect: fingerprinting canvas in HTML5. In: Proceedings of W2SP 2012, p. 12 (2012)
29. Regulation on Privacy and Electronic Communications. Proposal for a Regulation of the European Parliament and of the Council concerning the respect for private life and the protection of personal data in electronic communications and repealing Directive 2002/58/EC (Regulation on Privacy and Electronic Communications). Draft COM/2017/010 final - 2017/03 (COD):35 (2017). https://eur-lex.europa.eu/legal-content/EN/TXT/?uri=CELEX:52017PC0010
30. Rinaldi, G., Adamsky, F., Soua, R., Baiocchi, A., Engel, T.: Softwarization of SCADA: lightweight statistical SDN-agents for anomaly detection. In: Proceedings of the 10th IEEE International Conference on Networks of the Future (NoF) (2019). http://orbilu.uni.lu/handle/10993/40162
31. Transport Layer Security (TLS) Extensions (2020). https://www.iana.org/assignments/tls-extensiontype-values/tls-extensiontype-values.xhtml. Accessed 29 Jan 2020
32. Vastel, A., Laperdrix, P., Rudametkin, W., Rouvoy, R.: FP-scanner: the privacy implications of browser fingerprint inconsistencies. In: Proceedings of the 27th USENIX Security Symposium, p. 17 (2018)
33. Wagner, I., Eckhoff, D.: Technical privacy metrics: a systematic survey. ACM Comput. Surv. (CSUR) **51**(3), 1–38 (2018)
34. Waldron, R., Pozdnyakov, M., Shalamov, A., Langel, T.: Generic sensor API. Technical report, W3C, December 2019. https://www.w3.org/TR/generic-sensor/
35. Wilde, T.: Knock knock knockin' on bridges' doors — tor blog (2012). https://blog.torproject.org/knock-knock-knockin-bridges-doors. Accessed 03 Feb 2020
36. Zhang, J., Beresford, A.R., Sheret, I.: SensorID: sensor calibration fingerprinting for smartphones. In: 40th IEEE Symposium on Security and Privacy, pp. 638–655. IEEE (2019). https://doi.org/10.1109/SP.2019.00072

Author Index

Printed in the United States
By Bookmasters